PENGUIN COOKERY LIBRARY

MODERN BRITISH FOOD

Sybil Kapoor was born and brought up in the country. With no formal training she began her career as a cook in London, when she worked for Justin de Blank at the Institute of Contemporary Art. Over the next eleven years she worked in London and New York as a chef and restaurant consultant. On her return to London in 1986 she became head chef at Sally Clarke's restaurant and then at Café Kensington: a restaurant like Clarke's that specialized in serving modern food. It was during this period that she developed an interest in British cooking and the way it was developing.

In 1991 Sybil Kapoor was approached to join *Taste* magazine, of which she was later to become cookery editor. She embarked upon a new career of writing that has led her to contribute numerous articles to, among others, the *Telegraph* magazine, *You* magazine in the *Mail on Sunday*, *BBC Good Food* and *BBC Vegetarian Good Food*.

Modern British Food is her first book and has been shortlisted for the 1996 Michael Smith award.

MODERN
BRITISH FOOD
Sybil Kapoor

PENGUIN BOOKS

For Raju

PENGUIN BOOKS

Published by the Penguin Group
Penguin Books Ltd, 27 Wrights Lane, London W8 5TZ, England
Penguin Books USA Inc., 375 Hudson Street, New York, New York 10014, USA
Penguin Books Australia Ltd, Ringwood, Victoria, Australia
Penguin Books Canada Ltd, 10 Alcorn Avenue, Toronto, Ontario, Canada M4V 3B2
Penguin Books (NZ) Ltd, 182–190 Wairau Road, Auckland 10, New Zealand

Penguin Books Ltd, Registered Offices: Harmondsworth, Middlesex, England

First published by Michael Joseph 1995
Published in Penguin Books 1996
1 3 5 7 9 10 8 6 4 2

Copyright © Sybil Kapoor, 1995
Illustrations copyright © Neil Packer, 1995
All rights reserved

The moral right of the author has been asserted

Printed in England by Clays Ltd, St Ives plc

CONTENTS

ACKNOWLEDGEMENTS

I would like to thank Louise Haines, my editor, not only for all her help and patience but also for having given me the opportunity of writing this book. I would also like to thank Annie Lee for her painstaking work, Diana Miller for her wonderful photographs and Neil Packer for his beautiful illustrations. Of the many other people who have helped I have to thank my parents, Helen and Frederick Polhill, Nigel Slater, Arabella Boxer, Clarissa Dickson Wright, Viv Jawett, Louise Platt and everyone at Books for Cooks.

I should also like to thank all the authors and publishers who have kindly given me permission to quote from their books and use their recipes. These include Bantam Books, a division of Bantam Doubleday Dell Publishing Group, Inc., for permission to adapt the warm red cabbage salad recipe from *The Greens Cook Book* by Deborah Madison and Edward Espe Brown, copyright © 1987; The British Tourist Authority for various recipes from *British Cookery*; Robert Carrier for three recipes from *The Robert Carrier Cookery Course*, published by Sphere books; CPC (United Kingdom) Ltd for the Seville orange marmalade recipe; Philippa Davenport; David & Charles (1981) for a recipe for saffron bread from *The National Trust Book of Christmas and Festive Day Recipes* by Sara Paston-Williams; Sophie Grigson for allowing me to use various recipes from Jane Grigson's *English Food*, *Fish Cookery*, *The Fruit Book* and *Good Things*; Deh-Ta Hsiung; Alastair Little and Richard Whittington; Macmillan General Books for the date chutney recipe from Margaret Costa's *Four Seasons Cookery Book*; Jill Norman for an Elizabeth David quote in *An Omelette and a Glass of Wine*; Penguin Books Ltd for quotes from *Penguin Cordon Bleu Cookery* by Rosemary Hume and Muriel Downes and *How to be an Alien* by George Mikes; The Reader's Digest Association Ltd for two marmalade recipes from *The Cookery Year*; Katie Stewart; Robin Weir and Caroline Liddell. Lastly, thank you to Neal's Yard Dairy for generously giving me their cheeses to photograph.

INTRODUCTION

Everything from seared lemon chicken to greengage almond crumble comes under the broad umbrella of modern British food. For the last ten years we have been enjoying a culinary renaissance that has transformed not only our domestic cooking but also our shops and restaurants. This book is an attempt to capture the elusive nature of our food and try and place it in a historical context. The pace of change has been so rapid in the last twenty years, that it is hardly surprising that our national diet has also radically changed. Today you are just as likely to be served a salmon sashimi salad as roast beef and Yorkshire pudding at a dinner party.

With such a diverse diet, it is difficult to define what makes modern British food British. The revivalists appear to advocate a reinterpretation of Victorian dishes, steamed puddings, hearty stews and succulent roasts. While others, such as the supporters of classical haute cuisine, appear to dismiss the majority of British dishes as worthless. In reality, British food is, and always has been, a hotchpotch of culinary ideas. We have pilfered recipes from around the world and then subverted them to our own particular taste and needs. Even the ardent supporter of British cooking, Hannah Glasse, included French, Indian, Turkish, Italian and Portuguese influenced recipes in her wonderful book *The Art of Cookery Made Plain and Easy* in 1747. To generalize, modern British cooking is marked by its elegant simplicity and innovative use of ingredients. It is not what we cook, it is how we cook it. We prefer food with pure, fresh flavours where you can taste the original ingredients. Grilled sole with a delicate butter sauce or lemon jelly flavoured with gin. In recent years our meals have been simplified to fit in with pressurized lives and new ingredients and cooking methods have been skilfully adapted into our daily food. Thus avocado, bacon and roasted onion salad or stir-fried spring greens are becoming as British as pea soup and mashed potato.

Perhaps the greatest influence on any country's cooking is its basic produce. Britain acquired a deservedly bad reputation for much of her food after the war when she embarked on the eminently practical policy of producing large amounts of cheap food. Unlike many of our European counterparts we did not have many smallholders producing fine-tasting fruit, vegetables and cheeses. Instead we industrialized everything from bread and cheese to the size and shape of our woolly tomatoes. Happily, neither the manufacturers nor the farmers or retailers remained content with the status quo as public demand grew for better food. The most noticeable change can be seen in our supermarkets. Ten years ago it would have been impossible to imagine buying crème fraîche, red onions, fresh pasta or pot-grown herbs with any ease. Now our supermarkets excel in selling global ingredients and we in turn thrive on finding new ways of using them. It is an extraordinary thought that sweet peppers, avocados and courgettes were still a novelty in the sixties, while fresh herbs, chillies, ginger, limes, papayas and mangoes were not widely available until the eighties. More recently, many of our high streets have begun to show the first signs of a revival in specialist food shops as small entrepreneurs begin to produce superb foods from organic bacon to sheep's yoghurt or rye bread. No wonder our cooking has changed for the better.

But the increasing influence of ethnic restaurants, foreign travel and, of course, the media have all helped to broaden people's horizons. Television, radio, newspapers and books are brimming over with information. Their effect cannot be underestimated. Elizabeth David, Jane Grigson, Margaret Costa, Robert Carrier and Delia Smith (to name a few) have changed the way the British cook and have deeply influenced many of our food producers. Today many cooks will experiment with Italian, Chinese or Middle Eastern recipes. This open-mindedness to new ideas is a particularly British characteristic, but it should not be thought that we lose our national culinary identity as a result; in fact, the opposite is true. If you examine many modern dishes you will find that many owe a great deal to their past. Chicken, leek and spinach filo pastries can be traced back to chicken and leek pie, grilled pigeon salad has its roots in the old fashioned sweet and savoury salads, (pan-fried) green cabbage and bacon were traditionally stewed together, peach and ratafia ice cream can be found in Victorian ices. The list is endless.

There has also been much debate about whether the demands of modern living are destroying our cooking abilities. It seems to me that they are certainly changing the way we cook, but that this is not necessarily a bad thing, just different. Many of our slow-cooking dishes have been readapted so that they are quick and easy to prepare for small numbers. For example, duck is now more commonly sold ready-butchered as breasts and pan-fried or grilled rather than slowly braised or roasted. Yet minted peas are still tossed in its pan. The result is, if anything, more delicious as it has a fresher taste. Fast cooking has also led to an improvement in the quality of our raw produce as there is no disguising poor flavour with long, slow cooking or complicated sauces.

Another aspect of British cooking that has had to be redefined is seasonal food. In the past, each ingredient had its own distinct season even though some, such as cucumbers, were often eaten out of season as a luxury. Our ancestors varied their meals by using different foods rather than by changing their repertoire of recipes. Roast partridge became roast duck. Today, the vast majority of food (with a few notable exceptions) is available throughout the year, as almost anything can be imported or sold frozen when out of season. Consequently, many of the traditional lines between the gastronomic seasons have become blurred. Our solution has been to reinstate them in another way. We now change our cooking style (rather than our ingredients) according to the time of year. Summer meals are in the Mediterranean mode, winter meals revert back to heartier, more 'traditional' recipes.

Modern British food has taken many of its original elements and reordered them into a new style. Old partners such as salmon and cucumber have been adapted into recipes that allow for lack of time and informal eating habits. More recent introductions such as the sweet pepper or crème fraîche have been embraced with the same enthusiasm that our ancestors lavished on the pineapple or China orange. Our food has maintained its sense of elegance and sophistication, merely adjusting them according to the current fashion. In other words, a modern meal of pan-fried lamb with rocket salad and gooseberry elderflower fool is as British today as green pea purée, whitebait, vol-au-vent of chicken, saddle of mutton, green peas, new potatoes, strawberries in jelly or Napolitaine ice and stuffed mushrooms was in 1909.

This book is a very personal interpretation of modern British food. I have chosen dishes that I love to eat, but with such a large area to cover there are some glaringly obvious omissions and for these I apologize in advance. I have divided the book into the months of the year for several reasons. It allows the reader to capture that essentially romantic link between our variable weather and diet. Despite the erosion of our traditionally seasonal food, the majority of British cooks still anticipate particular foods at certain times of the year and, lastly, it is probably the most practical way to approach such an enormous and varied subject. However, I hope that among the following recipes, the modern cook will find something to suit his or her own taste.

CONVERSION TABLES

WEIGHTS

7.5g	¼oz	85g	3oz	340g	12oz	1.1kg	2½lb
15g	½oz	90g	3½oz	370g	13oz	1.4kg	3lb
20g	¾oz	115g	4oz	400g	14oz	1.5kg	3½lb
30g	1oz	140g	5oz	425g	15oz	1.8kg	4lb
35g	1¼oz	170g	6oz	455g	1lb	2kg	4½lb
40g	1½oz	200g	7oz	565g	1¼lb	2.3kg	5lb
50g	1¾oz	225g	8oz	680g	1½lb	2.7kg	6lb
55g	2oz	255g	9oz	795g	1¾lb	3.1kg	7lb
65g	2¼oz	285g	10oz	905g	2lb	3.6kg	8lb
70g	2½oz	310g	11oz	1kg	2lb 3oz	4.5kg	10lb
80g	2¾oz						

OVEN TEMPERATURES

Very cool	110°C	225°F	Gas ¼
Very cool	130°C	250°F	Gas ½
Cool	140°C	275°F	Gas 1
Slow	150°C	300°F	Gas 2
Moderately slow	170°C	325°F	Gas 3
Moderate	180°C	350°F	Gas 4
Moderately hot	190°C	375°F	Gas 5
Hot	200°C	400°F	Gas 6
Very hot	220°C	425°F	Gas 7
Very hot	230°C	450°F	Gas 8
Hottest	240°C	475°F	Gas 9

VOLUME

5ml		1 teaspoon	120ml		
10ml		1 dessertspoon	130ml	4.5fl oz	
15ml	0.5fl oz	1 tablespoon	140ml	5fl oz	¼ pint
20ml			155ml	5.5fl oz	
25ml			170ml	6fl oz	
30ml	1fl oz		180ml		
35ml			185ml	6.5fl oz	
40ml	1.5fl oz		200ml	7fl oz	
45ml			215ml	7.5fl oz	
50ml			225ml	8fl oz	
55ml	2fl oz		240ml	8.5fl oz	
60ml			255ml	9fl oz	
70ml	2.5fl oz		270ml	9.5fl oz	
75ml			285ml	10fl oz	½ pint
80ml			400ml	14fl oz	
85ml	3fl oz		425ml	15fl oz	¾ pint
90ml	3.5fl oz		565ml	20fl oz	1 pint
95ml			710ml	25fl oz	1 ¼ pint
100ml			850ml	30fl oz	1 ½ pint
105ml			1 litre	35fl oz	1 ¾ pint
115ml	4fl oz				

JANUARY

WINTER SOUPS
Beetroot and apple soup
Spiced spinach soup
Lentil soup

WINTER SALADS
Curly endive, bacon and egg salad
Warm red cabbage and apple salad
Soy honey prawn and watercress salad
Mixed winter leaves

PIES AND SAVOURY PUDDINGS
Partridge pie
Chicken, leek and spinach filo parcels
Venison pudding
Steak, grape and pigeon pie

WINTER VEGETABLES
Celeriac purée
Stir-fried spring greens
Red cabbage with cassis
Stewed cucumber

STEAMED PUDDINGS
Lemon raspberry surprise pudding
Nègre en chemise
Banana cinnamon pudding with toffee sauce
Steamed apple pudding

MARMALADE
Seville orange marmalade
Lime or lemon marmalade
Dundee marmalade

HOT DRINKS
Hot toddies
Buttered rum punch

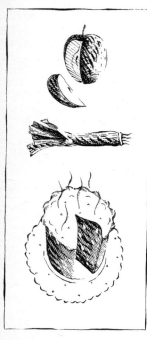

One of the delights of modern British cooking is just how much it varies from month to month. In the past, British cooks would serve their roasts, pies and puddings through summer and winter. Dishes were altered to encompass the produce of each season, but the fundamental repertoire changed little. Over the last forty years our cooking has slowly evolved into a far more varied, cosmopolitan style which we change and adapt through the year in response to both our mood and the climate.

One of the primary causes of this shift is that an incredible diversity of produce has become available to the ordinary cook throughout the year. Today it is much harder to gauge the seasons by produce. There are subtle differences, such as when Seville oranges slip into the shops in January, or game disappears, but a wide range of products such as cheese, meat or even fruit stay consistently good through the whole year. So modern cooks, perhaps unconsciously, have to express seasonality by their choice of recipes and use of ingredients.

January always brings a desire for simple food, as a reaction to the excesses of Christmas. Soups and salads now form an increasingly important part of our modern diet, especially as they conform to the currently fashionable criteria of being quick to prepare and healthy to eat. Salads in particular have undergone a radical change in the last few years, influenced in part by the liberal ideas of Californian cooking through the writings of Alice Waters, Wolfgang Puck and Deborah Madison. The germs of these new ideas first appeared, as with so many food fashions, on restaurant menus before they were taken up by food writers and home cooks. Winter salads are no longer a sad afterthought, but have become an integral part of the meal, eaten according to taste as a starter, main course or accompaniment. The supermarkets have responded to this revived interest by selling an ever-expanding variety of salad plants, herbs, vinegars and oils. As a result our salads are becoming distinctly sophisticated.

Vegetables have also undergone a small revolution in how they are cooked and served. Speed is of the essence, so happily we no longer have to suffer the boredom of preparing two or three dishes of plainly boiled vegetables to accompany each meal. Instead one vegetable will suffice, and since potatoes appear to no longer be *de rigueur*, the modern cook can choose from a wonderful range of winter vegetables. The only requirement is that the chosen vegetable is sensitively cooked to enhance its flavour. Thus spring greens can be stir-fried in sesame oil, while red cabbage can be simmered with crème de cassis and vinegar.

But the British appetite for steamed puddings and savoury pies remains unabated through the winter months – despite dietary good intentions, central heating and thermal underwear. These delicious creations have been updated with the passage of time, but they still take time to cook, even with the judicious use of the freezer and microwave. Although many of the ingredients have remained the same, modern taste dictates the use of subtle flavourings and lighter cooking methods. The days of laboriously boiling your fowl before shredding its flesh and making a velouté sauce from the stock for your pie filling have gone. Instead the meat is quickly pan-fried, along with the vegetables, before the pan is deglazed with wine and stock and thickened with cream.

There have always been certain recipes within British cooking that could be described as quintessentially British, and marmalade is just such a dish. Even today there are dozens of variations, from chunky Seville orange to delicate lime jelly. Although excellent ready-made marmalades can be bought, it is very easy to make at home and nothing can replace that deep glow of satisfaction every time you spread your toast with your own marmalade.

Perhaps another less obvious British dish is the hot toddy. Although rarely acknowledged these days, we still make excellent, hot alcoholic drinks at home. Family recipes, passed down through word of mouth, are remembered only when comfort is needed for the evils of the common cold. After all, there is nothing more soothing than a delicately spiced glass of steaming whisky flavoured with honey and lemon.

WINTER SOUPS

As soups are very popular all the year round, I have limited this section to puréed vegetable soups because they are so versatile for this time of year. Quick and easy to make, they can be thinned and simply garnished as an elegant starter or left thick and filling as an easy lunch or supper dish.

When I first began to cook professionally fourteen years ago it was still common practice in many private kitchens to add old cooked vegetables to mixed vegetable soups. Fortunately over the years this grim practice has died out and soup is regaining its position of honour on the table. The modern puréed soup is expected to have an intense fresh flavour and glowing colour. To achieve this, the vegetables are quickly cooked and are rarely extended with thickenings such as potatoes or flour. Even stock has become an optional addition, and cooks can decide whether they want vegetarian, home-made, ready-made or instant stock.

BEETROOT AND APPLE SOUP

Spiced apple soups have been made in Britain since medieval times, but this is a typical nineties interpretation with bold flavourings and wild colour. The crème fraîche is an essential ingredient and looks gorgeous swirled into the ruby soup. (Serves 4)

3 tablespoons vegetable oil
1 medium onion, diced
1 clove garlic, crushed
400g/14oz raw beetroot
3 dessert apples, for
   example Braeburn or Cox
565ml/1 pint chicken stock
   or water

salt and freshly ground black
   pepper
1 tablespoon finely chopped
   dill
4 tablespoons crème
   fraîche

Heat the oil in a heavy-bottomed saucepan and gently fry the onion and garlic until soft.

Meanwhile, scrub the beetroot under cold running water before slicing off their tops and tails and peeling them like potatoes. Roughly grate (use a food processor if you have one) and stir into the softened onion, ensuring that they are well coated in the oil. Cover and gently cook over a low heat for 5 minutes.

Peel and core the apples. Cut them into large chunks and stir into the softened beetroot. Cover and continue to cook for a further 10 minutes, stirring occasionally.

Add the water and bring to the boil. Lower the heat, season to taste and simmer, covered, for 30 minutes or until the beetroot is meltingly soft. Beetroot can vary in how long it takes to cook, so if it is tough, add a little extra water and simmer until soft. Liquidize the soup, adjust the seasoning to taste, and reheat.

Mix the dill with the crème fraîche and season lightly. Serve the soup and swirl some of the crème fraîche mixture into each plateful.

SPICED SPINACH SOUP

Curry powder is becoming a seasoning of the past, as an increasing number of cooks learn about Indian and Middle Eastern cookery. This soup belongs to the new category of ultra-fast food (provided you use ready-washed spinach). It is equally good served chilled in summer. (Serves 4)

400g/14oz cleaned spinach	½ teaspoon chilli powder
2 tablespoons vegetable oil	140ml/¼ pint buttermilk
1 medium onion, finely	285ml/½ pint whipping or
diced	double cream
2 fat cloves garlic, crushed	salt and freshly ground black
¼ teaspoon ground turmeric	pepper
½ teaspoon ground cumin	

Prepare the spinach (if unwashed) by carefully washing it in plenty of cold water. I find that spinach usually requires 3 separate washes to rid it of grit. Pull away the tough stalks and leave to drain in a colander.

Heat the oil in a large saucepan and gently fry the onion and garlic until they are soft, but not coloured. Add the spices and continue to fry over a low heat for a further 2 minutes. Then increase the heat and quickly add half the spinach. Allow this to wilt, stirring continuously to prevent it from catching, before adding the remaining leaves.

As soon as the spinach is soft and tender, which should be within 5 minutes, remove from the heat and add 285ml/½ pint of water and the buttermilk. Immediately liquidize and strain into a clean pan. Gently reheat before serving, add the cream and adjust the seasoning to taste. Do not allow the soup to boil or it may separate and will certainly lose its delicate colour.

LENTIL SOUP

In my family lentil soup was cooked in the traditional Scottish manner by simmering the lentils and vegetables in a huge saucepan with the leftover ham bone. However, since ham bones are not that prevalent in most modern homes, this is an updated version. If you like bacon flavour in your soup, fry four slices of finely diced back bacon with the vegetables and omit the garlic. (Serves 4)

2 tablespoons olive oil
1 medium onion, finely
   diced
2 carrots, finely diced
2 sticks celery, finely diced
1 clove garlic, crushed

225g/8oz red split lentils
1 litre/1¾ pints water,
   chicken or ham stock
salt and freshly ground black
   pepper

Heat the oil in a heavy-bottomed saucepan and gently fry all the vegetables and the garlic until they are soft.

Check the lentils for any stones and wash thoroughly. Add to the softened vegetables along with the water or stock. Bring to the boil, then simmer for 30 minutes until the lentils are soft.

Purée the soup in a liquidizer and strain to remove any celery fibres. Adjust the seasoning to taste, reheat and serve.

Note: If you are in a rush, leave the lentils to soak in some hot water while you prepare the vegetables. This will shorten the cooking time by about 10 minutes.

WINTER SALADS

Salads have had a chequered history in Britain. The first English recipe for a salad can be found in *Forme of Cury*, which was written around 1390. This set the trend for distinctly aromatic and hot (as in garlic and onions) salads that were dressed in oil and vinegar. As the centuries passed salads became increasingly complicated, with salamangundy forming an eighteenth-century precursor to the mixed hors d'oeuvre. The Edwardians ruined many of our salads by serving what seems to modern tastes to be distinctly unappetizing combinations of ingredients and coating them in heavy dressings. These were frequently thickened with cream, hard-boiled egg yolks or even mashed potatoes. A typical example can be found in the 1915 edition of Mrs Beeton's *Household Management*, where an Italian salad is made by mixing together equal quantities of cooked sliced carrots, turnips, potatoes and beetroot with cooked Brussels sprouts, French beans and cauliflower. These were then dressed in a tartar sauce, turned out of a basin mould, masked in aspic and garnished with tomatoes. I have the awful feeling that many of these salads were used as a means of using up over-cooked leftover vegetables. The Edwardians believed that if certain (most) vegetables were eaten raw they would ferment in the stomach, while garlic, leeks and onions were socially taboo through a fear of bad breath. The results can still be tasted in certain renowned London clubs, where delicacies such as Russian salad are unfortunately still served.

Despite this, good taste has survived and the salad is now more firmly part of our national diet than ever before. Many of the ingredients that we use today, such as blanched French beans, hard-boiled eggs, apples, red cabbage and watercress have been eaten in salads for centuries. But the combinations and methods of mixing have obviously changed.

One of the most noticeable developments has been the rise in popularity of the warm or 'wilted' salad. These are particularly good in winter, when a cold salad can seem less appealing. But another fundamental, if subtle, change is the increasing use of Eastern ingredients such as sesame oil or noodles in salads. It may be that this foreshadows a much more radical change in style for many familiar British dishes.

CURLY ENDIVE, BACON AND EGG SALAD

This salad is typical of the Anglo-French school of cooking that developed after Nouvelle Cuisine swept Britain in the early eighties. Ideally it should be eaten as soon as the eggs, bacon and croûtons are cooked, so that their warmth soaks into the lettuce leaves. It can be extended or altered to taste. (Serves 4)

Dressing
1 shallot, finely diced
2 tablespoons sherry or
    white wine vinegar
6 tablespoons olive oil
salt and freshly ground black
    pepper

Salad
1 curly endive or batavia
4 eggs
4 tablespoons olive oil
1 clove garlic, quartered

4 slices white bread, crusted
    and cut into cubes
3 tablespoons vegetable oil
225g/8oz smoked back
    bacon, diced

Optional additions
115g/4oz French beans,
    trimmed and lightly
    cooked, or 1 can
    sardines, drained and
    filleted

Whisk together the finely diced shallot with the sherry vinegar and olive oil. Season to taste and set aside.

Using a pair of scissors, trim the head of the curly endive as if it were a mop of hair, removing all the dark green ends and the tough outer leaves. Cut through the root and wash and dry the remaining leaves. Place in a large salad bowl.

Put the eggs on to cook in a small pan of cold water. Boil for 7 minutes, until the whites are firm. Meanwhile, heat the olive oil and garlic in a large frying pan. As soon as the garlic begins to sizzle, stir in the bread cubes and sauté until golden. Keep moving the croûtons around the pan to ensure that they colour evenly. on each side. Once they are ready, transfer them to some kitchen paper and sprinkle them with salt.

Clean the frying pan and add the vegetable oil. Once hot, fry the bacon until it is crispy and drain on kitchen paper.

As soon as the eggs are ready, peel and quarter them before adding them to the salad leaves with the croûtons and bacon. Quickly emulsify the dressing and pour over the salad (add the warm French beans or sardine fillets at this stage). Mix thoroughly, adjust the seasoning to taste, and serve immediately with lots of crusty bread.

WARM RED CABBAGE AND APPLE SALAD

I have adapted this recipe from *The Greens Cook Book* by Deborah
Madison with Edward Espe Brown, as it uses typically British ingredients
while at the same time perfectly illustrating the extraordinary influence
American chefs have had on certain aspects of British cooking. It should
be eaten as soon as it is cooked. (Serves 4)

115g/4oz soft goat's cheese, roughly diced	1 dessert apple, cored, quartered and thinly sliced
1 tablespoon finely chopped chives	30g/1oz walnut halves
2 tablespoons walnut oil	1–2 tablespoons balsamic vinegar
4 spring onions, finely sliced	salt and freshly ground black pepper
225g/8oz red cabbage, cored, quartered and finely sliced	

Place the goat's cheese and chives in a large salad bowl.

Heat the walnut oil in a large frying pan and quickly stir-fry the spring
onions and cabbage until they begin to wilt. At this stage add the sliced
apple, walnut halves, vinegar and seasoning to taste. Allow to heat
through and then toss into the cheese and chive bowl. Quickly mix and
serve warm.

SOY HONEY PRAWN AND WATERCRESS SALAD

Oriental influences with Western ingredients – perhaps this is British food of the future. (Serves 2 as a main course)

225g/8oz peeled cooked prawns
1 lime, juiced
1 fat clove garlic, crushed
1 dessertspoon runny honey
1 tablespoon soy sauce
2 tablespoons sesame oil
⅓ cucumber, peeled and diced to the same size as the prawns
2 little gem lettuces, roughly broken up
1 handful prepared watercress

Place the prawns in a large bowl and toss in a little of the lime juice. Make the dressing by whisking together the garlic, honey, remaining lime juice and soy sauce. Once the honey has dissolved, whisk in the sesame oil.

When ready to eat, add the cucumber, lettuce and watercress to the prawns. Give the dressing a final whisk and pour over the salad. Mix thoroughly and serve.

MIXED WINTER LEAVES

Throughout the winter months it is possible to buy a surprising variety of bitter-sweet winter chicory: white, red, curly endive, batavia and trevisse, a thin red chicory that curls like a feather at each leaf tip. These make excellent salads – so choose whatever looks best. (Serves 2)

3 handfuls chicory leaves
½ small red onion, cut into
   wafer-thin rings
½ Florence fennel bulb, finely
   sliced
scattering of fresh walnuts or
   hazelnuts, roughly
   chopped (optional)

1 clove garlic, crushed
1 tablespoon champagne or
   white wine vinegar
3 tablespoons walnut or
   hazelnut oil
salt and freshly ground black
   pepper

Trim, wash and dry the chicory leaves. Place in a large bowl with the onion, fennel and nuts.

Whisk together the garlic, vinegar and oil. Season to taste and dress the salad when you are ready to eat.

Note: If you are concerned about the heat of the onion, thinly slice it and soak it in iced water for 30 minutes. Pat dry and add to the salad.

PIES AND SAVOURY PUDDINGS

Pies and puddings have been a favourite British food for centuries.

The perfect manner in which the nutriment and flavour of an infinite variety of viands may be preserved by enclosing and boiling them in paste, is a great recommendation of this purely English class of dishes, the advantages of which foreign cooks are beginning to acknowledge. If really well made, these savoury puddings are worthy of a place on *any* table; though the decrees of fashion – which in many instances have so much more influence with us than they deserve – have hitherto confined them almost entirely to the simple family dinners of the middle classes. (Eliza Acton on savoury puddings, from *Modern Cookery*, 1855)

Much the same could have been said about savoury pies, except that every class of society enjoyed some form of pie, even the poor.

Lack of time is the problem that most modern cooks face today, and sadly there are no easy answers. Steamed puddings have become almost a luxury food, given the amount of time they take to steam. This can be lessened by cooking the fillings in advance and using smaller basins. They also reheat surprisingly well in the microwave, so glamorous hostesses can still avoid steamy kitchens if wished.

Pastry has also suffered from cooks wishing to spend less and less time in the kitchen. Filo pastry has become a fashionable alternative for some dishes, but despite popular belief I still feel that ready-made shortcrust or puff pastry is not as good as home-made. Have you ever read the ingredients list on a packet of frozen puff pastry? The best solution to lack of time, particularly with puff or rough puff pastry, is to make up more than you need and freeze the rest. (All the pastry recipes can be found in the Appendix, page 326. However, if you cannot bear the thought of making your own pastry, then buy frozen pastry rather than deprive yourself of the pleasure of eating pies and tarts.)

PARTRIDGE PIE

Plump little partridges are now being sold in some supermarkets, so this delicately flavoured game bird is becoming far easier to buy. This recipe can be adapted to pheasant or chicken if wished. (Serves 4)

4 partridges, cleaned	4 sprigs thyme
3 tablespoons vegetable oil	1 sprig parsley
4 tablespoons seasoned flour	345ml/12fl oz chicken (or partridge) stock
6 slices smoked back bacon, diced	170ml/6fl oz double cream
1 medium onion, finely diced	salt and freshly ground black pepper
2 cloves garlic, crushed	225g/8oz chilled puff pastry (see page 329)
2 carrots, cut into batons	½ egg beaten with 1 tablespoon milk
225ml/8fl oz dry white wine	
2 strips lemon peel	

Preheat the oven to 220°C/425°F/gas 7.

Neatly remove the 2 breast fillets of each partridge by cutting along the breast bone and down around the rib cage. Pull off any skin and cut into chunks. If you are confident about boning you can remove the legs and cut the meat away from the thigh bone, before skinning and dicing. The drumsticks are too small to worry about. Enthusiastic cooks can use the bones for stock.

Heat the oil in a large frying pan. Toss the partridge cubes in some seasoned flour, shaking off any excess, and fry until they are lightly coloured. Remove and place in a pie dish. You may need to add a little more oil at this stage. Once the frying pan is hot, quickly colour the bacon before adding the onion, garlic and carrots. Reduce the temperature and gently cook until they have softened. Add the white wine together with the lemon peel and herbs, and reduce the wine by half before adding the stock. Return to the boil, stir in the cream and let it bubble until the sauce has thickened a little. Pour over the partridge cubes and mix thoroughly, adjusting the seasoning to taste. If possible allow the mixture to cool before covering with pastry.

When you are ready to bake the pie, roll out the pastry on a lightly floured surface in roughly the same shape as your pie dish only larger. Cut a ribbon from the edge of the dough and press it firmly on to the rim of the pie dish. Brush this with a mixture of beaten egg and milk and place a pie vent in the centre of the filling. Loosely roll the pastry on to the rolling pin and lift on to the pie dish. Using a fork, firmly press around the rim so that the 2 pastries are glued together. Cut off the excess. Prick the lid with a knife, ensuring that the vent has a hole, and paint the crust with some more egg and milk.

Place in the centre of the preheated oven and bake for 35 minutes or until the pastry has puffed up and become golden. When you are serving, remember to fish out the herb sprigs.

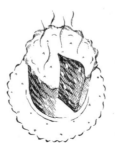

CHICKEN, LEEK AND SPINACH FILO PARCELS

Filo, or strudel pastry, can be bought frozen in most supermarkets. It still has a misleading reputation for being difficult to use but, as with all pastries, if a few simple rules are followed delicious results will ensue. Good quality filo pastry should have a silky smooth texture and each sheet should be paper-thin and easy to separate. If the pastry is crumbly or stuck together it has been stored badly. This happens surprisingly often, so once you find a good source and brand, stick to it.

Have all your ingredients ready before you begin to layer the pastry and keep the open pastry supple by covering it with a clean damp tea towel. Once the pastry packet has been opened, keep it tightly wrapped in the refrigerator for a day or two, but do not refreeze, as this will make it dry and crumbly. (Serves 2 – makes 6 parcels)

2 chicken breasts, skinned and boned	salt and freshly ground black pepper
2 tablespoons olive oil	1 leek, finely sliced
1 lemon, finely grated	170g/6oz cleaned fresh spinach
½ lemon, juiced	
1 clove garlic, crushed	70g/2½ oz melted butter
¼ teaspoon finely chopped thyme or lemon thyme	140g/5oz filo pastry

Preheat the oven to 220°C/425°F/gas 7.

Slice the chicken into thin strips. Mix these with the olive oil, lemon zest and juice, garlic, thyme and seasoning. Set aside to marinate while you prepare the remaining ingredients.

Bring a pan of water to the boil and add some salt. Place the sliced leek in a metal sieve and hold in the water for 2–3 minutes, until it turns bright green and begins to soften. Remove and cool under cold running water. Squeeze as much water out of the slices as you can and add them to the chicken.

Return the water to the boil and add the spinach. As soon as it has wilted, drain and cool under running cold water before squeezing dry. Finely slice the cooked spinach, squeeze once again and mix with the leeks and chicken.

Butter a baking sheet and clear a comfortable working space. Open your filo pastry sheets and keep them covered with a damp tea towel. You will need 18 squares, each measuring approximately 15cm/6 inches.

Each square has to be painted with melted butter and layered with another 2 sheets, each buttered in turn. When you have layered and buttered 3 squares, place ⅙ of the filling in the middle and gather together the edges, pinching at the neck to stick them together, so that the result looks like a stuffed brown paper bag with its edges pulled back. The filling should be completely sealed inside. Place each parcel on the baking sheet and once finished, brush with melted butter. This will help the parcels to colour evenly and become crispy as they bake.

At this point the pastries can be stored in the refrigerator until needed. Otherwise bake in the centre of the preheated oven for 20 minutes and serve immediately.

Note: Filo pastries can be made up to 12 hours in advance, provided their filling is not too wet. Bake when ready to serve.

VENISON PUDDING

Any stew suitable for a pie can be used as a filling for a pudding, and venison makes a deliciously rich one. Much of the deer now sold is farmed, which means that its meat is more tender than that of its wild cousins. But it is still a good idea to marinate the meat for at least 12 hours, as it is so lean. This has the added benefit of giving the dish a deeper, more complex flavour. I usually cook the stew the day before so as to lessen the cooking time of the pudding. (Serves 4)

Use a 850ml/1½ pint
   pudding basin
455g/1lb venison steak,
   trimmed of fat and cut
   into 2.5cm/1 inch cubes
225g/8oz suet pastry (see
   page 330)

Marinade
285ml/½ pint red wine
140ml/¼ pint port
1 medium carrot, roughly
   chopped
1 small onion, roughly
   chopped
1 outer stick celery, roughly
   chopped
4 juniper berries, lightly
   crushed
4 black peppercorns

2 strips orange peel
2 strips lemon peel
1 bay leaf
1 sprig rosemary
1 sprig parsley

Stew
5 tablespoons olive oil
1 small onion, finely sliced
1 clove garlic, crushed
1 large carrot, cut into
   rounds
5 tablespoons seasoned
   flour
285ml/½ pint water
salt and freshly ground black
   pepper
2 tablespoons redcurrant
   jelly

Mix the venison with all the marinade ingredients in a non-corrosive bowl. Cover and refrigerate for 12 hours. Pour the venison cubes into a colander set over a bowl. Save the juices and place the remaining marinade ingredients in a separate bowl.

Heat 2 tablespoons of oil in a casserole dish and fry the onion, garlic and carrot gently for 5 minutes. Remove from the heat when soft.

Heat the remaining oil in a frying pan. Toss the venison cubes in the seasoned flour, shaking off any excess, then fry in 2 batches until the meat has a good colour. Place the meat in the casserole dish and add the marinade vegetables and spices to the frying pan, stirring vigorously to remove any crusty bits from the bottom of the pan. Sauté for a good 5 minutes or until they are soft, then add 1 tablespoon of the seasoned flour and continue to fry for another 3 minutes. Add the water and the liquid from the marinade and bring to the boil. Bubble briskly until it has reduced by half and thickened.

Strain the reduced marinade over the meat and vegetables in the casserole dish, adjust the seasoning to taste and cover. Simmer gently for 1 hour, adding more water if necessary. Stir in the redcurrant jelly and cool until needed.

Follow the instructions for suet pastry on page 330, and boil the pudding in plenty of water for 2 hours. Be sure to keep the water level replenished with extra boiling water. When you are ready to turn the pudding out, remove it from the water and allow it to sit for a couple of minutes before removing the foil and greaseproof paper. Place a warm serving plate over the top and invert both together, giving a few gentle shakes until you feel the pudding slip out.

STEAK, GRAPE AND PIGEON PIE

Pigeon cooked in the classic British manner with beef tastes very similar to liver or kidney, which has always struck me as being rather disappointing, since you might as well cook kidneys instead. However, the addition of grapes, which have been used in British cooking since medieval times, brings out the sweet succulence of the pigeons and works surprisingly well with the beef. You can prepare the filling the day before if you wish. (Serves 4)

905g/2lb black or white grapes
3 tablespoons olive oil
340g/12oz trimmed chuck steak, cut into 2.5cm/1 inch dice
4–5 tablespoons seasoned flour
4 pigeon breast fillets, skinned and cut into 2.5cm/1 inch dice
15g/½ oz butter
1 medium onion, diced
2 cloves garlic, crushed
3 tablespoons warmed brandy
1 strip lemon peel
salt and freshly ground black pepper
2 tablespoons finely chopped parsley
225g/8oz shortcrust pastry (see page 327)
½ egg beaten with 1 tablespoon milk

Wash and stem the grapes and place in a non-corrosive saucepan with about 3 tablespoons of water to prevent them from catching. Cover and simmer over a gentle heat for about 10 minutes until they soften and burst. Then crush them with a potato masher or wooden spoon, so that they release as much juice as possible, and continue to simmer, covered, for another 5 minutes. Remove from the heat and strain the juice. You should have about 425ml/¾ pint.

While the grapes are cooking, heat the olive oil in a heavy-bottomed saucepan. Toss some of the beef in the seasoned flour and brown quickly in the oil. Set aside and continue with the remaining beef, followed by the pigeon. You may need to add a little more oil as you go.

Add the butter to the saucepan and gently fry the onion and garlic until soft. Return the meat to the pan, pour on the warm brandy and quickly set alight. Once the flames go out, stir in the grape juice, lemon peel and seasoning. Bring the casserole up to a simmer and cook very gently for 1 hour. Remove from the heat, skim off any excess fat and mix in the chopped parsley before pouring into a deep pie dish.

Preheat the oven to 220°C/425°F/gas 7.

When you are ready to bake, roll out the pastry in roughly the same shape as your pie dish only larger. Cut a ribbon from the edge of the dough and press it firmly on to the rim of the pie dish. Brush this with a mixture of beaten egg and milk and place a pie vent in the centre of the filling. Loosely roll the pastry on to the rolling pin and lift on to the pie dish. Firmly press the 2 pastries together. Cut off the excess pastry, prick the lid and brush with egg and milk.

Bake for 35 minutes or until the pastry has become crisp and golden.

WINTER VEGETABLES

January has a wide variety of vegetables, from sweet Canary cucumbers to interesting roots such as celeriac or salsify. From the eighteenth century, when gardening mania truly took hold of the British, the rich and middle classes have had a good range of vegetables to choose from throughout the year. Hannah Glasse, in her book *The Art of Cookery Made Plain and Easy* (1747), lists the following vegetables as available in January:

Many sorts of cabbages and savoys, spinach, and some colliflowers in the conservatory, and artichokes in sand. Roots we have as in the last month (carrots, parsnips, turnips, beets, skirrets, scorzonera, horse-reddish, potatoes, onions, garlick, shallots). Small herbs on the hot beds for sallads, also mint, tarragon, and cabbage lettice preserved under glasses; chervile, salary and endive blanched. Sage, thyme, savory, beet-leaves, tops of young beets, parsley, sorrel, spinach, leeks and sweet marjoram, marigold flowers, and mint dried. Asparagus on the hot bed, and cucumbers on the plants sown in *July* and *August*.

Even celeriac, which still suffers from the reputation of being a 'foreign' vegetable, was introduced at this time. According to Jane Grigson, Stephen Switzer, the garden designer and seedsman, first grew it here in the 1720s. However, despite its exquisite flavour, it has never enjoyed widespread popularity. Happily, with its increasing availability in supermarkets and greengrocers, modern cooks can at last appreciate celeriac as a supremely versatile vegetable that can be mashed into a fragrant purée, deep-fried into crinkly crisps or blanched and tossed into salads.

CELERIAC PURÉE

This is comfort food *par excellence*, so good it is hard to resist licking the saucepan. Its delicate celery-like flavour acts as a delicious foil to rich stews and pies. (Serves 4)

1 celeriac	1 small onion, finely diced
1 teaspoon vinegar or	2 cloves garlic
lemon juice	140 ml/¼ pint double cream
2 potatoes	salt and freshly ground black
40g/1½ oz butter	pepper

Wash the celeriac and cut away the tough roots and skin. Cut into large chunks and put in a large pan of cold salted water with a teaspoon of vinegar or lemon juice. Celeriac will discolour as soon as it is cut if it is not kept and cooked in acidulated water. Bring to the boil and cook for 25 minutes or until tender. Drain and leave in a colander for 5 minutes to dry out.

Meanwhile, peel the potatoes, cut into quarters and place in a pan of salted cold water. Bring to the boil and cook for 20 minutes or until soft. Drain and leave to steam for 5 minutes.

Melt the butter in a heavy-bottomed saucepan. Gently fry the onion and garlic for about 5–10 minutes, until very soft but not coloured. Add the cream and bring to the boil, then simmer for 3 minutes before adding the cooked celeriac and potato. Continue to cook over a low heat until the vegetables have absorbed some of the creamy juices and are meltingly soft.

Vigorously mash the vegetables and season to taste before beating with a wooden spoon until they form a fluffy purée. Celeriac purée has a softer consistency than mashed potato.

STIR-FRIED SPRING GREENS

Spring greens are much loved in Britain, although they suffer from a bad reputation through over-cooking. This is a typical East meets West nineties recipe that will woo a non-spring-green lover. Speed is of the essence, so make sure that all your ingredients are ready before you begin. The greens will turn a beautiful emerald colour and taste sweet and nutty. (Serves 4)

225g/8oz packet ready-prepared spring greens or 455g/1lb whole spring greens
3 tablespoons sesame oil
2 cloves garlic, crushed
3 tablespoons white sesame seeds

3 tablespoons soy sauce
3 tablespoons mirin or ½ tablespoon caster sugar mixed with 1 tablespoon water and 1 tablespoon sake or dry sherry

If you are using whole spring greens, remove the tough, dark green outer leaves and cut off the bottom of the stems. Roughly slice into wide strips and wash in several changes of cold water before leaving to drain in a colander.

Heat a large non-stick frying pan until very hot, then add the oil and as soon as it begins to smoke throw in the garlic and sesame seeds, which will immediately try and jump out again. At this stage add the greens and rapidly stir them around the pan. As soon as the sizzling begins to lessen, add the soy sauce and mirin. Allow them to bubble up, then remove from the heat and serve.

RED CABBAGE WITH CASSIS

I first cooked this recipe in New York in a Californian restaurant. But its use of ingredients seemed so quintessentially modern British that I have purloined it for this book. Just like spiced red cabbage, its flavour will improve the following day. (Serves 4)

3 tablespoons olive oil
1 small red cabbage, cored,
    quartered and finely
    sliced
1 clove garlic, crushed

3 tablespoons crème de
    cassis
2 tablespoons blackcurrant
    or balsamic vinegar
salt and freshly ground black
    pepper

Heat the oil in a medium heavy-bottomed saucepan. As soon as it is hot, add the cabbage and garlic and quickly stir around the pan to prevent it from burning. As soon as it has collapsed stir in the cassis, vinegar and seasoning. Reduce the heat, cover the pan, and gently cook for a further 15 minutes. If you prefer a more intense-flavoured cabbage add more cassis and vinegar to taste. Reheat when needed.

STEWED CUCUMBER

Stewed cucumber first appeared in the eighteenth century and was very popular, particularly out of season, so it seemed appropriate to include it here, especially as cucumbers are surprisingly sweet at this time of year. Traditionally, they were simmered in butter and then served in a creamy velouté sauce, so I have lightened the recipe. (Serves 6)

2 cucumbers
40g/1½oz butter
a pinch of caster sugar

salt and freshly ground black
    pepper

Peel the cucumbers and cut off each end, before slicing in half lengthways. Using a teaspoon, scrape out and discard the seeds. Slice each cucumber into thick sickle moons or cut at a slightly greater angle so that the curve is lengthened.

Just before you are ready to eat, melt the butter in a large frying pan and add the cucumbers with some sugar, salt and lots of black pepper. Keep moving them around the pan until they turn a lovely jade green, then remove and serve immediately as they lose their heat quickly and spoil if kept warm.

STEAMED PUDDINGS

The British feel very strongly about their steamed puddings and it would be impossible to choose from such a number of classics. So I have decided to illustrate the different methods behind cooking them and hope that enthusiasts will search out recipes for such gastronomical wonders as treacle sponge, Snowdon pudding (made with lemon marmalade), sticky date pudding or jam roly-poly. Try Eliza Acton, Jane Grigson, Margaret Costa or Delia Smith to begin with, as they certainly have recipes for the above.

Steamed puddings can be made in any number of different ways, so it is best to begin by dividing them into two categories – crust and batter. The former is usually made in exactly the same way as a savoury pudding, by lining a bowl with suet pastry and filling it with fruit such as spiced apples. The pastry is made with self-raising flour and can be enriched with butter. A crust can also be made with buttered bread instead – so there are no hard and fast rules.

Batter puddings vary even more in their methodology. A Christmas pudding, for example, is made from a stiff suet batter – although this can be lightened by the addition of breadcrumbs. A banana cinnamon pudding, on the other hand, is an example of a light sponge cake batter. These cake batters, which are made with butter (as opposed to suet), can be thickened with ground nuts or breadcrumbs instead of flour to produce moist, light puddings. Even the delicate lemon raspberry surprise pudding is a variation of a steamed pudding, because although it is not turned out, it is gently steamed in water in the oven. Incidentally, if you are ever cooking a large number of small puddings this is the best way of steaming them. Just cover each pudding in the normal fashion, place in a baking tray, half fill with boiling water and tightly cover the whole tray with foil.

LEMON RASPBERRY SURPRISE PUDDING

This is a deliciously tart variation of the classic lemon surprise pudding. Originally the surprise was finding a gooey lemon sauce hidden at the bottom of the dish, which is caused by the sponge mixture separating a little while cooking. These puddings are incredibly quick, need not be covered, and are equally good cold if you can keep them that long. (Makes 8 but perfect for 4 hungry people)

butter for greasing 8 small
    soufflé dishes
	2 large lemons, finely grated
	    and juiced

225g/8oz frozen raspberries	2 eggs, separated

2 tablespoons caster sugar
    or to taste
	55g/2oz self-raising flour,
	    sifted

55g/2oz butter, softened	140ml/¼ pint milk
115g/4oz caster sugar	

Preheat the oven to 190°C/375°F/gas 5 and butter the soufflé dishes. Toss the frozen raspberries in 2 tablespoons or so of caster sugar and place a single layer at the bottom of each dish.

Beat the butter, sugar and lemon rind in a large mixing bowl until pale, then gradually add the egg yolks. (I find it most effective to do this in a food processor, but I always transfer to a bowl for the remaining stages.)

Fold in half the flour, followed by half the milk. Then fold in the remaining flour and follow with the remaining milk, before mixing in the lemon juice. Quickly whisk the egg whites in a separate bowl until they stand in soft peaks and lightly fold them into your mixture, which should look like a runny soufflé mixture.

Spoon this over the raspberries, giving each dish a rap on the work surface to allow the batter to settle evenly and remove any air holes. The puddings will sink back as they cool, so fill to the brim. Place them in a shallow roasting tray and pour in 1cm/½ inch of hot water. Place them in the centre of the preheated oven and bake for 25 minutes. They will rise up and turn golden as they cook, forming a soft sponge which hides a gooey raspberry base.

NÈGRE EN CHEMISE

Nègre en chemise belongs to the breadcrumb and ground nut category of steamed puddings. Its romantic name is probably considered politically incorrect these days, but whatever you call it, it tastes wonderful. This recipe comes from an old, much loved, bespattered copy of *The Robert Carrier Cookery Course*. (Serves 4)

vegetable oil for greasing 4 × 170g/6oz basins	30g/1oz caster sugar
	4 eggs
115g/4oz trimmed white bread	2 egg yolks
	30g/1oz ground almonds
140ml/¼ pint double cream	115g/4oz bitter chocolate, melted
55g/2oz butter, softened	

Preheat the oven to its highest setting.

Place the base of one of the pudding basins on some greaseproof paper and draw 4 circles. Repeat with the top of the basin and cut out all the circles. Lightly oil the pudding basins and line their bottoms with the smaller paper circles. Check that they will fit into a roasting tray and boil up plenty of water.

Soak the bread in the cream for 5 minutes.

Place the butter and sugar in a food processor and beat until pale and fluffy. Add the softened bread and continue to process. Then gradually add the eggs, egg yolks and ground almonds. Finally, beat in the melted chocolate. If you are mixing this by hand the mixture may curdle, but do not worry, as the chocolate will bind it together.

Pour the pudding batter into the prepared basins. Neatly cover with the larger greaseproof paper discs. Take 4 squares of foil and make a pleat down the centre of each before tucking tightly around each pudding. Arrange them in the roasting tray and pour in enough boiling water to come half-way up their sides. Cover the tray with a large sheet of foil and place in the preheated oven to steam for 35 minutes.

The puddings can be served hot or cold. When ready, turn them out and top each one with lots of crème fraîche.

BANANA CINNAMON PUDDING WITH TOFFEE SAUCE

Many steamed puddings contain dried fruit or even diced apples. This is a modern variation. However, you can experiment by adding different fruit and spices if you keep the same balance of ingredients. Although I have given a recipe for toffee sauce, a simple custard (see page 194) could be served with the pudding instead. (Serves 6)

butter for greasing a 850ml/
  1½ pint basin
85g/3oz butter, softened
85g/3oz light Muscovado
  sugar
1 lemon, finely grated and
  juiced
1 teaspoon cinnamon
115g/4oz self-raising flour,
  sifted

2 eggs
2 medium bananas

Toffee sauce
115g/4oz butter
170g/6oz soft light brown
  sugar
140ml/¼ pint double cream
1 teaspoon vanilla essence

Place the base of the pudding basin on some greaseproof paper and draw a circle. Cut this out and lightly butter, along with the inside of the bowl, then line the bottom with the paper. Put in a saucepan and pour in enough water to come half-way up the basin. Remove, cover, and bring the water up to the boil.

Beat the butter with the sugar, lemon zest and cinnamon until fluffy, using a food processor (or by hand or with an electric beater). Then beat in half the flour, followed by 1 egg. Continue to beat, then add the remaining flour, the second egg and the lemon juice.

Peel the bananas and cut into small dice. Quickly fold them into the cinnamon mixture, so that they are evenly distributed. Pour this into the pudding basin and cover with greased, pleated foil. Steam in the covered saucepan for 1½ hours, replenishing the water regularly so that it never becomes too low. Turn out and serve piping hot with the toffee sauce.

While the pudding is cooking, make the sauce by placing all the ingredients in a heavy-bottomed pan over a low heat. Dissolve the sugar by stirring and bring the sauce slowly up to the boil. Once it has thickened and become a dark caramel colour, remove the pan from the heat. It can be stored covered in the refrigerator for 2 weeks at this stage. Just gently reheat when needed.

STEAMED APPLE PUDDING

While many of the batter steamed puddings are surprisingly light, this pudding will insulate you against the dampest cold, which, no doubt, was one reason for the sustained popularity of the steamed pudding in Britain. Try using other fresh fruit through the year, such as apricots, plums or gooseberries. These can be further enriched with a nugget of melted butter if you wish. (Serves 4)

Filling	Eliza Acton's richer
	pudding crust
30g/1oz raisins	115g/4oz self-raising flour
30ml/1 fl oz Calvados	pinch of salt
1 lemon, finely grated	30g/1oz cold butter, cut into
½ lemon, juiced	small dice
2 large Bramley apples	40g/1½oz shredded suet
pinch of ground cinnamon	(beef or vegetarian)
tiny pinch of ground cloves	70ml/2½ fl oz cold
6 tablespoons granulated	water (approx.)
sugar or to taste	

Soak the raisins in the Calvados – overnight if possible. Oil 4 small pudding basins. Place a large covered pan of water on to boil, checking the water level with the pudding basins before you begin.

Place the lemon zest and juice in a large bowl with the raisins and any remaining Calvados. Peel, core and dice the apples. Toss in the lemon juice. Mix in the spices and sugar to taste. Set aside while you make the pastry.

Sift the flour into a bowl with the salt. Add the butter and use your fingertips to quickly crumble it into the flour until it resembles fine breadcrumbs. Stir in the suet and then slowly add the water, mixing with a fork until a rough dough is formed. At this stage turn it out on to a floured surface and lightly knead into a soft ball. Divide the pastry into 6 balls. Thinly roll out the first 3 balls – be careful that they do not tear around the suet crumbs. Line the first 3 basins and cut away any excess folds. Add the trimmings to the remaining pastry, roll out 2 more balls and use the top of the unlined basin to cut out 4 lids. Finally, roll out the last ball and line the last basin. Fill each basin with the apples and cover with the lids. Lightly press these into the lining at the side, then, using a rolling pin, roll over the top to cut the pastry.

Cover with greased, pleated foil and place the basins in the boiling water. Cook for 1 hour, although if your pastry is thin you can get away with 45 minutes. Serve the puddings turned out of their basins with home-made custard (see page 194) or thick double cream.

MARMALADE

Until the seventeenth century the term 'marmalade' referred to a thick sweet fruit paste that was served as a sweetmeat. Originally, only quinces or 'marmelos' were made into 'marmelada', as this was the Spanish and Portuguese name and custom, but the term soon spread to include other fruits such as apples, cherries and apricots. In the seventeenth century, however, travellers such as Sir Kenelm Digby recorded their delight in the bitter orange preserves they found in Italy, and by the mid-eighteenth century orange marmalade began to be made in Scotland from Seville oranges and served for breakfast.

The fashion for eating marmalade gradually spread to Oxford and from there to the rest of the British Isles until it became a virtual institution. Today there are dozens of different marmalade recipes, ranging from jellied to chunky and using every imaginable citrus fruit.

Marmalade is easy to make if you have a few basic items, namely a jam pan, which will allow the marmalade room to bubble up, and either a clip-on thermometer or a refrigerator in which to chill a saucer. Thermometers bring confidence and allow the marmalade to cook for the minimum time, but you can also check whether a jam has set by placing a small blob on to a chilled plate and waiting for a couple of minutes. If a wrinkly skin forms when you lightly push it with your finger, it will set. In between each testing you should remove the pan from the heat. Just return it to the boil if you need to continue cooking.

The best time to buy Seville oranges is at the end of January. Choose fruit that is firm, unblemished and heavy for its size. Seville oranges are perfect for marmalade because their pith and pips contain a high level of pectin, which acts as a setting agent, and they are also highly acidic, which helps to release the pectin.

There are three basic methods for making marmalade, all of which are designed to release as much pectin as possible, but give different textures to the jam. I have given an example of each method, but the lime marmalade has quite a soft set and I would recommend saving some lemon or orange pips to add to the muslin bag for extra pectin. A good source of recipes for marmalade fanatics can be found in Reader's Digest's *The Cookery Year*, from which I have adapted the Dundee and the lime marmalades.

SEVILLE ORANGE MARMALADE

This sweet, almost jelly-like marmalade is based on an 1874 recipe from Frank Cooper, the firm that became famous for their Oxford marmalade. Citric acid is available from most chemists and helps to ensure a good set, as the acidity in Seville oranges varies each year. (Makes 2.7–3.1kg/6–7lb)

1.5kg/3½lb Seville oranges	1 teaspoon citric acid
3.4 litres/6 pints water	2.7kg/6lb granulated sugar

Thoroughly scrub clean the oranges and thinly peel, leaving the pith attached to the fruit.

Place 1.7 litres/3 pints of cold water in a saucepan. Finely slice the peel into shreds, adding it to the water as you go along to prevent it drying out. Stir in the citric acid and bring to the boil. Lower the heat and simmer for 1½ hours or until the peel is tender.

Cut the oranges into small pieces and place them with their pips, pith and pulp into another pan. Add 1.7 litres/3 pints of water, cover tightly, and simmer for 1½ hours to extract all the pectin.

Place a large sieve over a jam pan and strain the fruit pulp in batches to remove the pips and coarse tissue. The pith should look translucent by this stage. Clip the thermometer on to the side of the pan and mix in the softened peel with its juices. Bring to the boil and add the sugar, stirring over a low heat until it has dissolved.

Return the mixture to the boil and remove from the heat when it reaches 106°C/220°F, which should take around 15–20 minutes. As the setting point is reached the temperature should be reduced to prevent air bubbles setting in the finished marmalade. Stir immediately, then leave it to cool and settle for 30 minutes, stirring occasionally to distribute the peel evenly.

Pour into warm dry sterilized jam jars (see page 223) and cover with paper discs. Seal once cool.

LIME OR LEMON MARMALADE

Rose's introduced their lime marmalade in the thirties, and both lemons and limes have become a popular fruit for marmalade-makers. They make especially good additions to some puddings. (Makes 1.4kg/3lb)

| 680g/1½lb limes or lemons | 1.4kg/3lb preserving sugar |
| 1.7 litres/3 pints water | |

Thoroughly wash the fruit, then use a swivel potato peeler to remove the zest, leaving the white pith behind. Finely slice the zest and set aside in a couple of tablespoons of water to keep it soft. Cut the fruit in half and squeeze the juice. Pour into a preserving pan and add the zest.

Using a small sharp knife cut out the remaining pulpy centre of the fruit and finely chop, saving any pips. Add the pulp to the pan with the juice, then roughly chop the pith and tie it into a large square of muslin with any saved lemon pips. Place the bag along with all the water into the pan and bring to the boil over a low heat, before simmering for 2 hours or until the peel is soft and the mixture has reduced by half.

At this stage remove the muslin bag and clip the thermometer on to the side of the pan. Stir in the sugar, and once it has dissolved bring the mixture up to a full boil. Remove from the heat when it reaches 106°C/220°F, which should take around 15–20 minutes. Stir immediately and then leave it to cool and settle for 30 minutes, stirring occasionally to distribute the peel evenly.

Pour into warm dry sterilized jam jars (see page 223) and cover with paper discs. Seal once cool.

DUNDEE MARMALADE

This is my favourite chunky marmalade recipe – it has a gorgeous bitterness that I like in marmalade. It is also very easy to make, as the fruit is cooked whole and softened before being sliced into 'chunky' strips of peel. (Makes 2.3kg/5lb)

680g/1½lb Seville oranges
2 lemons
2 small oranges
1.7litres/3 pints water

1.4kg/3lb granulated sugar
1 heaped teaspoon black
    treacle

Wash all the fruit and place in a large pan with the water. Cover tightly, bring to the boil and simmer gently for 1½ hours, until the fruit is very soft and easily pierced with a knife.

Transfer the fruit to a bowl, leaving the cooking liquid in its pan. Once the fruit is cool enough to handle, slice it in half and with a spoon scrape out the pulp, pips and most of the pith into a bowl. Return these to the pan, making sure that the pulp is thoroughly mashed up. Bring back to the boil and reduce by half before straining into a jam pan.

Meanwhile, finely slice all the fruit skins into thin strips (or chunks) and add to the jam pan. Clip on the thermometer and return to the boil before mixing in the sugar and black treacle. Stir in the sugar until it has completely dissolved, then bring the marmalade up to the boil and allow it to reach setting point – 106°C/220°F – which should take about 10 minutes once the sugar has melted. Skim if necessary and then leave it to cool and settle for 30 minutes, stirring occasionally to distribute the peel evenly.

Pour into warm dry sterilized jam jars (see page 223) and cover with paper discs. Seal once cool.

HOT DRINKS

January is the month when the cold, damp darkness penetrates everywhere, and over the centuries the British have very sensibly developed
hundreds of delicious hot alcoholic drinks to keep these nasty elements
out and all foul infections at bay. Everyone has their own recipe, which
nowadays is usually a variation of a hot toddy using whisky, whereas in
the past brandy or rum were more commonly used as a base.

HOT TODDIES

There are many variations of this one drink. Some use lemon juice, others
lemon slices, while yet others add Angostura bitters instead of spices. My
favourite recipe combines a dessertspoon of honey with the juice of ½ a
lemon in a large tumbler. Add 2–4 cloves (depending on how sore your
throat is, as cloves act as a mild anaesthetic) and a large measure of
whisky. Finally, boil a kettle and top up the glass with scalding water.

Note: Always leave a metal spoon in the glass if you are adding a hot
liquid, to prevent it from cracking.

BUTTERED RUM PUNCH

While I was researching an article on cold cures for *Taste* magazine, I
discovered that all bartenders have their own special cold cures which are
whisked together on demand for sniffling customers. This recipe comes
from Jorge Gonzalez Dominguez, who was then working at the Lanesbor-
ough. It was too good to leave out.

Mix together in a glass tumbler 2 teaspoons of brown sugar with a large
measure of dark rum, a slice of lemon, into which 4 cloves have been
stuck, a cinnamon stick (which you can stir with), and 1½ teaspoons of
butter. Then top up to taste with boiling water and stir until the sugar
and the butter are dissolved.

FEBRUARY

CHILLIES
Avocado, bacon and roasted onion salad
Honey and chilli chicken in lettuce leaves
Guinea-fowl stuffed with spiced apple
Spiced pork dumplings and cabbage

SCALLOPS AND SOLE
Scallops with Chambéry thyme sauce
Fricassée of sole with winter vegetables
Grilled Dover sole with tarragon butter

FAST CHICKEN
Blue cheese rosemary chicken
Seared lemon chicken
Chicken and mushroom ragout

TARTS
Leek, bacon and blue cheese tart
Spinach, red onion and crème fraîche tart
Cardamom pear tarte Tatin
Mrs Beeton's lemon tart

SORBETS
Mango clementine sorbet
Apple and rosewater sorbet
Seville orange sorbet

QUICK PICKLES AND CHUTNEYS
Quick spiced plums
Sweet and sour cucumber
Date chutney

There is a subtle change of emphasis in British cooking in February, as an increasing number of traditional dishes are set aside in favour of lighter recipes. Hearty stews and pies are replaced by salads, tarts and sorbets. Whether this is because the shops are so temptingly full of imported exotics or whether it is because everyone is fed up with winter, it is difficult to know, but the fact is that by St Valentine's Day, much of our food conveys a promise of spring.

The last months of winter have traditionally been a period of scarcity, as supplies slowly diminish. Nothing could be further from the truth these days, as modern cooks are spoilt for choice by the supermarkets, which continue to import new ingredients each year. It is hard to believe that chillies, coriander, ginger and mangoes only became widely available in the eighties. Even peppers and avocados were a novelty in the sixties. As a result, cooks have had to look abroad for ideas on how to adapt these foods into our diet. We have no references for such exotics in our own culinary culture and assimilation takes time and understanding. Older recipes are gradually being updated, such as spiced apple stuffing, while an increasing number of new dishes, like honey chilli chicken, are being introduced.

However, there are many factors that shape a nation's diet. New technology inevitably changes how and what we cook, as do new farming practices. Just as chilled and iced recipes became *de rigueur* in the twenties with the introduction of the domestic fridge, so it could be argued that it is the recent influx of ice-cream machines, and highly influential television series such as Delia Smith's cookery programmes, that have been responsible for the sudden popularity of home-made ices. In much the same way the arrival of the humble battery-fed hen has completely changed our attitude towards chicken. No longer active, battery-fed hens have lost their flavour and their tough muscles, while at the same time becoming a cheap, everyday meat. Cooks no longer want to spend time mid-week gently simmering their fowls, and the new chickens taste better quickly cooked. Modern recipes for marinating, grilling and pan-frying have replaced the old – and a new period of experimentation has begun.

As British cooks have widened their horizons to new cuisines and new ingredients over the last ten years, so they have become less dependent on rigidly following classic French recipes. In other words, in my opinion, modern British cooks are losing some of their old insecurities as to their abilities and becoming far more creative and innovative. This is easily illustrated with modern British tarts. In restaurant or home you are just as likely to be served leek, bacon and blue cheese tart or spinach and red onion tart as quiche lorraine or French onion tart. And domestic cooks are given further incentive to experiment with the increasing availability of superb ingredients such as crème fraîche or red onions in many supermarkets. Even sweet tarts are being reappraised. The currently fashionable tarte Tatin, for example, is now cooked with pears or peaches as well as apples and flavoured with delicate spices and liqueurs.

One area where the British remain vigorously traditional is in their choice of fish. Despite the arrival of swordfish, parrot fish et al, they like their familiar varieties. Prawns, scallops and sole have remained popular for centuries, although our culinary repertoire has broadened considerably. It seems that the more expensive the fish the more simply we will serve it. So whereas prawns may be added to Oriental salads and stir-fries, expensive scallops or sole are more likely to be plainly fried or grilled and served with a piquant butter sauce.

Curiously, although the British have acquired the reputation for enjoying bland food, they have always made incredibly spicy pickles and preserves. Keen pickle-makers can usually find something delectable to pickle every month of the year. February is a particularly good month for dates, as they are often very cheap at this time of year. They make a delicious, Branston-like pickle that will be ready to open and enjoy in the summer.

CHILLIES

Chillies have long been a part of the British diet, although they have also always been regarded with some suspicion:

> Now we have heard how Mrs Sedley had prepared a fine curry for her son, just as he liked it, and in the course of dinner a portion of this dish was offered to Rebecca. 'What is it?' said she, turning an appealing look to Mr Joseph. 'Capital,' said he. His mouth was full of it; his face quite red with the delightful exercise of gobbling. 'Mother, it's as good as my own curries in India.'
>
> 'Oh, I must try some, if it is an Indian dish,' said Miss Rebecca. 'I am sure everything must be good that comes from there.'
>
> 'Give Miss Sharp some curry, my dear,' said Mr Sedley, laughing. Rebecca had never tasted the dish before. 'Do you find it as good as everything else from India?' said Mr Sedley.
>
> 'Oh, excellent!' said Rebecca, who was suffering tortures with the cayenne pepper.
>
> 'Try a chili with it, Miss Sharp,' said Joseph, really interested.
>
> 'A chili,' said Rebecca, gasping. 'O yes!' She thought a chili was something cool, as its name imported, and was served with some. 'How fresh and green they look!' she said, and put one into her mouth. It was hotter than the curry; flesh and blood could bear it no longer. She laid down her fork. 'Water, for Heaven's sake, water,' she cried. (Thackeray, *Vanity Fair*)

However, it seems that British tastes are changing as a large proportion of us enjoy an extraordinary range of spicy flavours from fragrant Thai curries to ultra-hot pizzas. Until recently you could buy only green or red chillies, but now it is possible to buy named varieties such as the mild Anaheim chillies or the ultra-hot habeneros. Inevitably, this influx of new produce will mean further experimentation with recipes.

Used sensibly, chillies heighten other flavours, but they should be treated with caution as two chillies from the same variety can vary widely in heat. This heat comes from a chemical called capsaicin, which is found mainly in the white ribs and seeds. As some people are allergic to capsaicin, care should be taken when cutting chillies. Touch them only with the tips of your fingers, and wash your hands thoroughly afterwards. Avoid touching your eyes for at least an hour after washing your hands.

AVOCADO, BACON AND ROASTED ONION SALAD

Avocado and bacon have accompanied one another in salads for some time, but the addition of home-made chilli sauce adds another dimension to this salad. The roasted onions and bacon can be eaten warm or at room temperature. (Serves 4)

1 red pepper, seeded and quartered	225g/8oz smoked back bacon, diced into 1cm/½ inch squares
1 red chilli	
1 lime, juiced	3 tablespoons vegetable oil
1 tablespoon crème fraîche	½ curly endive
	½ radicchio
salt and freshly ground black pepper	2 tablespoons balsamic vinegar
2 medium red onions, halved	6 tablespoons olive oil
1 tablespoon olive oil	2 ripe avocados

Preheat the oven to 180°C/350°F/gas 4.

Prepare the chilli sauce by placing the pepper quarters skin side up under a hot grill with the whole chilli. Grill until the skins begin to blister, turning the chilli so that it is evenly grilled. Place in a covered bowl and leave until they are cool enough to handle.

Peel the peppers and place them in a food processor. Gently peel the chilli before pulling away its stalk and removing the seeds with a knife. Depending on the heat of the chilli, add half or all of it to the pepper quarters and process to a purée. Add the lime juice, fold in the crème fraîche, and season to taste.

Toss the prepared onions in 1 tablespoon of olive oil, season and bake in the preheated oven for 30 minutes until they are soft and lightly caramelized. When the onions are ready, fry the bacon dice in the vegetable oil until crispy. Drain on kitchen paper and place in the bottom of a large mixing bowl with the salad leaves. Whisk together the balsamic vinegar and olive oil and season to taste.

Toss the leaves and bacon in half the dressing and divide between the 4 plates. Halve, stone and peel the avocados before cutting into long slices. Place these in the mixing bowl and gently coat with the remaining vinaigrette. Arrange them prettily among the leaves with the red onion halves. Drizzle with the chilli sauce and serve.

HONEY AND CHILLI CHICKEN IN LETTUCE LEAVES

Serve as a new-wave spicy starter or as a light main course. (Serves 4)

4 skinned and boned chicken breasts	4 tablespoons vegetable oil
1 small egg white	115g/4oz salted cashew nuts
1 tablespoon cornflour	12 tiny dried red chillies
2 cloves garlic, crushed	12 spring onions, cut into chunks
2 tablespoons runny honey	8 cup-shaped radicchio or iceberg lettuce leaves
2 tablespoons rice vinegar	
2 tablespoons soy sauce	

Cut the chicken into large chunks. Beat the egg white with the cornflour and then mix in the chicken with half the garlic. Cover and chill until needed.

Stir the honey into the vinegar and soy sauce. Set aside.

When ready to serve, heat a large non-stick frying pan. Add 3 table-spoons vegetable oil and heat until smoking. Add the chicken in 2 batches, stirring all the time, and remove as soon as the meat has coloured.

Wipe the pan clean, add a further 1–2 tablespoons of oil and heat until very hot. Quickly stir-fry the cashew nuts until they begin to colour and then remove with a slotted spoon. Add the chillies with the remaining garlic and the spring onions. Rapidly stir-fry, then return the nuts and chicken to the pan before stirring in the honey soy mixture. Bring the sauce up to the boil, let it reduce a little, and spoon into the lettuce leaves, allowing 2 per person.

GUINEA-FOWL STUFFED WITH SPICED APPLE

This is a modern interpretation of an old recipe, where to save time the bird is portioned and stuffed under the skin. The stuffing itself has chillies, lime and coriander instead of lemon zest and parsley and complements the delicate flavour of the guinea-fowl. (Serves 4)

1 guinea-fowl	2 tart apples, peeled, cored
2 tablespoons olive oil	and roughly grated
1 fat shallot, finely diced	1 tablespoon finely chopped
1 clove garlic, crushed	coriander
1 red chilli, seeded and	salt and freshly ground black
finely diced	pepper
1 lime, finely grated and	1 tablespoon vegetable oil
juiced	

Prepare the guinea-fowl by cutting around each thigh socket and removing its legs. Cut each leg in half at the drumstick joint and then, following the bone, run your knife down the length of each leg and thigh. Keeping the knife close to the first thigh bone, gently cut the flesh away from it until you can ease the bone out. Repeat with the remaining 3 pieces.

Now turn your attention to the bird and cut down one side of the breast bone, working your way around the rib cage and down to the wing socket. Each breast should come away with the wing attached. Remove this. Then, ensuring that the skin is well stretched over the meat, cut each breast in half, at a slight angle so that the 2 halves are roughly the same size. It is important to keep as much of the skin attached as possible, as you are going to push the stuffing under the skin.

Heat the oil in a small frying pan and gently fry the shallot, garlic and chilli until soft, then thoroughly mix with the lime zest and juice, grated apple, coriander and seasoning.

Carefully loosen a small piece of skin on one of the guinea-fowl portions and stuff the apple mixture under the skin. Push it down so that it covers the meat evenly and then repeat with the remaining pieces. The meat can be covered and refrigerated until needed.

Twenty minutes before you wish to cook, turn the grill on to its highest setting. At the same time remove the guinea-fowl from the refrigerator to allow it to come back to room temperature. Season and very lightly oil it. Place it skin side up under the grill and cook for 7 minutes or until the skin is bubbling and turning crispy. Then turn over and cook for another 7 minutes or so. Return it skin side up and cook for another couple of minutes just to crisp up the skin. Serve immediately.

SPICED PORK DUMPLINGS AND CABBAGE

Another example of traditional ingredients being turned around to create a new dish. Pork and cabbage have been cooked together for centuries, but by adapting Eastern flavourings this old partnership is rejuvenated. Serve with steamed rice and sweet and sour cucumber (see page 65) (Serves 3)

Pork dumplings
4 spring onions, roughly chopped
2 cloves garlic, roughly chopped
½ teaspoon roughly chopped root ginger
1 green chilli, seeded and roughly chopped
1 small carrot, roughly diced
4–6 button mushrooms, trimmed and roughly diced
340g/12oz minced pork
2 tablespoons soy sauce
1 tablespoon mirin
1 lemon, finely grated
3 tablespoons vegetable oil

Broth
1 dessertspoon cornflour
7 tablespoons cold water
3 tablespoons soy sauce
3 tablespoons sake
3 tablespoons mirin
2 tablespoons vegetable oil
2 cloves garlic, crushed
1–2 green chillies, seeded and finely diced
½ small green cabbage, cored and thickly sliced

Place the spring onions, garlic, ginger, chilli, carrot and mushrooms in a food processor and give a few quick whizzes until they are finely chopped. Otherwise finely chop by hand. Mix in the minced pork, soy sauce, mirin and lemon zest – the mixture will be a little sloppy.

Heat the oil in a large frying pan and fry a small patty of pork to test its seasoning. Add more soy, mirin or chilli according to taste. Once you are happy, shape the meat into 30 small balls. Fry them briskly, turning regularly so that they colour evenly, and remove to a bowl.

Mix together the cornflour, water, soy sauce, sake and mirin.

Wipe out the pan and then heat a further 2 tablespoons of oil. Once the oil is smoking, quickly stir-fry the garlic and chilli for 10 seconds, before returning the pork balls to the pan. Continue to fry for 30 seconds. Add the cabbage, cook for a further 30 seconds, then add the cornflour mixture. Allow this to come up to the boil and bubble vigorously for 2 minutes, so that the sauce thickens slightly and the pork is cooked through. Remove and serve immediately.

SCALLOPS AND SOLE

The cold seas around Britain are rich in sweet-flavoured, slow-growing crustacea and fish. Sadly, much of this is exported to the discerning Europeans. Despite this, it is possible to buy excellent fish in Britain – provided you have a good fishmonger. The unpredictable nature of fishing makes fish a harder product to sell in the supermarkets, and much of their stock has been previously frozen. While this is acceptable with prawns, it gives a lower quality for other items such as scallops and Dover sole.

The best scallops are collected by divers. Dredging indiscriminately gathers up the scallops with sand and other small sea creatures, damaging their delicate shells and filling them with silt. Most frozen scallops are dredged. We have two types of native scallops – the King or Great scallop and the Queen scallop. The latter are much smaller (and cheaper) and reputedly have a sweeter flavour. In either case they are very easy to cook, provided you follow two simple rules: if you are frying or grilling them, sear over a very high heat until just cooked. However, if you are poaching scallops, simmer them gently over a low heat until just cooked but still meltingly tender.

Dover sole is adored by the British, who advocate serving it plainly grilled above all other methods of cookery. Even the French – so often revered by us in culinary matters – are denigrated for ruining the aristocratic Dover sole with complicated sauces and stuffings. That being said, we have a long history of adding its firm flesh to simple fricassées. This is still a useful way of extending Dover sole, and a delicately flavoured sauce can enhance its taste.

SCALLOPS WITH CHAMBÉRY THYME SAUCE

It is worth the expense of buying scallops for just a few mouthfuls of seared, sweet succulence. Happily, there are now plans to develop scallop beds off the coast of Scotland, so hopefully this delicious bivalve will become more widely available and perhaps cheaper. (Serves 4)

1 shallot, finely diced	salt and freshly ground black
1 large sprig thyme	pepper
285ml½ pint Chambéry or a	20 scallops, cleaned
similar dry vermouth	1 tablespoon lemon juice
3 tablespoons double	1 tablespoon finely chopped
cream	chervil
225g/8oz cold butter, diced	pinch of finely chopped
3 tablespoons olive oil	thyme

Begin by making the sauce. Place the shallot, thyme sprig and Chambéry in a small non-corrosive saucepan and boil vigorously until the liquid has reduced down to 3 tablespoons. Remove the thyme.

Add the double cream and return to the boil, then reduce the heat to low and gradually whisk in the butter. Do not let the sauce boil at this stage. If you have a thermos flask, rinse it with some hot water then pour in the hot sauce and seal. Otherwise, set your saucepan in a tray of hot but not boiling water.

Heat a non-stick frying pan until very hot. Add the oil and while it is heating season the scallops. Sear them in batches over a high heat. They should become almost caramelized on the outside, while remaining sweetly tender inside. Quickly add the lemon juice and toss the scallops in this before serving.

Stir the finely chopped herbs into the butter sauce and pour over the scallops.

FRICASSÉE OF SOLE WITH WINTER VEGETABLES

The term fricassée has become interchangeable with ragout and frequently means different things to different cooks. In the seventeenth century it referred to meats that had been boiled together in a broth, but by the eighteenth century it could be applied to fish, chicken or even hard-boiled eggs. These were usually initially fried in butter before being cooked in a thickened sauce. Over the centuries everything from asparagus to sweet-breads was fricasséed. Some were dainty messes, exquisitely flavoured with cream, lemon, mace or nutmeg, while others were unpleasant, floury dishes. The British were famed for their predilection for floury sauces, for, as Heinrich Heine wrote in his *English Fragments*: 'Heaven preserve any Christian man from their sauces, which consist either of one-third flour and two-thirds butter, or according to the taste of the cook, one third butter and two-thirds flour.' This is a delicate updated version, without flour, that is good with any firm-textured white fish. If wished the sole need not be fried before being added to the sauce, in which case leave it to simmer for a few minutes before adding the watercress. (Serves 3)

2 large Dover sole, skinned and filleted (save the skin and bones)	1 sprig parsley
	2 black peppercorns
	Fricassée
Stock	3 tablespoons olive oil
285ml/½ pint white wine	1 leek, finely sliced
1 small onion, studded with a clove	1 small stick celery, finely sliced
1 stick celery, roughly sliced	170ml/6 fl oz double cream
½ leek, the white part only, roughly sliced	115g/4oz watercress (discard the tough stems)
1 bay leaf	fresh nutmeg

The stock can be made the day before if wished. If you are preparing the fish yourself, begin by skinning the fish as described in the following recipe. Then, using a sharp flexible knife, run the blade down the length of the sole's backbone, before slowly working around the bump of backbone and down along the line of the flat bones until you reach the fins. If you stick to the bones and use small strokes with your knife the fillet will just fall away. Repeat with the other side before turning the fish over.

Cut the 8 fillets into thick strips or 'gougons'. Cover and chill until needed.

Rinse the fish trimmings under cold running water. Break up the bones and place them in a non-corrosive saucepan with the white wine, 565ml/1 pint of cold water, the vegetables, herbs and peppercorns. Bring this slowly to the boil, but as soon as it begins to bubble, lower the heat and simmer gently for 30 minutes. Skim off any scum that is thrown up while the stock is cooking. Strain the stock into a clean saucepan and boil vigorously until it is reduced to 140ml/¼ pint. Cover and chill until needed.

When ready to cook, heat the oil in a non-stick frying pan. Lightly season the fish and fry the gougons until they are just cooked. Remove with a slotted spoon.

Add the sliced leek and celery to the pan and fry gently for 2 minutes. Pour in the reduced stock and bring to the boil before whisking in the cream. Return to the boil and allow the cream to reduce and thicken a little before returning the fish to the pan with the watercress. Adjust the seasoning to taste and simmer for 1 minute. Just before serving, lightly grate a small amount of nutmeg over the pan. Stir this in and serve.

GRILLED DOVER SOLE WITH TARRAGON BUTTER

(Serves 4)

1 tablespoon finely chopped parsley	2 teaspoons tarragon or champagne vinegar
2 tablespoons finely chopped chives	salt and freshly ground black pepper
2 tablespoons finely chopped tarragon	4 Dover sole, 170–225g/ 6–8oz each
115g/4oz butter, at room temperature	2 tablespoons olive oil

Begin by beating the herbs into the butter. Add the vinegar, and season to taste. Roughly shape the butter into a sausage on some wet greaseproof paper and roll it into a smooth cylinder. Chill until needed. Alternatively, wrap in clingfilm and twist both ends until the butter is pushed into a smooth sausage.

Preheat the grill to its highest setting and brush the grid with oil to help prevent the fish from sticking.

Do not worry if the fish is unskinned – it is very easy to remove. Cut a nick at the tail end, gently insert the handle of a teaspoon under the skin, and lift it up. Then, using a cloth to protect your hands and give you extra grip, pull the skin very hard towards the head of the fish. It will peel off. Repeat with the other side. The fish should then be trimmed around the edges and the tail snipped. Traditionally, the head is left on, but I prefer to remove it, rather than be stared at by grilled eyes.

Brush all the fish with olive oil (or clarified butter if you wish). Lightly season and place under the grill. Cook each side for 4–5 minutes.

Just before you remove the fish from the grill, cut the herb butter into neat discs and place on each sole. As soon as it begins to melt, remove the fish and serve.

FAST CHICKEN

Before the era of the battery hen, chickens were a full-flavoured luxury food that needed gentle cooking to make it tender. The arrival of the cheap, sedentary battery hen changed our diet for ever. The market was flooded with tasteless, oven-ready birds and carefully portioned packs of tender chicken thighs, legs, breasts and fillets. This new form of cheap meat demanded new methods of cooking and new recipes to enhance its flavour and succulence.

Stews and ragouts were updated by shortening the cooking times and simplifying the sauces. The old-fashioned English chicken cutlet – fried and crumbed – was given succulence and flavour by the addition of a layer of cream and mustard between the chicken and breadcrumbs. At the same time recipes were sought from China, the Middle East, India and the Mediterranean. These ideas are still in the process of being subverted into the British culinary repertoire, but it has become commonplace for many families to stir-fry or curry their chicken. In the same way cooks have begun to experiment with different marinades and stuffings for pan-fried and grilled chicken pieces.

As the market has grown, so the consumer is being offered more and more choice from corn-fed, free range, organic and specialist breeds of chicken. Some of these varieties are no longer cheap, but ultimately it is up to the customer to decide on which they prefer – happy, flavoursome chickens or their cheaper, battery-fed cousins.

BLUE CHEESE ROSEMARY CHICKEN

With the increasing use of chicken pieces, it is important to find new ways of adding succulence and flavour to them. A popular method is to place a stuffing, such as cheese, under the skin. As the chicken cooks this will melt, basting and flavouring the meat as it does so. (Serves 4)

115g/4oz Dolcelatte cheese, mashed	4 chicken breasts or thighs, boned but with skin left
large pinch of finely chopped rosemary	on
salt and freshly ground black pepper	1 tablespoon olive oil

Mash the cheese with the rosemary and a little black pepper. Loosen the skin on one side of each chicken breast or thigh and push a quarter of the cheese under it, pressing on the skin to spread the cheese out over the meat. Cover and chill until needed.

Preheat the grill to its highest setting. Place a heavy cast-iron plate under the grill to heat through. Season the chicken and lightly rub with olive oil before placing on the plate and grilling for 7 minutes on each side. Serve with a salad and chips or warm crisps.

SEARED LEMON CHICKEN

Quick marinades are the perfect solution for preventing chicken from becoming boring. This recipe has Middle Eastern influences and makes an excellent telly supper dish. (Serves 2)

2 chicken breasts, boned and skinned	*Garnish*
2 cloves garlic, crushed	Greek yoghurt
1 small lemon, finely grated and juiced	salt and freshly ground black pepper
2 tablespoons Greek yoghurt	2 little gem lettuces
salt and freshly ground black pepper	6 spring onions, roughly sliced
1 tablespoon olive oil	cucumber or tomato slices
	4 large or 6 small pitta breads

Preheat the grill to its highest setting.

Cut the chicken into large chunks and mix in a small bowl with the garlic, lemon zest and juice, yoghurt and seasoning. Marinate for 30 minutes.

Meanwhile, prepare the remaining ingredients. Thin some yoghurt to a pouring consistency with a little cold water and season to taste with salt and pepper. Assemble all the salad ingredients.

When you are ready to serve, sear the chicken in a tablespoon of olive oil in a very hot non-stick frying pan. As soon as one side is sealed, turn over and cook until the meat is flecked golden. At the same time place the pitta bread under the grill and turn once it is warm.

Slit open the warm pitta bread and stuff with some lettuce leaves, spring onions, cucumber or tomatoes and hot chicken. Drizzle with the yoghurt and eat immediately.

CHICKEN AND MUSHROOM RAGOUT

The art of making a modern chicken ragout lies in lightly cooking your fowl. The chicken pieces are quickly sealed over a high heat and then removed until the dish is assembled and virtually ready to eat. At this stage they are returned to the pan and gently simmered for a few minutes, so that they stay tender and succulent. Overcooking a modern chicken will turn its flesh firstly to rubber and then to shreds. (Serves 4)

4 boned and skinned
 chicken breasts, roughly
 diced
3 tablespoons seasoned
 plain flour
3 tablespoons olive oil
1 small onion, finely diced
2 cloves garlic, crushed
140g/5oz mixed mushrooms
 (shiitake, oyster and
 brown cap)
115ml/4 fl oz dry white
 wine

2 strips lemon peel, without
 any white pith
115ml/4 fl oz chicken stock
285ml/½ pint double cream
1 tablespoon finely chopped
 parsley
½ tablespoon mixed finely
 chopped thyme and
 chervil
salt and freshly ground black
 pepper

Lightly coat the chicken cubes with the flour. Heat the oil in a large frying pan and quickly sear the chicken in batches. Set aside.

Add the onion and garlic to the pan, loosening any chicken debris and adding a little more olive oil if necessary. Gently fry until soft.

Wipe the mushrooms clean and remove the stems of the shiitake and oyster mushrooms. Rip them into large chunks. Trim the brown caps (or button mushrooms) and thickly slice. Add all the mushrooms to the softened onion and fry briskly. As soon as they are beginning to soften and release their juices, add the white wine, lemon peel and chicken stock. Reduce by half and then add the cream. Allow it to reduce and thicken a little before returning the chicken to the pan.

Cook for a further 3 minutes, then remove the lemon peel and add the herbs and seasoning.

Note: Ragout has become another name for a stew. In the early eighteenth century a ragoo was considered to be a highly seasoned dish that was cooked in the French manner.

TARTS

The ubiquitous watery quiche was served for years at dreadful parties and is still obtainable in many restaurants that specialize in serving lunch to the office worker. The reason that this cheap creation is so dank is that the custard is made with whole eggs and milk (rather than egg yolks and cream) and processed rubbery cheese. To make matters worse, it is usually baked in a thick, sweet-tasting pastry. As to the filling – whoever thought of putting broccoli, sweetcorn and carrots into tarts? A true tart should have a thin crisp shell of pastry and be filled with harmonious ingredients that are baked in a creamy custard flavoured with wonderful cheeses.

Everyone has a different way of making pastry and if your method works, stick to it. I usually make my shortcrust pastry when I need it and instead of allowing it to rest for 30 minutes I immediately roll it out. I then leave it to chill while I prepare the other ingredients. I always bake my tarts blind, as I find that this gives a crisper pastry.

LEEK, BACON AND BLUE CHEESE TART

Of the modern mode; the blue cheese cuts the sweetness of the leeks and gives the tart a lovely rounded flavour. (Serves 4)

225g/8oz shortcrust pastry (see page 327)	85g/3oz Dolcelatte or other blue cheese
225g/8oz smoky back bacon	1 whole egg
2 tablespoons olive oil	1 egg yolk
3 leeks, finely sliced	170ml/6 fl oz double cream
	salt and freshly ground black pepper

Preheat the oven to 220°C/425°F/gas 7.

Roll out the pastry on a lightly floured surface into a 30cm/12 inch circle and loosely wrap around the rolling pin. Hold the pin over a 23cm/9 inch tart dish and carefully unroll, gently pressing the pastry into place. Prick the bottom with a fork, press some aluminium foil or greaseproof paper into the middle, and fill with rice or old dried beans before chilling for 30 minutes.

Place the tart in the centre of the preheated oven and bake blind for 15 minutes. Remove the covering and continue to bake for another 5–10 minutes, until the pastry has become dry but not coloured and has lost that raw sweaty look. As soon as you have removed the pastry case reduce the oven temperature to 200°C/400°F/gas 6.

While the pastry is cooking, remove the fat from the bacon and cut into small cubes. Heat the oil in a large frying pan and gently fry the bacon for 5 minutes. Meanwhile, thoroughly wash the sliced leeks and add to the bacon. Continue to cook for another 4 minutes or until just soft, then remove from the heat.

Purée the cheese in a food processor with the egg and egg yolk. Alternatively, vigorously mash the cheese by hand before beating in the eggs. Stir in the cream and season to taste. Be careful that you do not over-salt, as both the cheese and the bacon are quite salty.

When the tart case has cooled a little, fill with the bacon mixture and pour in the blue cheese custard, making sure that it seeps through all the leeks. Return to the oven and continue to bake for a further 25 minutes or until the filling puffs up and turns golden brown.

SPINACH, RED ONION AND CRÈME FRAÎCHE TART

Red onions have a sweeter flavour than ordinary onions, but if you cannot find them don't worry – just use white onions but cook them until they are meltingly soft and sweet. However, you must use fresh spinach, for example the kind that is sold ready-washed in pillow packets, as its flavour is so much better than frozen. (Serves 4)

225g/8oz shortcrust pastry (see page 327)	1 egg yolk
1 large red onion, finely diced	200ml/7 fl oz crème fraîche
2 tablespoons olive oil	salt and freshly ground black pepper
185g/6½oz cleaned spinach	2 tablespoons finely grated Parmesan cheese
1 whole egg	

Preheat the oven to 220°C/425°F/gas 7.

Roll out the pastry on a lightly floured surface into a 30cm/12 inch circle and loosely wrap around the rolling pin. Hold the pin over a 23cm/9 inch tart dish and carefully unroll, gently pressing the pastry into place. Prick the bottom with a fork, press some aluminium foil or greaseproof paper into the middle, and fill with rice or old dried beans before chilling for 30 minutes.

Place the tart in the centre of the preheated oven and bake blind for 15 minutes. Remove the covering and continue to bake for another 5–10 minutes, until the pastry has become dry but not coloured and has lost that raw sweaty look. As soon as you have removed the pastry case reduce the oven temperature to 200°C/400°F/gas 6.

Gently fry the onion in the oil until soft, then set aside. Bring a pan of salted water to the boil and add the spinach. As soon as it changes colour remove, drain, and cool under running cold water. Squeeze out as much liquid as you can, then roughly chop the spinach and add to the onions.

Mix together the egg, egg yolk, crème fraîche and seasoning. Stir the onions and spinach into the custard and pour into the cooled pastry case. Sprinkle with the cheese and return to the oven. Bake for a further 25 minutes or until golden and slightly risen.

CARDAMOM PEAR TARTE TATIN

The tarte Tatin became very fashionable in the eighties, popularized by the likes of the Roux brothers and Marco Pierre White. Initially made with apples, chefs soon began to experiment with other fruits such as pears and peaches. The subtle addition of ground spices can add a lovely flavour to these gorgeous puddings.

There are only 2 things you need to make a tarte Tatin – one is a cast-iron omelette pan and the other is confidence. I avoided making them for years, fearing they would not caramelize or that they would get stuck in the pan or, worse still, completely collapse. The reality is that it does not matter what the tart does, it will still taste absolutely delicious, and hundreds of chefs have had to carefully unstick a pear or apple segment from the pan and neatly re-arrange the tart, mopping up excess juice, so fear not. (Serves 2–4, depending on greed)

Use a 18cm/7 inch cast-
    iron omelette pan
225g/8oz puff pastry (see
    page 329)
6 green cardamom pods
55g/2oz granulated sugar

55g/2oz butter, softened
2 tablespoons Poire William
    liqueur (optional)
1 tablespoon lemon juice
3–4 ripe pears

Preheat the oven to 220°C/425°F/gas 7.

Roll out the pastry on a lightly floured surface. Then, using a plate that is slightly larger than your pan as a template, cut out a circle of pastry, lightly prick with a fork, and chill while you prepare the remaining ingredients.

Lightly crush the cardamoms so that you can remove the black seeds. Discard the green husks and then, using either a pestle and mortar or a rolling pin, roughly crush the seeds. Mix half of them with the sugar and set the remaining half aside. Using your fingers, press the butter on to the base of your frying pan until it coats it evenly. Evenly sprinkle the sugar over the butter and set aside.

Place the Poire William and lemon juice in a mixing bowl. If you are not using any alcohol, add a little extra lemon juice to help prevent the fruit from discolouring. Peel 1 pear at a time, cutting it into quarters and removing the seeds and tough core. Thoroughly coat in the lemon juice and then repeat with the remaining fruit.

Tightly pack the pears in a circle in the frying pan, ensuring that their more attractive rounded sides are pressed lightly into the sugar. Fill the centre with the roundest pear and then place on a medium high heat. The pears will shrink slightly, so do not be afraid to add another slice or two as they cook.

Stand over the pan at this stage, moving it around slightly if one area is browning faster than another. As soon as the sugar has caramelized, scatter with the remaining cardamom seeds and remove from the heat. Quickly press the pastry circle on to the pears, tucking the edges down the side of the pan, then place in the centre of the oven.

Bake in the preheated oven for 25 minutes or until the pastry is a beautiful golden colour and well risen. Do not worry if some of the caramelized juices bubble out. Remove from the oven and allow to sit for 5 minutes. Then take a slightly larger plate, press against the pastry and invert the pan, giving a good shake. The tart should slip out, juices and all. Serve hot with lots of thick double cream.

MRS BEETON'S LEMON TART

Lemon tart became one of the favoured restaurant puddings of the late eighties. It has since slipped back from this prime position, but is still much loved by pudding eaters. As it is such a classic among sweet tarts I have decided to include an earlier recipe that Jane Grigson credits in *Good Things* to Mrs Beeton. I usually make it with a plain shortcrust pastry, as the filling is very rich (Serves 4)

225g/8oz shortcrust pastry (see page 327)	1½ tablespoons double cream
1 lemon, finely grated and juiced	2 egg yolks
55g/2oz caster sugar	30g/1oz ground almonds
	55g/2oz melted butter

Preheat the oven to 200°C/400°F/gas 6.

Roll out the pastry and line a 23cm/9 inch tart dish. Prick the bottom with a fork, line with weighted paper, and chill for 30 minutes.

Place the tart in the centre of the preheated oven and bake for 15 minutes. Remove the covering and continue to bake for another 5–10 minutes, until the pastry has become dry but not coloured and has lost that raw sweaty look. Reduce the oven temperature to 170°C/325°F/gas 3.

Beat together all the remaining ingredients until smooth. Pour them into the pastry case and bake in the centre of the oven for 35 minutes, until speckled brown and slightly risen. Serve warm or cold with cream.

SORBETS

Sorbets are very easy to make, even without an ice-cream machine. In their most basic form they are a mixture of fruit juice, sugar and water. There are hundreds of permutations and perfectionists may follow these, but for the happy-go-lucky cook just remember that the more alcohol you add the less firmly your sorbet will set. If you are making it by hand, pour the chilled liquid into a shallow plastic container, cover and place in the fast freeze compartment of your freezer. Every 30–40 minutes, mash up the ice crystals with a fork until the mixture has set into a sorbet. If it freezes too hard, allow it to soften a little in the fridge.

There are many different kinds of ice-cream makers on the market, but the best are those that freeze and churn at the same time. The mixture can be made in advance, chilled and then left to churn for about 30 minutes before being stored in the freezer. The tradition of serving ices in winter as well as summer originated in the nineteenth century, when they were served as part of the evening refreshments at balls. It still feels very luxurious to eat a delicately flavoured ice inside, while it is cold and frosty outside.

MANGO CLEMENTINE SORBET

Minimum effort for maximum tropical effect. (Serves 4)

285ml/½ pint freshly squeezed clementine juice	1 lime, juiced 285ml/½ pint mango juice icing sugar

Mix together the clementine, lime and mango juice. Adjust the sweetness with icing sugar to taste. Most mango juice is sold sweetened, so it is very important to taste the mixture before you add any icing sugar. Cover and chill.

Churn in the normal manner in your ice-cream maker. Transfer to the freezer and leave to firm up for a further hour.

APPLE AND ROSEWATER SORBET

The addition of rosewater to this recipe gives it a delicious fragrance. Rosewater can be bought from the pharmacy in a chemist or from some supermarkets. (Serves 4)

2 strips lemon peel	455g/1lb dessert apples such
1 lemon, juiced	as Cox's
285ml/½ pint water	115g/4oz granulated sugar
	2 tablespoons rosewater

Put the lemon peel, lemon juice and water in a non-corrosive pan. Peel and core the apples and cut into small cubes. Place in the pan, cover and simmer gently until the apples have disintegrated. Add the sugar to taste, stirring it into the warm apples. Remove the peel and purée the mixture. Cover and chill.

Flavour the cold apple purée with rosewater and measure the mixture. Add enough cold water to bring it up to 565ml/1 pint and churn in the normal manner in your ice-cream maker. Transfer to the freezer and leave to firm up for a further hour.

Note: It is best to eat this recipe within 1–2 days of making, as the flavour of the rosewater lessens in time.

SEVILLE ORANGE SORBET

I have adapted this recipe from *Ices*, a wonderful book for ice-cream lovers by Caroline Liddell and Robin Weir. It has an incredibly intense flavour. (Serves 6)

255g/9oz granulated sugar	1 lemon, juiced
285ml/½ pint hot water	2 tablespoons Cointreau
6 Seville oranges	

Place the sugar and hot water in a saucepan over a low heat and stir until the sugar has dissolved. Leave to cool.

Wash the oranges and finely zest or grate 2 of them. Juice all 6 oranges and add to the sugar syrup along with the orange zest, lemon juice and Cointreau. Measure this and, if necessary, add enough cold water to bring it up to 740ml/26 fl oz. Cover and chill.

Churn the cold orange syrup in the normal manner in your ice-cream maker. Transfer to the freezer and leave to firm up for a further hour.

QUICK PICKLES AND CHUTNEYS

The British are still a nation of pickle-eaters – everything from onions to dates is put into jars with exotic spices, sugar and vinegar and then eaten with great relish for the rest of the year. However, for many there seems to be increasingly less time to make up these tart preserves. So I have included two quick recipes that should give immediate gratification to pickle addicts. The sweet and sour cucumber is not a true pickle since it is for immediate consumption, but it will satisfy those cravings for a sweet yet acid relish.

QUICK SPICED PLUMS

This recipe can be applied to other fruits, such as apples or pears – just alter the spices to your taste. Try it with roast duck or an apple version with pork. The flavours will develop overnight, but if stored in a sterilized container in the fridge, this pickle will last for at least 6 months. (Serves 4)

225g/8oz granulated sugar	6 black peppercorns
115ml/4fl oz water	1 strip lemon peel
1 stick cinnamon	455g/1lb ripe plums
3 star anise	3 tablespoons white wine
1 red or green chilli	vinegar
3 cloves	

Place the sugar in a non-corrosive saucepan with the water, spices and lemon peel, and dissolve over a low heat. Bring to the boil and bubble vigorously for 3 minutes.

Meanwhile, wash, stone and quarter the plums. Add the plums to the boiling syrup and simmer gently for 10 minutes. Stir in the vinegar, transfer hot to a clean container, and leave to cool. Cover and chill.

SWEET AND SOUR CUCUMBER

This quick pickle is very addictive. It comes from Deh-Ta Hsiung's *The Home Book of Chinese Cookery* and is one of my favourite recipes. (Serves 4)

1 cucumber, peeled	2 tablespoons rice vinegar
salt	3 tablespoons caster sugar

Cut the cucumber in half lengthways and slice thinly. Toss in plenty of salt and leave for 5–10 minutes. Discard the bitter juices, but do not rinse the cucumber. Add the vinegar and sugar, mix well and eat immediately.

DATE CHUTNEY

This lovely recipe comes from Margaret Costa's *Four Seasons Cookery Book*. Use fresh as opposed to dried dates for this recipe. They are usually cheap and plentiful in the shops and can be stoned in a matter of minutes. Never use a food processor to finely dice the ingredients, as they will turn to sticky mush. Either chop by hand or push through a mincer.

905g/2lb stoned fresh dates	565ml/1 pint white wine vinegar
455g/1lb finely diced onions	30g/1oz allspice berries
55g/2oz salt	55g/2oz mustard seeds
1 teaspoon ground ginger	455g/1lb granulated sugar
½ teaspoon cayenne pepper	

Finely chop the dates and place in a non-corrosive preserving pan with the onions, salt, ginger, cayenne pepper and one-third of the vinegar. Tie the allspice berries and mustard seeds in a piece of muslin and add. Gently simmer this mixture until thick.

In a separate pan dissolve the sugar and remaining vinegar. Add to the chutney and continue to simmer until thick. Meanwhile, wash your jam jars in hot soapy water, then rinse thoroughly and dry in a very low oven to sterilize them. (Alternatively, use them hot but dry from the dishwasher.) Once the chutney is ready, pot while piping hot and place a wax disc on top. Allow to cool, then tightly seal. Label and date.

MARCH

PANCAKES
Lemon and sugar pancakes
Crêpes Suzette
Blinis and caviar
Buttermilk griddlecakes with honey bananas

SPRING GREENS
Sea kale with browned butter
Green cabbage with bacon
Blanched curly kale
Stir-fried purple sprouting broccoli

WILD SALMON
Lime-cured salmon
Salmon filo parcels
Grilled salmon fillets with cucumber vinaigrette

RABBIT
Rabbit fricassée
Grilled rabbit with chive mustard butter
Dorset fried rabbit and onions

CREAMS AND WHIPS
Syllabub
Apple snow
Bavarois
Burnt cream

JELLIES
Rhubarb jelly
Lemon gin jelly
Plum jelly

March is a difficult month for modern cooks. Such is our capacity to enjoy new foods that it irks us to suffer the same produce for too long, and March is just such a month. Nothing seems to change. Only the superabundance of greens hints that spring food will soon arrive. It is a period that demands ingenuity and imagination to liven up daily meals.

Of course, this is not a problem with puddings – the British thrive on creating delicious messes out of nothing. Our love of creams, whips and jellies stretches back over the centuries and the principles behind them have changed little since the sixteenth century. Recipes for apple snow, syllabub and thickened cream date back to this period and have never gone out of fashion. Jellies and whips, though, have suffered from the instant packet market, which has wooed many cooks away from the delights of a home-made jelly. Fortunately, the revival of interest in British food has led chefs to recreate jellies, subtly flavoured with alcohol, such as rhubarb and Cointreau, or lemon and gin.

Even in March there are some delicacies about – wild salmon, for example. Its season runs from January to October (depending on where you fish). Fashion has dictated that salmon should be poached or baked whole and served with an unctuous sauce such as mayonnaise or hollandaise. But tastes are beginning to change as cooks are able to experiment more freely with cheaper, farmed salmon. Salmon is often now filleted and quickly seared or grilled, before being served with a tart vinaigrette-based sauce. Lightly cured salmon, especially gravad lax, has become a very popular appetizer and is even sold ready sliced in vacuum packs.

Rabbit also seems to be enjoying a revival, as it has been reintroduced by the supermarkets. Safely de-bunnified into neatly packaged joints – simply labelled as farmed or wild – it makes a good alternative meat. Like salmon, rabbit has been food for both kings and paupers at different times in its history. Many of our rabbit recipes are heavily influenced by the French, our usual model for *haute cuisine*, and we still flavour it with mustard, bacon, cider and chives. Modern farmed rabbits benefit from being marinated, but can be cooked as quickly as chicken.

Spring greens are also being subjected to the supermarkets' marketing departments in an attempt to make them more appealing. Gone are the days of buying an armful of muddy greens and picking through them for a handful of jade green hearts. Now you can buy ready sorted, washed and sliced greens in clear pillow packets. They look so healthy it is hard to resist. As a result many British cooks are learning for the first time how to cook their greens. Faster methods are applied to traditional partnerships, so that boiled ham and greens becomes pan-fried bacon and cabbage; while new influences are sought to transform the like of bitter curly kale into elegant side dishes.

March does enjoy at least one occasion for feasting – depending on how the ecumenical calendar falls – Shrove Tuesday or Easter and Mothering Sunday. For convenience I have dealt with the latter two events in April. Shrove Tuesday always falls between 2 February and 8 March. Pancakes have traditionally been cooked on Shrove Tuesday since Saxon times. It is commonly believed that they were made on this day to use up all the eggs and dairy produce before the Lenten fast began the next day, as such foods were forbidden during Lent. Whatever the reason, pancakes are still much loved and as popular as ever. Indeed, fashions change little as to what is deemed a good pancake, sugar and lemon having been served with a thin crêpe-like pancake for well over a hundred years. As for the puffy little pancakes currently regarded as a recent American import, these have Celtic origins – griddle cakes have been cooked since time immemorial. They were often served as a type of bread, in much the same way as crumpets are eaten today. Even their name is a derivative from a 'kaak of bread' that was cooked on a griddle or pan.

PANCAKES

For the cook pancakes fall into two main categories: thin delicate discs of batter and small fat, puffy cakes that contain a raising agent such as yeast, baking powder or egg whites. The flours and liquids that make the batter of either type vary immensely, from buckwheat flour to cornmeal and buttermilk to beer.

To make pancakes successfully you need a small heavy frying pan that conducts the heat evenly and does not stick. I use an old cast-iron omelette pan that has become proved by years of use for crêpes, and a non-stick frying pan for blinis and griddle cakes.

If you are making thin pancakes you must ensure that your batter is lump-free before you begin to cook. Strain it if in doubt. It is also a good idea to add a little oil or melted butter to the batter, as this helps to stop the pancakes sticking as they cook. It is not necessary to allow the batter to rest before cooking. Some writers maintain that this gives the batter greater elasticity, allowing it to flow across the pan, but in my opinion it makes little difference. Lastly, if your pancakes tear very easily the batter is either too thin or contains too few eggs – adjust accordingly, remembering that the thinner the batter the more delicate the crêpe.

LEMON AND SUGAR PANCAKES

This is the traditional Shrove Tuesday pancake recipe. (Makes 12 pancakes)

115g/4oz plain flour	1 tablespoon liqueur
pinch of salt	(depending on what you
pinch of caster sugar	have to hand, for example
1 egg	Calvados)
170ml/6 fl oz milk	vegetable oil for frying
55ml/2 fl oz water	extra caster sugar
1 tablespoon vegetable oil	2 lemons, each cut into 8
	wedges, pips removed

Sift the flour, salt and sugar into a bowl and make a well in the centre.

Lightly beat the egg and pour into the well. Mix together the milk and water and slowly add to the egg, beating with a wooden spoon. Gradually incorporate the flour from the sides of the bowl. Beat until smooth.

Stir in the oil and alcohol. Strain through a fine sieve into a jug.

Heat a small (15cm/6 inch) heavy frying pan and rub with a thick wedge of oil-soaked kitchen paper. When the pan is very hot and well greased, pour in about 2 tablespoons of the batter and rotate the pan so that it is evenly coated in a thin layer. As soon as the batter begins to set and form small bubbles, loosen the edges with a greased palette knife and flip over. Cook for another minute or so, then slip the pancake on to a warm plate and cover with a cloth.

Grease the pan once more and repeat. Any excess batter can be poured back into the jug. As soon as the pancakes are cooked, serve with lots of caster sugar and lemon wedges.

Note: Savoury pancakes can be made using this recipe if you exclude the sugar and the liqueur. Variations can be made by adding finely chopped herbs to the batter or even flavoured oils such as sesame. Thin pancakes also freeze well.

CRÊPES SUZETTE

Although crêpes Suzette were originally invented at the turn of the century for the Prince of Wales, they have about them a glamorous aura of the sixties, when everything was flambéed. Despite this, they are a classic that firmly belongs in the British culinary repertoire – after all, one of the high street supermarkets is selling a ready-made version, next door to its bread and butter pudding. The following recipe is adapted from *The Robert Carrier Cookery Course.* (Serves 4)

12 sweet pancakes (see
   previous recipe)

Orange butter
115g/4oz butter, softened
55g/2oz caster sugar
2 large oranges, finely
   grated and juiced
3 tablespoons orange
   liqueur

To flame
1 level tablespoon caster
   sugar (optional)
2 tablespoons orange
   liqueur
2 tablespoons brandy

Place all the orange butter ingredients together in a large, heavy-bottomed frying pan. Gently heat and simmer briefly until slightly reduced.

Add 1 pancake at a time to the frying pan. Once it is in the pan, carefully fold it half and then in half again, using a spoon and fork. Push to the side of the pan and repeat with the remaining pancakes. This method ensures that they become well coated in the buttery juices.

Sprinkle the pancakes with the sugar, pour on the alcohol, and standing well back, immediately light with a match. If you leave it too long the alcohol will become too absorbed into the juices to catch alight. Give the pan a couple of good shakes and wait for the flames to die down before you serve.

BLINIS AND CAVIAR

Surprisingly, buckwheat flour has been used in English pancake cookery for at least two centuries. Elizabeth David gives a strange 1817 recipe called Bockings, which she traces back to the *Modern Domestic Cookery and Useful Receipt Book* by Elizabeth Hammond. Apparently these yeast-risen pancakes were closer to Welsh crumpets than pancakes, but nevertheless, very good. It seems that buckwheat was grown in the Midlands, mainly as pheasant and poultry feed, and somehow slipped into the local cooking. Mrs Beeton, on the other hand, gives a bizarre recipe for buckwheat cakes, which use both brewer's yeast and bicarbonate of soda to aerate them.

Today, Russian-style blinis have taken the place of Bockings and such like. Although most commonly served with caviar, they are extremely good served with smoked salmon or gravad lax. The following recipe is adapted from Jane Grigson's *Fish Cookery*. (Serves 6)

225g/8oz plain flour	*To cook*
115g/4oz buckwheat flour	vegetable oil or clarified
1½ teaspoons easy-blend	butter (see page 107)
dried yeast	
425ml/¾ pint lukewarm milk	*To serve*
3 large eggs, separated	285ml/½ pint sour cream
salt	(minus the 3 tablespoons
1 teaspoon caster sugar	needed above)
3 scant tablespoons melted	caviar, to taste (Beluga,
butter	Oesetra or even salmon
3 scant tablespoons sour	caviar)
cream	

Sift the plain flour and half the buckwheat flour into a large warm mixing bowl. Mix in the yeast and make a hole in the centre. Pour in the milk and then, using a wooden spoon, gradually incorporate the flour from the sides of the bowl. Beat until smooth. Cover with clingfilm and leave to rise in a warm place for 3 hours.

Beat in the remaining buckwheat flour and leave covered in a warm place for another 2 hours. It will rise once again.

Beat the egg yolks with the salt, sugar, butter and sour cream and mix into the batter.

Whisk the egg whites until stiff in a clean bowl and then, using a metal spoon, fold into the batter. Cover once more and leave for 30 minutes.

Although the batter will continue to rise, it is quite stable and can be left covered in the refrigerator provided it has plenty of space in its bowl. The coldness will slow down its expansion and you can safely leave it for a few hours.

When you are ready to make the blinis, preheat the oven to low. Heat a large, heavy-bottomed (preferably non-stick) frying pan over a medium high heat. Wipe the pan with some oil. (If you want ultra-rich blinis, add some clarified butter to the pan and use this to grease the pan. The blinis will soak it up as they cook.)

When it is hot drop a spoonful of batter on the pan for each pancake, allowing plenty of space between each blini, as they will spread out a little as they are cooking. When they have puffed up and show tiny bubbles, flip them over and cook them for a few minutes more − they should turn a beautiful deep golden brown. Keep them warm in the oven until you have finished cooking.

Quickly arrange the finished pancakes on individual plates and top with spoonfuls of sour cream and caviar.

BUTTERMILK GRIDDLE CAKES WITH HONEY BANANAS

These belong to the Scottish school of pancakes, which are often cooked with a rising agent. For maximum fluffiness, they must be cooked as soon as the batter is mixed. Any fruit topping can be used, depending on the time of year. (Makes 24 pancakes, serves 6)

Fruit topping
6 tablespoons runny honey
1 lemon, grated and juiced
1 orange, grated and juiced
6 bananas, sliced

Batter
215g/7½oz plain flour
70g/2½oz wholewheat
    flour

½ teaspoon salt
½ teaspoon bicarbonate of
    soda
2 teaspoons baking powder
1 large egg, beaten
1 tablespoon melted butter
455ml/16 fl oz buttermilk
crème fraîche, to taste

Heat the honey in a saucepan with the grated zest and juice of the lemon and orange. As soon as it has melted add the sliced bananas and simmer gently for 3 minutes.

Sift all the dry ingredients into a large bowl. Make a well and add the beaten egg and melted butter. Gradually beat in the buttermilk until the batter is smooth.

Use any large heavy-bottomed frying pan. Place over medium high heat and grease well. Once it is sizzling hot, pour (or spoon) the batter on, in small dollops, cooking about 3–4 cakes at a time, depending on the size of your pan. They will spread out a little as they are cooking. When they have puffed up and show tiny bubbles, flip then over and cook them for a few minutes more. Serve each portion of pancakes with a generous spoonful of the hot bananas and a large dollop of crème fraîche.

SPRING GREENS

Cooking greens has undoubtedly been a British failing. Smollett, in *Humphry Clinker*, wrote of London cooking: 'Perhaps, you will hardly believe they can be so mad as to boil their greens with brass half-pence, in order to improve their colour; and yet nothing is more true. Indeed, without this improvement in the colour, they have no personal merit. They are produced in an artificial soil, and taste of nothing but the dunghills, from whence they spring . . .' Happily we are improving in all forms of vegetable cookery, aided in part by our need for fast food. After all, who has time to boil their greens to a slime these days? As with much of our food, Mediterranean and Asian influences have introduced new ideas to traditional dishes, transforming lowly greens into fragrant accompaniments.

I have included sea kale in this section, because although strictly speaking we do not eat it as a green, it is one of the first spring delicacies and can be eaten as an accompaniment to roast meat in much the same way as greens.

SEA KALE WITH BROWNED BUTTER

Sea kale grows wild along the coastline of Britain. It can grow into a large, celery-like plant, unless it is kept blanched and regularly trimmed. It has a fresh, sweet flavour, with a hint of celery. The delicate fronds and stalks are eaten either raw or cooked. Locals used to pile up pebbles around the wild plants to keep out the sun and then snip the white stalks as a spring delicacy. The Victorians then adopted it, cultivating hundreds of sea kale plants in their massive kitchen gardens and serving it like asparagus or with the juices from a roast joint of lamb or beef. After the Second World War it went out of fashion, despite the fact that it is easy to grow. Some of the supermarkets have tried, unsuccessfully, to sell it as a luxury vegetable, but plants are obtainable from many good nurseries. (Serves 4)

225g/8oz butter	sea salt and freshly ground
4 handfuls of sea kale stems	black pepper

Begin by clarifying the butter. Place it in a heavy-bottomed saucepan and melt over a low heat. Allow the butter to separate and let the pale yellow froth bubble up and form a head. Leave to simmer for 15 minutes.

Line a sieve with some clean muslin, kitchen paper or a J-cloth and place over a clean bowl. Carefully pour the clear butter through the cloth, holding back the froth until the very end. Discard any milky liquid at the bottom of the melted butter. Leave the clear butter to drip through the cloth and throw away the froth.

The butter should be a beautiful buttercup yellow. Pour as much butter as you need for the sea kale into a small clean pan and refrigerate the remainder. (It is wonderful for cooking fish and making curries.) Gently heat the clarified butter over a medium heat until it begins to turn a lovely golden brown and releases a nutty smell. Immediately remove from the heat, as it will continue to brown as it cools.

Meanwhile, quickly immerse the sea kale stems in a pan of boiling salted water and cook for a minute, or until they are *al dente*. Drain, and serve piping hot, drizzled in the brown butter with a sprinkling of black pepper.

GREEN CABBAGE WITH BACON

Cabbage and bacon have, through necessity, been a staple food for the poor for centuries. Despite this, the two flavours complement each other beautifully, as this modern interpretation illustrates. (Serves 4)

1 small green cabbage (any variety, including Savoy) 170g/6oz smoked back bacon	3 tablespoons olive oil 2 cloves garlic, crushed

Remove the tough outer leaves of your cabbage. If it is quite clean, cut into quarters and remove the tough white core of each section. Roughly slice, place in a colander and wash thoroughly. However, if it is muddy or looks as though it might be hiding the odd slug or snail, begin by submerging it in a sink full of salted cold water and swish it about before you begin quartering. After all, there is nothing worse than finding a sliced slug!

Remove the fat from the bacon and cut into small lardons.

When ready to serve, heat the olive oil in a frying pan and colour the bacon. As soon as it no longer releases any water, add the garlic and continue to fry for another minute. Increase the heat to full and add the sliced cabbage. Stir continuously to prevent the cabbage from catching, and as soon as it has collapsed, season to taste and serve. The cabbage will take about 3–4 minutes to cook.

BLANCHED CURLY KALE

Curly kale has a strong cabbagey taste that to non-enthusiasts needs careful handling. This simple Japanese-influenced salad enhances the slightly peppery nature of the kale while bringing out its sweetness. It is not for the stewed greens traditionalists. (Serves 4)

170g/6oz prepared curly
   kale
salt

Dressing
1 clove garlic, crushed
pinch of finely chopped root
   ginger

pinch of sugar
large pinch of chilli flakes
   (optional)
1 tablespoon soy sauce
1 tablespoon rice vinegar
3 tablespoons walnut oil

Place the sliced curly kale in a large pan of boiling salted water and cook for 3 minutes, then drain and immediately cool under cold running water. Once the kale is cold, squeeze out the water and place in a mixing bowl. Pull the squashed leaves back into shape.

Whisk together the dressing ingredients and pour over the kale. Toss and serve as a side dish.

STIR-FRIED PURPLE SPROUTING BROCCOLI

At this time of year there suddenly appear packets of leafy thin purple sprouting broccoli. It is delicious stir-fried with chilli, turning a luminous green as it cooks. (Serves 4)

255g/9oz purple sprouting broccoli	½ teaspoon rice vinegar
2 tablespoons vegetable oil	2 cloves garlic, crushed
6 small red dried chillies	1–2 tablespoons soy sauce
	½ teaspoon sugar (optional)

Trim the stalks of the broccoli, removing any yellow leaves and cutting out any scars, before washing thoroughly. If any of the stems are too thick, slice them into elegant strips.

Heat the oil until very hot in a large, heavy-bottomed frying pan. Add the chillies, and when they begin to sizzle and deepen in colour, stand back and quickly add the vinegar. The frying pan will spit and sizzle for a few seconds and you will suddenly inhale a huge amount of chilli. Despite this, immediately add the garlic and broccoli.

Stir-fry for a further 2–3 minutes, then add the soy sauce and sugar (if wished), check the seasoning and serve.

WILD SALMON

To many, salmon has become less of a luxury with the advent of the
farmed salmon. Despite this, it is widely agreed that wild salmon have a
better flavour and texture than their farmed cousins. This is hardly
surprising when one considers that the one- to three-year-old young
salmon (or smolts) have swum back to the Atlantic, from their river
nursery, and then stayed out in the ocean for at least another couple of
years, enjoying an active life with a varied diet.

  Like all fish, salmon benefits from being cooked on the bone, but since
many modern cooks have become timid of fish bones, an increasing
quantity of salmon is sold neatly filleted and portioned. I suspect that
small families are also changing cooking habits, as it can take a long time
for two people to eat their way through even part of a salmon. However,
if you want to bake a whole salmon turn to page 218 and use the recipe
for cold sea trout – just serve it immediately if you want hot salmon.

LIME-CURED SALMON

All sorts of flavourings can be used when curing salmon at home, but it is important to get the correct ratio of salt and sugar to fish weight. As a golden rule allow 35g/1¼oz for every 905g/2lb of fish fillet. The herbs, spices or citrus zest can then be added to taste.

If you have a small refrigerator or only want to make a limited amount, either buy a small side of salmon or a segment of the fish's torso and ask the fishmonger to fillet this for you. Always make sure that the skin is left on, otherwise it is extremely difficult to slice later. If you are using two pieces, sandwich them together with the gravad lax filling. In either case, once the salmon flesh has been coated with the sugar salt mixture, generously wrap it up in clingfilm, before laying it in a large dish (to catch any juices) and placing heavy weights on top. If you are using the single fillet, place it in the dish flesh side down. (Serves 6–8)

905g/2lb salmon fillet	3 limes, finely grated
35g/1¼oz granulated sugar	1 tablespoon vodka or gin
35g/1¼oz coarse sea salt	
freshly ground black	
pepper, to taste	

Trim the side of salmon by removing any fins and cutting away any thick white bands of creamy fat at the edges. Run your fingers gently over the fish. You will normally feel the tips of a few small bones in the centre of the fish. Using a pair of tweezers, pull these out. If left in they make it harder to slice the salmon cleanly.

Mix together the sugar, salt, pepper and lime zest. Rub the flesh of the salmon with the vodka and evenly spread the sugar mixture over. Wrap in clingfilm, place in a shallow dish and cover with a heavily weighted plate. Leave in the fridge for 24 hours, turning once.

Thinly slice the cured salmon, just as for smoked salmon, leaving a green edge on each slice. Serve with a simple salad or with finely cut buttered brown bread.

Note: If you wish to make a traditional gravad lax, replace the lime zest with 3 generous tablespoons of finely chopped dill and replace the vokda or gin with aquavit or brandy. Finely chopped tarragon or lightly crushed coriander or fennel seeds also make elegant variations.

SALMON FILO PARCELS

The modern British answer to a fast fish pie. Simple but good. (Makes 6 parcels)

Filo parcels

455g/1lb salmon fillet, skinned

2 tablespoons olive oil

1 lemon, finely grated

½ lemon, juiced

1 teaspoon finely chopped dill

salt and freshly ground black pepper

70g/2½oz melted butter

140g/5oz filo pastry

Sauce

1 tablespoon finely chopped dill

1 lemon, finely grated

4 tablespoons sour cream

salt and freshly ground black pepper

Preheat the oven to 230°C/450°F/gas 8.

Slice the salmon into 5mm/¼ inch thick strips. Mix these with the olive oil, lemon zest and juice, dill and seasoning. Set aside to marinate while you prepare the remaining ingredients.

Butter a baking sheet and clear a comfortable working space. Unwrap your filo pastry sheets and keep covered with a damp tea towel. You are going to need 18 squares, each measuring approximately 15cm/6 inches. Each square has to be painted with melted butter and layered with another 2 sheets, each buttered in turn. When 3 squares are layered and buttered, place ⅙ of the filling in the middle and gather together the edges, pinching at the neck to stick them together, so that the result looks like a stuffed brown paper bag with its edges pulled back. The filling should be completely sealed inside. Make 1 parcel at a time, placing it on the baking sheet once finished, so that the pastry remains soft. Then brush all 6 with melted butter, so that they will brown evenly and stay crisp while cooking.

At this point the pastries can be stored in the refrigerator until needed. Otherwise bake in the centre of the preheated oven for 20 minutes and serve immediately.

Make the sauce by mixing together the dill, lemon zest and sour cream. Season to taste and serve with the filo parcels.

GRILLED SALMON FILLETS WITH
CUCUMBER VINAIGRETTE

Salmon fillets must be lightly cooked, so that they remain succulent. If possible use a stove-top cast-iron ribbed grill to get a delicious crust, otherwise pan-fry instead. The current restaurant fashion of serving salmon with a simple vinaigrette that has been flavoured with herbs and finely diced tomatoes and olives or cucumber is perfect for the domestic cook. Such sauces not only enhance the natural sweetness of the salmon, but are also very quick and easy to make. (Serves 6)

6 small salmon fillets
2 tablespoons olive oil
salt and freshly ground black
  pepper

Vinaigrette
1 shallot, finely diced
1 teaspoon finely chopped
  tarragon

1 teaspoon finely chopped
  chervil
1 cucumber, seeded and
  finely diced
2 tablespoons rice wine
  vinegar
6 tablespoons olive oil

Heat the stove-top grill until it is smoking and brush with some oil. Rub the salmon fillets with a little oil and then season. Grill them flesh side down first, neatly marking them with golden grill lines, then turn over and grill until their skin is crispy. Allow 5 minutes per side, depending on their thickness.

Place the shallot, herbs and cucumber in a bowl. Whisk together the vinegar and oil and pour over the cucumber. Season to taste and transfer to a small jug. Serve with the fish.

RABBIT

Rabbits were introduced to Britain by the Normans and were bred for their delicate flesh in specially constructed warrens by the nobility. So good were they considered to be that Henry VIII had to introduce a close season to protect them from being over-hunted in the wild. Since then they have fluctuated in popularity, suffering in recent years from their cuddly bunny image rather than from the fear of myxomatosis.

Rabbits can still be divided into two categories – wild and farmed. Wild rabbits have a slightly gamey flavour and can vary in toughness, depending on their age. The darker the meat, the older they are likely to be. Older wild rabbits should be quickly seared and then gently stewed. It is also wise to look out for any shot, as the rabbit, like any hunted game, may contain some. Farmed rabbits have pale pink flesh that has a delicate, almost chicken-like flavour. As all rabbit meat is very lean, it has a tendency to be dry so it is a good idea to marinate it. Farmed or young wild rabbit should be cooked quickly to retain its juicy succulence.

If you are given a whole rabbit, ask your butcher to skin, gut and joint it for you, rather than bravely confront it as E.M. Delafield does in her *Diary of a Provincial Lady*, when she decides with the onset of the Second World War to learn how to cook:

October 21st: Aunt Blanche tells me very seriously to have nothing whatever to do with rabbits. Breakfast scones if I like, mayonnaise sauce and an occasional sweet if I really must, but *not* rabbits. They can, and should, be left to professional cooks.

Could say a great deal in reply, to the effect that professional cooks are anything but numerous and that those there are will very shortly be beyond my means – but remember in time that argument with the elderly, more especially when a relative, is of little avail and go to the kitchen without further discussion.

Quite soon afterwards am wishing from the bottom of my heart that I had taken Aunt Blanche's advice.

This gives place, after gory and unpleasant interlude, to rather more self-respecting frame of mind, and Mrs V. (the cook) tells me approvingly that I have now done The Worst job in all Cooking.

Am thankful to hear it.

Rabbit-stew a success, but make my own lunch of scrambled eggs.

RABBIT FRICASSÉE

This richly flavoured creamy fricassée can be adapted to chicken or even sweetbreads. Either ask the butcher to bone a whole rabbit for you or buy a selection of rabbit joints from the supermarket and bone them yourself. The legs are boned in exactly the same way as chicken or guinea fowl legs (see page 46). (Serves 4)

1 rabbit, jointed and boned

Marinade
4 tablespoons olive oil
140ml/¼ pint dry cider
1 lemon, finely grated
2 cloves garlic, crushed
1 bay leaf
3 sprigs parsley
4 sprigs thyme
3 black peppercorns

Fricassée
3 tablespoons olive oil
16 small pickling onions
170g/6oz smoked back
    bacon, cut into lardons
2 cloves garlic, crushed
285ml/½ pint chicken stock
285ml/½ pint dry cider
285ml/½ pint double cream
½ teaspoon finely chopped
    thyme
salt and freshly ground black
    pepper

Mix the rabbit pieces with all the marinade ingredients. Cover and chill for at least 4 hours.

When you are ready to cook take the rabbit pieces from their marinade, removing any bits that are sticking to them, and lightly season. Discard the marinade.

Heat the oil in a large heavy-bottomed frying pan. Quickly brown the rabbit and set aside. Reduce the heat a little and add the onions. Keep these moving around the pan to ensure that they colour evenly. Once they have turned a beautiful golden colour, add the bacon lardons and the garlic. Allow these to lightly colour then pour in the stock and cider and increase the heat. Boil vigorously until they have reduced by two-thirds.

At this stage, reduce the heat and stir in the cream and thyme. Simmer gently for a few minutes until the sauce has thickened a little, then return the rabbit to the pan. Adjust the seasoning to taste and simmer for a further 5 minutes before serving.

GRILLED RABBIT WITH CHIVE MUSTARD BUTTER

Use a farmed rabbit for this recipe. Ideally it should be grilled on a stove-top cast-iron ribbed grill, but you can pan-fry it instead. Wonderful with crispy potato cakes (see page 286) and a simple salad. The rabbit should be marinated for at least 24 hours, but improves with longer. Saddles are easy to bone, but if you are worried ask your butcher to bone them instead. (Serves 4)

4 rabbit saddles, skinned	**Butter**
	½ tablespoon whole-grain
Marinade	mustard
8 tablespoons olive oil	1 tablespoon Dijon mustard
8 tablespoons dry white	4 tablespoons finely
wine	chopped chives
4 sprigs tarragon	115g/4oz butter, at room
4 sprigs thyme	temperature
4 sprigs parsley	2 teaspoons tarragon
2 shallots, roughly chopped	vinegar
2 cloves garlic, roughly	salt and freshly ground black
chopped	pepper
4 black peppercorns	

To bone the rabbit saddles, work your knife along the spine, then slowly cut down one side of it, underneath the plump fillet of meat. Keep your knife in touch with the rabbit bones as you do so, until the knife re-emerges on the other side of the fillet. Repeat on the other side of the spine, to remove the other fillet.

Mix together all the marinade ingredients and then add the rabbit fillets. Coat well, cover and chill.

Prepare the butter by beating the mustards and herbs into the softened butter. Add the vinegar, salt and pepper to taste. Place the mixture on to some wet greaseproof paper. Roughly shape it into a sausage and roll in the paper. Keep rolling it gently until it forms a perfect cylinder without any air bubbles. Chill until needed.

When ready to serve, heat the greased stove-top grill until it is very hot. Remove the rabbit fillets from their marinade, wipe off any herbs, shallot or garlic, and lightly season. Strain the marinade and reserve for basting the fillets as they cook.

Grill the fillets for 3 minutes on each side. The rabbit should be just cooked through, so that the juices run clear, but it is still juicy – exactly like a chicken.

Allow the fillets to rest in a warm place while you prepare the butter sauce. Bring 2 tablespoons of water up to the boil in a small saucepan and very quickly whisk in the flavoured butter, never allowing the mixture to come to the boil. Cut the fillets into oval slices and arrange on each place. Serve with the sauce.

DORSET FRIED RABBIT AND ONIONS

This is an updated version of a traditional Dorset recipe for farmed rabbit. Originally the rabbit joints were quickly blanched in boiling water to tenderize them before being chilled and coated in egg and breadcrumbs, while the onions were used as a basis for a creamy rabbit gravy. This is much the same method as Eliza Acton recommends for crumbing chicken. Modern animals do not need such vigorous treatment and most people prefer lighter, more piquant dishes. I owe the idea of delicately flavouring a sweet-sour onion relish with fennel seeds to Kit Chan, who invented this recipe for a different dish. (Serves 4)

Fried onions
55g/2oz butter
2 large onions, finely sliced
1 clove garlic, crushed
1 teaspoon fennel seeds
1 dessertspoon red wine
    vinegar
2 tablespoons granulated
    sugar
salt and freshly ground black
    pepper

Fried rabbit
2 tablespoons finely
    chopped parsley
1 tablespoon finely chopped
    chives
1 teaspoon finely chopped
    thyme

1 dessertspoon finely
    chopped tarragon
6 tablespoons double
    cream
1 egg yolk
1 tablespoon smooth Dijon
    mustard
1 tablespoon English
    mustard
salt and freshly ground black
    pepper
1 farmed rabbit, jointed and
    boned
3 tablespoons seasoned
    flour
225g/8oz soft white
    breadcrumbs
6 tablespoons vegetable oil

Melt the butter over a low heat in a heavy-bottomed pan. Add the onion, garlic and fennel seeds and slowly cook until meltingly soft. Add the vinegar, sugar and seasoning and adjust to taste. Continue to cook for a further 5 minutes, until the vinegar and sugar have become absorbed by the onions. This can be re-heated whenever needed.

Meanwhile, mix together the finely chopped herbs, cream, egg yolk and mustards. Season and set aside.

Lightly coat the rabbit joints in the seasoned flour before dipping them in the mustard mixture. Then completely cover each piece with the breadcrumbs, pressing them firmly in. Cover and chill until needed.

When ready to serve, heat half the oil in a large frying pan. When sizzling hot, add the rabbit and fry over a medium heat for about 20 minutes or until golden brown and tender. Drain on kitchen paper, sprinkle with a little more salt if necessary, before serving with the warm fried onions.

CREAMS AND WHIPS

It is hard to know when we began eating creams, whips, jellies and blancmanges, but certainly the latter two were very popular, if different, in medieval times. Blancmanges, for example, were made from a mixture of white sweet and savoury foods. However, whereas our syllabubs and creams have retained their popularity through the ages, our jellies and blancmanges have borne the brunt of poor cooking, just as Mr Pooter experienced in *The Diary of a Nobody*, by George and Weedon Grossmith (1892):

> November 18. I told Sarah not to bring up the *blanc-mange* again for breakfast. It seems to have been placed on our table at every meal since Wednesday . . .
>
> In spite of my instructions, that *blanc-mange* was brought up again for supper. To make matters worse, there had been an attempt to disguise it, by placing it in a glass dish with jam around it. Carrie asked Lupin if he would have some, and he replied: 'No second-hand goods for me, thank you.' I told Carrie, when we were alone, if that *blanc-mange* were placed on the table again I should walk out of the house.

SYLLABUB

According to Dorothy Hartley, syllabub was made by mixing Sille (a wine from an area of the champagne country) with frothing cream to make a Bub (Elizabethan slang for a bubbling drink), hence Sille Bub. In its simplest form, milk was drawn direct from the cow's udder into a bowl of wine, forming a natural froth. (Serves 4)

1 large lemon, finely grated and juiced	2 tablespoons brandy
115g/4oz caster sugar	285ml/½ pint double cream
140ml/¼ pint sherry	freshly grated nutmeg, to taste

Place the lemon zest and juice in a large mixing bowl with the sugar, sherry and brandy. Leave for 30 minutes to allow the sugar to dissolve.

Add the cream and gently begin to whip until the mixture becomes thick and fluffy. Transfer to serving glasses and chill for about 8 hours. The liquid should separate and the alcoholic mixture is then supped through the cream. Just before serving, quickly grate some nutmeg on the top of each portion. Delicious with sponge biscuits or macaroons.

APPLE SNOW

This is such a bizarre British dessert that I had to include it, although I have made it a little more grown-up with the addition of Calvados. These lighter-than-air whipped childhood puddings have their roots in the sixteenth century, when the wondrous properties of whipped egg white were discovered. (Serves 4)

4 cooking apples, peeled, cored and cut into chunks	4 tablespoons water
	2 tablespoons Calvados
	3 tablespoons chilled double cream, lightly whipped
1 lemon, finely grated	
115g/4oz sugar or to taste	1 large egg white

Gently simmer the apples with the lemon zest, sugar and water until they have disintegrated into a mush. Cool, then purée. Add the Calvados and chill, covered.

Once cold, fold in the whipped cream. Whip the egg white until it forms soft peaks and then fold into the apple mixture. Serve immediately, with little biscuits.

BAVAROIS

The bavarois has become the modern interpretation of many cold cream puddings. The following recipe is an adaptation of a greengage and yoghurt bavarois from *Jane Grigson's Fruit Book* where the two creamy mixtures were layered together. It is an excellent way of using up frozen currants, raspberries and plums before the new season's fruits arrive. (Serves 6)

Fruit bavarois	Yoghurt bavarois
455g/1lb frozen	225ml/8fl oz Greek
blackcurrants or other	yoghurt
fruit	85g/3oz vanilla sugar
170g/6oz sugar	1 sachet (1 tablespoon)
2 tablespoons water	powdered gelatine
1 sachet (1 tablespoon)	225ml/8fl oz double
powdered gelatine	cream
225ml/8fl oz whipping	
cream	

Begin by making the fruit bavarois, as this takes longer to set. Place the blackcurrants in a non-corrosive pan with the sugar and water. Cover and gently cook for 20 minutes or until the currants are soft. Purée the currants and then push through a sieve.

Meanwhile, sprinkle the gelatine over 3 tablespoons of very hot water in a small bowl. Leave to sit for 5 minutes and then stir. If it has not completely melted, place the bowl in a shallow pan of simmering water and heat gently for a further few minutes. Stir the warm gelatine into the warm puréed berries and set aside to cool.

Once the currants are cold, whip the cream until it forms soft peaks and fold into the currant mixture.

Immediately begin to make the yoghurt bavarois by preparing the gelatine in exactly the same way as above. While it is cooling, sweeten the yoghurt to taste and whip the cream. Then gently fold the lukewarm gelatine into the yoghurt, followed immediately by the whipped cream.

By this stage both mixtures should be close to setting – test by seeing if a spoon will leave a trail for a few minutes. Carefully swirl the yoghurt bavarois into the blackcurrant bavarois, ensuring that the mixture remains vividly striped and does not become blended. Immediately ladle into tall glasses and chill, covered, until set.

BURNT CREAM

Burnt cream is more commonly known as crème brulée in Britain, no doubt following our long-standing predilection for giving dishes French names to make them sound more fashionable. I do not know whether the idea for a caramelized sugar-topped custard originated here or in France, but certainly by 1769 Mrs Raffald had included a recipe for 'burnt cream' in her book *The Experienced English Housekeeper*.

Whatever you call it, this dish is far easier to make than is often believed – you simply require confidence, patience, and ideally a blow torch to ensure that the sugar burns evenly. Blow torches can be bought from your local DIY shop and are simple to operate. Be sure to follow the manufacturer's instructions carefully and keep out of the way of children.

Luxurious fruit variations can be made in the summer by placing raspberries, blueberries or currants in the bottom of each dish and covering with the cool custard. (Serves 4)

1 small vanilla pod, split	1–2 tablespoons caster sugar
565ml/1 pint double cream	or to taste
4 egg yolks	3–4 tablespoons demerara
	sugar, to cover

Place the vanilla pod in the cream and gently heat to scalding point. Cover and leave to infuse for 30 minutes.

Whisk the egg yolks with the sugar in a large bowl until pale and creamy. Slowly add the warm cream, beating all the time. Strain and pour the mixture into a clean saucepan.

Return to a low heat (vanilla addicts can return the pod at this stage to ensure that the brulée is liberally flecked with vanilla seeds) and keep stirring the custard until it begins to thicken. If you feel that the custard is getting too hot, just lift the pan off the heat and continue to stir. Gradually you will feel the custard thickening. Once it begins to become thick and velvety, remove from the heat and continue to stir until it cools a little. Place over a bowl of iced water if wished. Strain once again and pour into 4 ramekins.

Cover and chill. Before serving, evenly sprinkle the top of each crème brulée with demerara sugar and caramelize with the flame of a blow-torch. I have done this under a hot grill, but it gives a less even caramel, slightly more granular and crunchy.

JELLIES

Glistening wobbly clear jellies are coming back into fashion and can now be found on the menus of many restaurants, such as London's Bibendum or the Greenhouse. Jellies have been in serious decline since their heyday in Victorian Britain, when they were displayed in wondrous mounds on banqueting tables, set upon elegant long-stemmed dishes of silver or crystal. Mrs Rundell (1853) warns that 'the shape of the moulds used for jellies and creams is a matter of importance in the appearance of the entremets of a handsome dinner. They should be high and nearly of the same size. If jelly or cream sinks flat on the dish, it has a poor and shabby appearance.' Mrs Beeton gives dozens of recipes, the most wonderful of which is a golden jelly with tiny pieces of gold leaf suspended in a wine jelly.

Jellies are very simple to make if you remember that to every 565ml/ 1 pint of liquid you will need one sachet or 11g/0.4oz of gelatine. The simplest jelly can be made from the excess juice of poached fruit. But they are transformed into refreshing, sophisticated puddings with the addition of alcohol or spices.

The texture of a jelly is dependent on the amount of gelatine added. Many people prefer soft and shimmering jellies, which need to be set in wineglasses or glass bowls for added support. If you wish to turn a jelly out of a mould then reduce the proportion of liquid to gelatine to prevent the jelly from collapsing under its own weight. This is also wise if the weather is hot or if you wish to dice the jelly up and serve it as a glittering crystalline mass with lashings of double cream or crème fraîche.

Gelatine is most commonly sold as powder in sachets. It is extracted mainly from calves' feet and pigs' knuckles, so never serve it to a vegetarian. Agar-agar, a seaweed extract, is the best alternative, but take care to experiment and adjust your recipes as it does not set so firmly. For lump-free jellies, place a few tablespoons of very hot liquid into a small cup or bowl. Evenly sprinkle with the gelatine powder and leave to soak for 5 minutes, then gently stir. If it is not completely melted, place the cup in a shallow pan of water and simmer until the granules have dissolved. Never allow it to boil. Slowly add some of the remaining fruit/ wine liquid until the two solutions are the same temperature, before mixing together.

RHUBARB JELLY

Forced rhubarb is in season in March, and makes the most exquisite pink jellies. (Serves 4)

905g/2lb rhubarb (prepared weight)	1 sachet (1 tablespoon) powdered gelatine
225g/8oz granulated sugar	4–6 tablespoons Cointreau
285ml/½ pint water	

Trim the rhubarb, discarding the tops and bottoms. Wash and cut into very small chunks. Place in a non-corrosive pan with the sugar and water. Bring up to the boil, cover, and simmer for 10 minutes or until the rhubarb is meltingly soft.

Meanwhile, put 3 tablespoons of very hot water into a small bowl and sprinkle with the gelatine. Leave for 5 minutes, then stir. If it does not completely melt, place the bowl in a shallow pan of simmering water and simmer until the gelatine dissolves.

Strain the rhubarb and set aside the pulp to make a fool. Measure the rhubarb syrup. You will need 565ml/1 pint, so add extra water if necessary, before stirring in the Cointreau. Mix the melted gelatine into the warm syrup. Transfer to a large covered bowl and chill until the jelly is nearly set. Then, using a large whisk, vigorously beat the jelly until it bubbles up into a frothy mass, reminiscent of pink blancmange. Pour into 4 wineglasses, lightly cover and leave to set in the fridge.

LEMON GIN JELLY

Lemon and orange jellies first appeared on our tables in the eighteenth century, when they were flavoured with wine and set with hartshorn or calves' feet. This is not a jelly for children. It has an intense lemony flavour with a kick. (Serves 6)

200ml/7fl oz lemon juice	8 cloves
(about 5 large lemons)	285ml/½ pint water
finely pared peel of 2	70ml/2½fl oz gin
lemons	1 sachet (1 tablespoon)
285g/10oz granulated sugar	powdered gelatine

Place the lemon juice, lemon peel, sugar, cloves and water in a saucepan. Dissolve the sugar over a low heat and allow to cool for 10 minutes. Strain through a muslin-lined sieve and add the gin.

Place 3 tablespoons of hot water into a cup and sprinkle the gelatine over it. Leave to soak for a few minutes, then place in a pan of simmering water. Add some of the lemon syrup. Once both solutions are the same temperature, mix together and pour into a pretty bowl. Refrigerate until needed.

PLUM JELLY

Japanese plum wine (*ume*) has the most exquisite taste – pure plum – that once sipped is hard to renounce. It is becoming more widespread, but can certainly be bought from Japanese and Asian shops. This is a new wave recipe where Eastern ingredients are wedded to a Western recipe. (Serves 4)

905g/2lb juicy plums	1 sachet (1 tablespoon)
170g/6oz sugar or to taste	powdered gelatine
2 star anise	140ml/¼ pint plum wine
285ml/½ pint water	

Quarter and stone the plums so that they release plenty of juice while they cook. Add the sugar, star anise and water. Simmer gently until the plums are cooked and have released lots of juice.

Strain the juice from the plums. These can be puréed later for a fool. Measure the juice and, if necessary, add enough water to bring it up to 425ml/¾ pint. Stir in the plum wine and allow to cool.

Place 3 tablespoons of hot water into a cup and sprinkle the gelatine over it. Leave to soak for a few minutes and then place in a pan of simmering water. Add some of the plum syrup. Once both solutions are the same temperature, mix together and pour into a glass bowl. Refrigerate until needed.

APRIL

WILD SPRING FOOD
Nettle soup
Dandelion salad
Candied primroses and violets

LOBSTER, CRAB AND DAB
Lobster salad
Cornish crab pasties
Pan-fried dab with capers

LAMB
Roast lamb with mint sauce
Redcurrant sauce
Pan-fried lamb with rocket
Grilled lamb cutlets with green flageolets

NEW POTATOES
Jersey Royals with mint
Potato salad 1
Potato salad 2

EASTER BAKING
Hot cross buns
West Country saffron bread

CHOCOLATE
Hot chocolate
Chocolate bread and butter pudding
Chocolate praline pots

Until the arrival of the railways Britain was divided into gastronomical regions in much the same way as France or Italy. Local food for the poor and middle classes was defined by their occupations and the availability of ingredients. Lancashire, for example, became famous for its cheap, slow-cooking urban dishes of hot-pot, steak and cow heel, lobscouse and tripe and onions – dishes that evolved from the demands of long working hours and poor wages. But the increase in communications and transport steadily eroded the relative isolation of these areas, introducing such foods and recipes to every region of the country. Thus Lancashire hot-pot became part of the national repertoire. Of course, regional tastes do still differ, influenced as they are by climate and culture, but these differences are becoming less clearly defined as the years go by.

Today, the term traditional food tends to refer either to certain mainstays such as roast meat or bread and butter pudding, or to a particular, almost simplistic approach to ingredients. Thus, boiled lobster served with mayonnaise, or new potatoes cooked with mint and tossed in butter, could be called traditional. This particular form of British cookery is quite prevalent in April. This is partly because many of the early spring delicacies such as lamb, Jersey potatoes, crabs and lobsters all taste delicious cooked in this 'traditionally' simple manner. Easter, like Christmas, also demands traditional cooking to satisfy individual family customs such as serving hot cross buns on Good Friday or roast lamb on Easter Sunday.

Despite these family occasions, the British are eating far less red meat than in the past. The weekly roast is in decline and we are demanding a greater variety of smaller, fast cooking cuts. This in turn has led to the adoption of Continental methods of butchery in many shops. Carcasses are no longer cut into large joints, rather they are butchered along their muscle seams to produce small lean cuts of meat that will not toughen as they cook, since the muscles cannot pull against one another as they heat and shrink. This has allowed modern cooks to adapt Continental recipes, so that plainly grilled lamb chops served with a gravy and several vegetables are becoming a dish of the past, dropped in favour of marinades, piquant butters and a simple composite side dish such as flageolet beans.

The British passion for chocolate has remained unabated since its first introduction in the seventeenth century. Most modern cooks have at least one favourite chocolate dish which is faithfully cooked for special occasions. The last few years have seen the gradual introduction of very high-quality dark chocolates from Europe. These *grand cru* chocolates have a superb flavour and a much higher cocoa content than your ordinary chocolate bar. Although their availability is very limited, there has been a renaissance in chocolate-making and even the plain supermarket bars are beginning to be improved. Naturally, this means better and more reliable results for the cook.

WILD SPRING FOOD

Historically, early spring has also always seen high prices due to the scarcity of home-grown produce, although these days it is more likely to be due to the cost of importation or growing under glass. As a result, many cooks would gather large quantities of wild produce as soon as it appeared. Stinging nettle tops and dandelions offered a welcome change from a dull winter diet and provided a valuable source of vitamins and minerals.

After the war, wild food slipped out of fashion, representing to many the trials of cooking with rationing rather than one of the great pleasures of country walks. However, the media's romantic longing for the 'idyllic country life' has brought it back into vogue. Wild greens like hop tops or garlic mustard have become the latest in food in delicatessens, while sloe custards, bramble jellies and nettle soup are appearing on many fashionable menus. For the home cook some of these recipes may seem rather recherché, but they are no different from making elderflower syrup or sloe gin, for example.

Before picking any wild food make sure that you properly identify whatever you pick, to ensure that it is safe to eat. Only pick where the plant is abundant and never take all its fruit, flowers or leaves. Never pick where pesticides have been sprayed and avoid picking on busy road verges, as these will be very polluted. Lastly, never uproot any plant as this is illegal.

NETTLE SOUP

Nettles have been eaten in Britain since prehistoric times. But as the old broths and puddings are a little spartan for modern tastes, I have adapted this elegant soup recipe from Alastair Little and Richard Whittington's book *Keep It Simple*.

Nettles should be picked when the plants are still small and tender, as after June the leaves undergo a chemical change, making them unpleasantly bitter. (Serves 4)

55g/2oz young stinging-nettle leaves	3 leeks, finely diced
3 tablespoons olive oil	285ml/½ pint chicken stock
1 small onion, finely diced	285ml/½ pint double cream
1 medium potato, finely diced	salt and freshly ground black pepper

Wearing rubber gloves, thoroughly wash the stinging-nettles in plenty of cold water. Strip the leaves from their stems, discarding any damaged or eaten ones. Wash the leaves once more, then spin dry and weigh.

Heat the olive oil in a heavy-bottomed saucepan and gently fry the onion until meltingly soft. Stir in the diced potato and cover. Keep a watchful eye on the potatoes, stirring them regularly to prevent them from catching. After about 3 minutes add the leeks, and as soon as they begin to wilt pour in the chicken stock. Bring to the boil, then simmer for 20 minutes or until the potatoes are very soft.

Stir in the nettle leaves and cook for a further minute. Remove from the heat and immediately liquidize, otherwise the soup will turn a nasty green. Add the cream, strain, and season to taste. Reheat carefully, making sure the soup does not boil. Incidentally, this soup is very good served cold like vichyssoise.

DANDELION SALAD

Young dandelion shoots make a pleasant addition to green salads with their bitter, chicory-like flavour. If you would like them sweeter, just blanch a few plants in the vegetable garden by placing a flower-pot on top like a rhubarb cloche. Alternatively, arrange your leaves in a glass of cold water and leave for 12 hours before eating. Never pick the leaves after a dandelion has flowered, as they will be very bitter. (Serves 4)

1 generous handful young dandelion leaves	1 heaped teaspoon whole-grain mustard
1 curly endive heart	1 tablespoon white wine vinegar
12 quail's eggs	3 tablespoons olive oil
140g/5oz smoked back bacon	salt and freshly ground black pepper
2 tablespoons vegetable oil	
1 clove garlic, crushed	

Trim and wash the salad leaves, spin dry and place in a large salad bowl.

Put the quail's eggs in a pan of cold water, bring to the boil, then turn off the heat and leave for 30 seconds. Place under the cold tap and peel as soon as they are cool enough to handle. The whites will be hard-boiled while the yolks will be slightly soft. Cut in half and add to the leaves.

Remove the fat from the bacon and cut into lardons. Heat the vegetable oil in a small frying pan and fry the bacon until crispy. While the bacon is cooking, whisk together the garlic, mustard, vinegar and olive oil. Season to taste.

Add the bacon to the dandelion leaves and quickly pour the dressing into the frying pan. Warm it over a high heat and immediately add to the salad. Mix thoroughly before serving.

CANDIED PRIMROSES AND VIOLETS

Crystallized flowers have been popular since Elizabethan times, when they were used to decorate both sweet and savoury dishes. There is still something magical about capturing their fragrance and colour in sugar. Primroses and violets are the first flowers of the year suitable for candying, but you can crystallize marigolds, cowslips (if they are specially grown in a garden – wild cowslips are a protected species), elderflowers, apple blossom, borage flowers, roses and cottage pinks later in the year. Whichever edible flower you use, make sure that you use only the petals.

The flowers

Pick newly opened flowers early in the morning, just after the dew has dried. Try and cut them with their stalks attached and never pick any that have been sprayed or are diseased. Gently dip each flower into a bowl of cool water to remove any little insects and then lightly shake and place in a bowl of water in a cool, shady place until the petals have completely dried.

Once they are dry, remove the petals from the flower-heads and snip off any green parts. Then, depending on whether you wish to use them in the next couple of days or preserve them for two months, choose one of the following methods:

Egg white method

The sugared petals will keep for 2–3 days.

> 1 lightly beaten egg white
> caster sugar

Using a fine clean paintbrush, carefully paint the petals and sprinkle with caster sugar to ensure that they are completely coated in a white frosting. Strew the flower petals on to a sheet of greaseproof paper and leave in a warm place to dry. Store in an airtight container when they have dried.

Gum arabic method

Gum arabic is available from most chemists and the sugared petals should keep for up to 2 months in an airtight container.

> 1 teaspoon gum arabic   caster sugar
> 30ml/1fl oz water

Mix together the gum arabic and water in a small basin and place in a pan of simmering water. Stir until the gum arabic has dissolved, then leave to cool.

Paint the petals in the cold mixture and coat with sugar. Continue as in the previous method.

LOBSTER, CRAB AND DAB

April brings the first native lobsters and crabs of the season and the last of the dabs – small fine-tasting flat fish that can be served instead of plaice and sole. Ironically, many of the lobsters we buy are Canadian. This is because the Canadian fisheries have a sound fishing policy that enables them to farm their stock efficiently, control their prices and export cheaply. But the majority of our crab meat still comes from our native brown crabs, although we export most of our spindly-legged, sweet-fleshed spider crabs and dark velvet crabs to Europe. The current fashion for serving food simply has benefited the delicate flavours of all three fish, so that the rich Edwardian recipes for lobster Newburg or gratin of crab are rarely seen today.

LOBSTER SALAD

Lobster salad is still a classic British dish. The essential ingredients are a freshly boiled lobster and mayonnaise – plain, or flavoured with herbs, lemon or even Pernod. The salad can be made as simple or as complicated as you wish. Delicious served with hot new potatoes. (Serves 4)

Mayonnaise	Salad
2 egg yolks	4 small boiled and cleaned
salt and freshly ground white	lobsters
(or black) pepper	2 fat cos lettuce hearts
1 tablespoon lemon juice	12 small spring onions
140ml/¼ pint sunflower oil	2 bunches radishes
140ml/¼ pint olive oil	1½ limes, cut into 8 wedges

Make the mayonnaise by placing the egg yolks, a pinch of salt and the lemon juice in a food processor. Whizz until they turn pale and frothy. Then slowly add the 2 oils, in a slow constant stream, until you achieve a thick pale mayonnaise. Season to taste and transfer the mixture to a serving bowl. Alternatively whisk by hand.

Extract the meat from the lobsters by twisting off their claws and legs. Crack these open and carefully pull out their meat. Then split each lobster in half lengthways. Discard the white gills (to be found in both halves of their heads), the sand sack and the intestinal canal that runs down the length of each lobster. Finally, gently lift out the meat from their tails.

Separate all the lettuce leaves and divide between 4 plates. Arrange the 2 tail halves of each lobster among the lettuces with the 2 claws and any extra meat. Tuck the spring onions and radishes into the salad and garnish with lime wedges. Serve the mayonnaise separately. Repeat with the remaining plates and serve immediately.

CORNISH CRAB PASTIES

Cornish pasties were originally made in every conceivable size and filled with every imaginable filling, from apples to pilchards. Cornish fishermen, farmers and miners would take them to work for their midday meal. Even the poorest of families would make them, flavouring potatoes or breadcrumbs with onions as a filling. The only essential rules to follow for a good Cornish pasty are that the filling should be moist and succulent rather than wet or too dry and that it should never be minced. (Serves 6)

Pastry
455g/1lb plain flour
½ teaspoon salt
115g/4oz lard, diced
115g/4oz butter, diced
1 beaten egg, to glaze

Filling
1 small leek, finely diced
1 tablespoon butter

115g/4oz monkfish fillet,
   finely diced
225g/8oz mixed crabmeat
1 lemon, grated and juiced
1 tablespoon finely chopped
   parsley
pinch of thyme
¼ teaspoon cayenne pepper
salt and freshly ground black
   pepper

Sift the flour and salt into a large mixing bowl. Add the lard and butter and lightly rub into the flour until it forms fine crumbs. Then add enough cold water to form a soft dough and knead for a couple of minutes. Wrap and chill for 30 minutes.

Preheat the oven to 200°C/400°F/gas 6 and grease a baking sheet.

To prepare the filling, first fry the leek in butter until it is soft, then mix with all the remaining ingredients and season to taste.

Roll out the pastry on a lightly floured surface to about 3mm/⅛ inch thick and, using a small plate as a template, cut out 6 circles, each 15cm/6 inches in diameter. Brush the rim of each circle with some beaten egg and arrange 1½ tablespoons of the filling in the middle. Bring the 2 halves of each circle over the top of the filling. Firmly pinch together and crimp to form a scalloped crest. Pierce a tiny hole on either side to allow the steam to escape and brush with beaten egg.

Bake in the preheated oven for 20 minutes then turn the oven down to 180°C/350°F/gas 4 and bake for a further 20 minutes. Serve hot or cold.

PAN-FRIED DAB WITH CAPERS

Dab are very endearing little rough-skinned flat fish – despite the fact that their name was used as a term of contempt in Lincolnshire. As they are not always available, it is sensible to order these fish from your fishmonger. They should always be skinned before cooking. (Serves 4)

115g/4oz butter
8 dab, skinned and trimmed
seasoned plain flour
2 tablespoons small capers,
   rinsed

3 tablespoons finely
   chopped parsley
1 lemon, juiced

Begin by clarifying the butter. Melt the butter in a small pan over a low heat. As soon as a pale scum has risen to the top, remove from the heat and skim. Carefully pour the clear butter into a bowl, discarding the milky liquid at the bottom of the saucepan. Pour half the butter into a large frying pan and place over a moderate heat. Dip the fish into the seasoned flour and fry for about 3 minutes on each side. Remove the fish to a warm place and add the remaining butter. As soon as it turns a golden brown, add the capers and lemon juice. Once the sizzling has subsided, add the parsley and pour over the fish. Serve immediately.

LAMB

Lamb is traditionally eaten in the spring when aged between four and eight months, after which it unofficially turns into hogget. Hogget yields more meat to the bone than lamb, but its texture is slightly coarser. Hoggets eventually turn into mutton, which is now available only from small specialist producers scattered around the country. These days farmers rear their lambs from early spring through to midsummer.

Although roast lamb is still a favourite Easter dish, symbolizing the innocence of Christ, roast meat in general is being eaten less and less. It is said that this is because family life no longer follows the old rituals of a sit-down roast dinner on Sunday, cold meat on Monday . . . but it may also be that British tastes are changing. After all, a roast joint may take time to cook, but it requires surprisingly little work.

ROAST LAMB WITH MINT SAUCE

The French may scoff, but as every Briton knows, mint sauce is the perfect accompaniment to roast lamb. Happily, home-made mint sauce is one of the easiest sauces to make and tastes much better than the lurid green paste you can buy in jars. (Serves 4)

1.5kg/3½lb leg of lamb
1 lemon, juiced
85g/3oz softened butter
generous pinch of cayenne
  pepper
salt and freshly ground black
  pepper

Mint sauce
3 tablespoons finely
  chopped mint
1 tablespoon boiling water

2 teaspoons caster sugar
3 tablespoons white wine
  vinegar

Traditional gravy
2 tablespoons plain flour
425ml/¾ pint hot lamb stock
  (bought or home-made)
140ml/¼ pint dry white
  wine
salt and freshly ground black
  pepper

Preheat the oven to 200°C/400°F/gas 6.

Rub the lamb leg with the lemon juice then coat liberally with the butter. Season with cayenne pepper, salt and black pepper. Arrange on a roasting tray and place in the centre of the preheated oven. Roast for 1 hour 20 minutes if you like your meat rare, 1 hour 35 minutes for medium rare and 1 hour 48 minutes if you prefer it well done. Baste regularly with the melted butter in the roasting pan.

Meanwhile, mix together the mint, water and sugar. Allow to cool, then add the vinegar and leave for 1 hour before serving.

Transfer the joint to a clean dish and leave to rest in a warm place for 15–20 minutes. This makes it more succulent, as the juices are re-absorbed into the meat.

While the meat is resting, prepare the gravy. Pour off any excess fat, leaving about 2 tablespoons in the pan along with the meat's juices. Place the roasting pan over a moderate heat and sprinkle with 2 tablespoons plain flour. Blend the flour into the juices and allow to cook through for a couple of minutes. Using either a wooden spoon or a whisk, gradually stir in the hot stock, followed by the wine, until it forms a smooth liquid. Vigorously boil for 5 minutes, stirring all the time, until it thickens a little. Season to taste.

Strain the gravy into a warm sauce-boat and serve with the lamb.

Note: Lamb can also be served with simple sweet-sour jellies such as redcurrant or apple and rowanberry jelly, or with sauces that are made with jellies such as the following:

REDCURRANT SAUCE

A slightly more delicate variation of this sauce can be made by using home-made whitecurrant jelly with white port.

4 tablespoons redcurrant jelly	1 tablespoon lemon juice
1 tablespoon port	salt and freshly ground black pepper

Place the redcurrant jelly, port and lemon juice in a small pan. Melt the jelly over a low heat, season to taste, and serve hot in a sauce-boat.

Note: Whitecurrant jelly is made in exactly the same way as redcurrant jelly.

PAN-FRIED LAMB WITH ROCKET

The traditional greens that were once served with a roast are now served as a tart salad with quickly seared lamb. Although this may seem a lengthy recipe, it is actually very simple to make. Rack of lamb is easy to bone, but if you are worried ask your butcher to do it for you. (Serves 6–8)

2 short cut pairs of best end lamb (also sold as 4 French trimmed racks of lamb), boned and stripped of fat and sinew

Marinade
½ bottle dry white wine
12 sprigs thyme
4 shallots, roughly chopped
140ml/¼ pint olive oil
6 black peppercorns

Dressing
1 shallot, finely diced
2 tablespoons sherry vinegar

6 tablespoons olive oil
salt and freshly ground black pepper

Sauce
140ml/¼ pint dry white wine
285ml/½ pint lamb stock (bought or home-made)
115g/4oz butter, diced

Salad
225g/8oz rocket
1 large packet plain salted crisps

Trim the lamb fillets of any fat and remove the fine blue skin by running a sharp knife just underneath it. Mix together the marinade ingredients and coat the lamb fillets. Cover and chill for 12–24 hours.

Just before serving, make the dressing by whisking together the shallot, vinegar and olive oil and seasoning to taste.

Remove the lamb from the marinade and cut into thick slices. Heat a tablespoon of olive oil in a non-stick frying pan over a high heat. Season the lamb slices and quickly sear on each side. Keep these warm while you make the sauce. Deglaze the frying pan with the white wine. Allow this to bubble down, then add the stock and simmer until it reduces a little and tastes good. Turn the heat down, then whisk in the cold butter, remove from the heat.

Place the rocket in a large bowl and quickly toss in the dressing before gently mixing in the crisps.

Arrange the lamb on warmed individual plates, leaving half of each plate free. Pour on the sauce. Arrange the salad in a large pile on the other side of each plate and serve immediately.

GRILLED LAMB CUTLETS WITH GREEN FLAGEOLETS

The British have become very adept at adopting foreign ideas. Their love of French food knows few bounds, and one of the benefits of this adoration is the increasing availability of French produce such as dried flageolet beans instead of their nasty tinned counterparts. (Serves 4)

12 trimmed lamb cutlets

Marinade
1 clove garlic, chopped
2 sprigs parsley
4 sprigs thyme
2 tablespoons olive oil
3 tablespoons dry
  white wine

Beans
225g/8oz dried green
  flageolet beans
2 cloves garlic, crushed
4 shallots, finely diced
3 tablespoons olive oil

225g/8oz ripe tomatoes,
  peeled and chopped
4 tablespoons dry white
  wine
2 tablespoons finely
  chopped parsley
1 teaspoon chopped thyme
2 teaspoons caster sugar
salt and freshly ground black
  pepper

Thyme butter
1 shallot, finely diced
1 teaspoon chopped thyme
1 teaspoon balsamic vinegar
115g/4oz softened butter

Put the lamb cutlets in a shallow dish. Mix together the garlic, parsley, thyme, olive oil and white wine and pour over the cutlets, rubbing the marinade into them. Cover and leave in the fridge for 8 hours. At the same time soak the beans in plenty of cold water.

Rinse the beans and place in a pan with plenty of fresh cold water. Bring to the boil, skim, and boil for 10 minutes, before reducing the heat. Simmer for about 1½ hours or until the beans are tender.

Meanwhile, fry the garlic and shallots in the olive oil until soft and golden. Add the diced tomatoes to the shallots, and simmer for a few minutes before adding the white wine.

As soon as the beans are cooked, drain and add to the tomatoes. Simmer gently for 15 minutes, then add the finely chopped herbs and season to taste with the sugar, salt and pepper.

To make the thyme butter, beat together the finely chopped shallots, thyme, vinegar and butter. Season to taste and set aside.

Preheat a cast-iron ribbed grill and season the cutlets. As soon as the grill is very hot, sear each side of the cutlets. They should still be pink and juicy inside. Brush with the thyme butter and serve with the hot beans.

NEW POTATOES

Potatoes are enjoying a well-deserved renaissance as the supermarkets have begun to sell more and more unusual varieties, among them many old breeds that had almost disappeared for good. Nowadays, the early Jersey Royals are followed by Charlottes, Belle de Fontenay and Pink Fir Apples as they each come into season through the summer.

Yet our manner of cooking potatoes has changed little to accommodate their different flavours and textures. Perhaps it is just too soon. So I have limited this section to three of the simplest British recipes for new potatoes.

JERSEY ROYALS WITH MINT

The perfect way to eat these fragrant tubers. (Serves 4)

455g/1lb small Jersey	6 sprigs mint
Royals	butter, to taste
1 teaspoon salt	

Thoroughly wash the potatoes in plenty of cold water. Then, following your usual practice, either meticulously scrub each potato to remove the papery delicate skin or simply remove any dirt. Place in a pan of salted cold water with 3 mint sprigs. Bring to the boil over a moderate heat and boil for 10 minutes or until tender when pierced.

Drain the potatoes and place in a china bowl with the fresh mint sprigs prettily tucked in among them. Cut the butter into dice and scatter over the hot potatoes so that it coats them all as it melts. Serve with extra sea salt.

POTATO SALAD 1

The great art in making a good potato salad is to toss the potatoes hot into their dressing. This way all the flavours seem to melt into one another. I have to admit that I adore potato salad made with Hellman's mayonnaise, though you can, of course, make your own. If you do, be sure to add plenty of mustard. (Serves 4)

455g/1lb new potatoes	salt and freshly ground black
4 spring onions, finely sliced	pepper
6 tablespoons mayonnaise	

Cook the potatoes as described in the previous recipe, then quickly slice them and toss while still hot into a large bowl with the spring onions and mayonnaise. Season to taste. Leave to cool – if you can – and serve with a crisp green salad and cold salmon, chicken or ham.

Note: If you like peeled potatoes but hate skinning them, boil them in their skins and quickly peel them while they are hot.

POTATO SALAD 2

This piquant salad is gorgeous served warm with spicy sausages. (Serves 4)

455g/1lb new potatoes, scrubbed	½ tablespoon whole-grain mustard
1 shallot, finely diced	2 tablespoons sherry vinegar
1 tablespoon finely sliced chives	6 tablespoons olive oil
½ tablespoon finely chopped parsley	salt and freshly ground black pepper

Boil the potatoes in plenty of cold salted water until tender. While they are cooking whisk together the diced shallot, chives, parsley, mustard, vinegar and olive oil. Season to taste.

Drain the potatoes, allow to steam for a couple of minutes, then halve and toss in the vinaigrette. Adjust the seasoning to taste.

EASTER BAKING

Modern cooks are not so committed to home baking as their ancestors. This may be due to lack of time, lack of knowledge, or the variety of breads and cakes available to them in the shops. However, although their numbers may have diminished, many domestic cooks still enjoy making the occasional cake or bun, especially for festivities such as Easter. Happily, science has moved on and cooks can now buy a form of dried yeast that needs only to be mixed in with other dry ingredients. Gone are the worries about whether or not the yeast is live – bread-making has become easy.

As there are too many Easter breads and cakes to mention here, I have decided to limit the section to just two favourites – hot cross buns and saffron bread. Hot cross buns as we know them only appeared after the Reformation. Originally all dough was marked with a cross before it went into the oven to ward off any evil spirits that might prevent it from rising. This practice was considered 'popish' so was banned except on Good Friday, when the appearance of a cross was felt to be appropriate – hence our delectable buns.

Another ancient Lenten bread that dates back to around the early sixteenth century is saffron bread. According to Sara Paston-Williams, from whom the following recipe comes, it was commonly eaten in the West Country for Easter, although it has now spread across the country.

HOT CROSS BUNS

The dough can be mixed the day before and left covered overnight in the fridge. Just continue as normal when you are ready to cook them. (Makes 8–10)

455g/1lb plain flour	55g/2oz melted butter
55g/2oz caster sugar	170ml/6fl oz tepid milk
1 teaspoon salt	1 egg, beaten
1 teaspoon ground cinnamon	85g/3oz currants
1 teaspoon ground mixed spice	55g/2oz mixed candied peel
½ teaspoon ground nutmeg	85g/3oz marzipan
½ teaspoon ground mace	*Glaze*
2 teaspoons easy-blend dried yeast	3 tablespoons granulated sugar
	4 tablespoons water

Sift the flour, sugar, salt and spices into a large mixing bowl. Thoroughly mix in the yeast. Mix together the melted butter and the milk. Make a well in the centre of the spiced flour and pour in the milk along with the beaten egg, currants and candied peel. Draw the flour into the mixture and mix until the dough leaves the sides of the bowl clean.

Turn the mixture out and knead for 5 minutes or until the dough feels silky and resilient to touch. Wash the bowl in very hot water and quickly dry. Return the dough to the bowl and cover with clingfilm. Leave to rise for 90 minutes in a warm place. It should double its size. If it has not, leave until it does.

Preheat the oven to 200°C/400°F/gas 6 and grease 2 baking sheets. Turn the dough out and lightly knead once again. Divide into 8–10 pieces. Shape into smooth round buns and space evenly on the baking sheets. Lightly cover with some clingfilm.

Roll out the marzipan and cut into strips. Press 2 of these into each bun so that each is marked with a marzipan cross. Cover again and leave to rise for 35 minutes or until the buns have risen and look puffy. Dissolve the sugar and water over a low heat and set aside until needed.

Bake the buns in the preheated oven for 20 minutes. Remove from the oven, place on a cooling rack and brush while warm with the sugar syrup to give them a deliciously sticky appearance.

WEST COUNTRY SAFFRON BREAD

(Makes 1 loaf)

large pinch of saffron
  strands
285ml/½ pint milk
455g/1lb plain flour
½ teaspoon ground mace
1 teaspoon ground
  cinnamon

½ teaspoon salt
170g/6oz cold butter, diced
2 teaspoons easy-blend
  dried yeast
85g/3oz caster sugar
170g/6oz currants
55g/2oz chopped candied
  peel

Crumble the saffron strands into the milk and scald. Leave the milk to infuse for 30 minutes.

Sift the flour, spices and salt into a mixing bowl. Rub the butter into the flour until it forms fine crumbs, then mix in the yeast, sugar, currants and candied peel. Pour the milk into the flour and mix until it forms a soft dough. Turn out and lightly knead before returning it to a large clean bowl. Cover and leave in a warm place until it has doubled its size.

Preheat the oven to 180°C/350°F/gas 4 and grease a 20cm/8 inch cake tin.

Turn the dough out and lightly knead before shaping into a ball so that it neatly fits the cake tin. Bake in the preheated oven for 1 hour or until it is well risen and golden. Leave to cool in its tin before turning out. Serve sliced, either fresh with clotted cream or toasted with lashings of butter.

CHOCOLATE

Chocolate has been a national passion since its introduction in the mid-seventeenth century. Chocolate houses such as White's (which quickly became a gentlemen's club to protect its members from gambling with riff-raff) were founded to drink this new nectar, while many of the coffee houses added it to their menu. Our obsession was further encouraged in the nineteenth century by the Quakers, who founded some of the great chocolate factories such as Cadbury's, Fry's and Rowntree to help encourage teetotalism.

Today any serious chocolate buyer should always read the label of a chocolate bar first. A premium chocolate will have over 50 per cent cocoa solids and will use cocoa butter rather than cocoa butter substitutes. It should contain natural (as opposed to artificial) vanilla. The best chocolates state which variety of cocoa beans has been used – but many are blended. These chocolates should not taste particularly sweet and the flavour should develop in the mouth, just like a fine wine.

HOT CHOCOLATE

Hot chocolate was originally made by whisking together grated chocolate, claret, egg yolks and sugar, while the very rich added cinnamon, pepper, cloves, aniseed, almonds, orange flower water, vanilla pods and milk to their whisked chocolate. By the eighteenth century Sir Hans Sloane, who was Queen Anne's physician, recommended that it be drunk with milk, rather than water, as a sound nutritional drink. Apparently he sold his recipe to a London apothecary, who later sold it to the Cadbury brothers. These days high-quality drinking chocolate has to be made at home. (Serves 3–4)

285ml/½ pint single cream
115g/4oz good bitter
    chocolate, for example
    Valrhona, roughly grated

565ml/1 pint milk
caster sugar, to taste

Heat the cream over a low heat without letting it boil. Whisk in the chocolate and stir until it has completely melted.

Meanwhile, heat the milk to scalding point in a separate pan. Once the chocolate has melted, whisk in the milk and sweeten to taste.

CHOCOLATE BREAD AND BUTTER PUDDING

Bread and butter pudding has enjoyed an enthusiastic revival in the eighties. Here is my chocoholic version. If you cannot buy Selkirk Bannock, use another lightly fruited bread or brioche. (Serves 6)

55g/2oz sultanas	2 whole eggs
6 tablespoons dark rum	3 egg yolks
425ml/¾ pint milk	55g/2oz caster sugar
425ml/¾ pint double cream	155g/5½oz good dark
1 split vanilla pod	chocolate, broken into
55g/2oz butter, softened	small pieces
400–500g/14–18oz Selkirk	
Bannock, sliced	

Soak the sultanas in half the rum overnight.

Gently heat the milk, cream and split vanilla pod in a saucepan to scalding point, then immediately remove from the heat and leave to infuse for 30 minutes.

Preheat the oven to 180°C/350°F/gas 4 and liberally butter a large ovenproof dish that is at least 5cm/2 inches deep.

Spread the remaining butter over the bread slices. Neatly line your dish with slightly overlapping bread slices and strew them with the rum-soaked sultanas. Cover with another overlapping layer of buttered bread.

Whisk the eggs, egg yolks and sugar until they are pale and frothy. Return the milk pan to the heat and gently warm. Remove the vanilla pod and stir in the chocolate. As soon as it has melted, slowly pour the mixture into the beaten eggs, whisking all the time. Stir in the remaining rum and pour the chocolate custard through a strainer over the bread. Leave to soak for 15 minutes.

Bake in the centre of the preheated oven for 30–40 minutes until it is just set and golden brown. Serve warm or cold, with crème fraîche or double cream.

CHOCOLATE PRALINE POTS

Another favourite combination – chocolate and nuts. (Serves 4)

115g/4oz blanched hazelnuts and/or almonds	30g/1oz butter
115g/4oz granulated sugar	3 eggs, separated
3 tablespoons water	a pinch of salt
200g/7oz good dark chocolate	

Preheat the oven to 180°C/350°F/gas 4. Lightly oil a baking sheet and set aside while you roast the nuts.

Roast the nuts until they turn golden brown and smell gorgeous. Melt the sugar with the water in a heavy-bottomed pan over a low heat. As soon as the sugar begins to caramelize, turning a delicate gold, stir in the roasted nuts. Coat them thoroughly and cook for a further 1–2 minutes, so that they deepen in colour. Pour on to the greased baking sheet and leave to cool and harden. Once cold, remove the praline and place in a polythene bag. Crush with a rolling pin until it forms fine chips. Measure out 115g/4oz of praline and store the remainder in an airtight container for future use.

Place the chocolate and butter in a bowl over a pan of simmering water and slowly melt. Beat the egg yolks in a large bowl until pale and thick. Mix in the praline and the melted chocolate.

Whisk the egg whites and salt in a large bowl until they form soft peaks. Fold a couple of spoonfuls of whipped egg white into the chocolate mix to slacken it. Then, using a metal spoon, swiftly fold in the remaining egg whites and pour into 4 small soufflé pots. Chill until needed.

MAY

SUMMER SALADS
Grilled goat's cheese salad
Spring beetroot salad
Salmon sashimi salad

ASPARAGUS
Asparagus with butter
White asparagus vinaigrette
Asparagus soup
Asparagus tartlets

PASTA
Broad bean and bacon tagliatelle
Roasted pepper and pasta salad
Pappardelle with ceps

DUCK
Duck breast with mint peas
Marinated duck breast
Soy roast duck salad

HERBS
English herbal salad
Lemon balm pistachio sauce
Tarragon chicken salad

CHERRIES AND APRICOTS
Warm cherry salad
Flambéed cherries
Apricot rosewater pie

SUMMER DRINKS
Pimm's
White wine cup

The common image of British food, come rain or shine, has been dominated by stodgy, Edwardian recipes. Yet the average British family would be somewhat startled if they were served 'fried fillets of plaice, beef roll, salad, gooseberry pudding, butter, cheese, bread and biscuits' for lunch on a warm summer's day as suggested in the 1915 edition of Mrs Beeton's *Household Management*. In reality our national repertoire of recipes is in a constant state of flux as food fashions come and go, changing the national diet as they do so. However, the vogue for Mediterranean food, which effectively began with Elizabeth David, has gradually eroded these old-fashioned notions of British summer food, shaping it into its modern form. May marks a turning point in the culinary year, when light, simple dishes return to the table, and warming stews and puddings are put away with the winter woollies.

Slowly but surely Mediterranean cooking has influenced the way we eat and how we cook in summer. It has become fashionable to have ultra-simple daily meals consisting of just one dish, such as pasta with broad beans and bacon or duck breasts cooked with peas. Olive oil has become essential, along with the once frowned-upon garlic and herbs. An appreciation of good food has become modish once more and many cooks, their confidence growing, are widening their horizons to embrace culinary influences from further afield. But it is important to remember that, as in all cultures, new ideas are never replicated exactly; rather they are adapted and subverted to the national taste to create modern food.

The British have embraced with open arms, new ways of serving pasta –

it fits so perfectly into modern life. Pasta has been cooked for aristocratic tables since the late fourteenth century, but although it was accepted by the middle classes in the nineteenth century, its popularity was limited until recently. But a combination of influential food writers and broadcasters, foreign travel, improved home produce and a need for quick easy food has created a demand for all kinds of pasta dishes. Our summer recipes will range from the orthodox Italian-influenced wild mushroom sauces to the 'new wave' cherry tomato vinaigrettes.

Salads are another area that has benefited from the Mediterranean influence. Gone are the post-war days of wilted lettuce with the obligatory tomato quarter, cucumber slice and hard-boiled egg. Now it is socially acceptable to serve salads as sophisticated starters, light main courses and piquant side dishes. Cooks are constantly demanding better quality produce and consequently the supermarkets are improving both the range and quality of many of their foods. It is now possible to buy a large range of specialist oils, vinegars and cheeses, as well as a wide variety of fruit and vegetables. The influx of these ingredients has allowed both professional and domestic cooks to reinterpret some of their traditional recipes to create delicate new dishes, such as young beetroot dressed in herbs and nut oils.

The abundance of fresh herbs is another sign of impending summer. Although they can be bought throughout the year, they begin to appear in quantity only in May. It is odd to contemplate the fact that in 1955 (according to Elizabeth David) fresh herbs were hard to come by unless you grew them. This is strange, because the British have traditionally used a great many herbs in their cooking, right up to the turn of the century. Delia Smith attributes their demise to industrialization and the difficulties of transport, but perhaps it was also due to a change in the nation's taste. Whatever the reasons, these days it is hard to find a savoury recipe that does not use herbs.

The arrival of May signifies the beginning of the English asparagus season, and British good taste still dictates that a simple approach is the best way to prepare it. May also brings the first imported cherries and apricots of the season. Modern recipes using these differ little from their predecessors, but sadly, puddings are often relegated to special occasions and weekend cooking.

Another food that is traditionally associated with the end of May is duck. Domesticated ducks were often eaten in the early summer to vary a diet that some carnivores considered dull without game. Nowadays duck is good throughout the year, but our taste in the matter of serving it has changed. In the past it was either stuffed and roasted or gently simmered in stock and served with delicacies such as stewed peas or green cabbage. Even glazed turnips were initially fried with the duck. Modern cooks are hesitant at carving whole ducks (especially outside the privacy of their own kitchen) and many prefer to buy quick-cooking duck breasts instead. Consequently many of our traditional recipes are being adapted to suit sautéed duck breasts while recipes for roast duck are exploiting other methods. Chinese-influenced recipes in particular are becoming popular, with the increasing availability of spices and good-quality soy sauces.

May would not be complete without the first cool glass of Pimm's or iced wine cup of the summer. These fragrant alcoholic drinks appear with the first warm day and are an essential part of outdoor entertaining. They are bound by few social rules as to when they should be served – the only essential rule being that the imbiber should be wary of their potency.

SUMMER SALADS

How one learns to dread the season for salads in England. What becomes of the hearts of the lettuces? What makes an English cook think that beetroot spreading its hideous purple dye over a sardine and a spoonful of tinned baked beans constitutes an hors d'oeuvre? Why make cold salmon, woolly enough anyhow by midsummer, look even less appetizing than it is by serving it on a bed of lettuce leaves apparently rescued from the dustbin? What is the object of spending so much money on cucumbers, tomatoes and lettuces because of their valuable vitamins, and then drowning them in vinegar and chemical salad dressings?

So wrote Elizabeth David in 1955 in her introduction to hors d'oeuvre and salads in *Summer Cooking*, before going on to educate British cooks on the art of salad-making. Happily, such days are long gone, modern salads having become an essential part of the British diet throughout the year. These days, salads can incorporate ideas from all over the world, depending on the cook's prediliction. Cosmopolitan dinner parties are just as likely to feature a dainty British interpretation of salmon sashimi for an appetizer as they are a grilled goat's cheese salad.

GRILLED GOAT'S CHEESE SALAD

Grilled goat's cheese salad is a little like a latter-day prawn cocktail. Simple to make, it became one of the popular restaurant starters in the early nineties, its arrival coinciding with the renaissance in British cheeses. (Serves 4)

4 × 115g/4oz British goat's
cheeses
heart of a red oak-leaf
lettuce
heart of a green oak-leaf
lettuce
15g/½oz roughly chopped
walnuts

1 clove garlic, crushed
1 tablespoon runny honey
2 tablespoons lemon juice
3 tablespoons walnut oil
salt and freshly ground black
pepper

If possible buy small individual rounds of soft goat's cheese, otherwise choose a goat's cheese log (removing any rind) and cut into 2.5cm/1 inch thick discs. Lay them on greaseproof paper and chill until you need them.

Preheat the grill to its highest setting.

Trim and wash the lettuces. Spin and place in a large mixing bowl with the walnut pieces. Whisk together the garlic, honey and lemon juice before slowly adding the walnut oil. Season to taste.

Lightly season the goat's cheese with freshly ground black pepper and place on a greased baking sheet under the grill. Keep an eye on them.

Toss the salad with the dressing and arrange in a small circle on each of the 4 serving plates. As soon as the cheese begins to colour and melt, carefully remove with a fish slice and place in the centre of each salad. Serve immediately. It is wonderful eaten with walnut bread.

Note: **Vary the lettuces according to what is best at the time of shopping.**

SPRING BEETROOT SALAD

Until you have tasted tiny home-grown beetroot, it is hard to understand the British penchant for tossing them into salads, particularly as they stain everything in sight a lurid pink. But freshly dug young beetroot are like small scented sugar lumps – delicious. Gardeners can also grow yellow and white beetroot, which make the most beautiful salads. If you are cooking a mixture of colours, cook and dress them separately and mix at the last moment to preserve their separate colours. This salad can be eaten warm or cold. (Serves 4)

455g/1lb young raw
  beetroot
salt
1 shallot, finely diced
1 teaspoon finely chopped
  tarragon
½ tablespoon finely
  chopped chervil
½ tablespoon finely
  chopped parsley

1 tablespoon finely sliced
  chives
2 tablespoons white wine
  vinegar
3 tablespoons walnut oil
3 tablespoons hazelnut oil
freshly ground black pepper

Scrub the beetroot clean and trim off their roots and leaves. (The latter can be used like a spinach green, if wished.) Place in a pan of salted cold water and bring up to the boil. Cook over a moderate heat for 20–30 minutes, until the beetroot are tender. Drain, and as soon as they are cool enough to handle, peel off their skin, which should loosen and come away if you rub your thumb and fingers over them. Wear rubber gloves if you don't want pink hands!

While the beetroot are cooking make the vinaigrette. Place the finely diced shallot and herbs in a mixing bowl, add the vinegar, then whisk in the 2 nut oils. Season to taste and toss over the warm peeled beetroot. Serve warm or cold. Gorgeous with cold roast ham and hot new potatoes.

SALMON SASHIMI SALAD

Japanese cooking has had a long, if subtle, influence on modern cookery, beginning with Nouvelle Cuisine. However, with the increasing availability of Japanese ingredients many domestic cooks are now able to explore dishes that were previously served only in modern British restaurants. (Serves 4)

340g/12oz salmon fillet or tuna fillet (sashimi grade)	1 tablespoon rice vinegar
12 thin spring onions	3 tablespoons sesame oil
2 bunches watercress	1 lemon, cut into 8 wedges
1 teaspoon caster sugar	1 teaspoon wasabi
1 tablespoon soy sauce	horseradish paste

Finely slice the salmon – just like smoked salmon. Neatly arrange on a plate that is covered with clingfilm. Cover and chill while you prepare the rest of the salad.

Wash and trim the spring onions, just snipping off the tops of their leaves. Bring a small pan of water to the boil and quickly immerse the spring onions for about 30 seconds. Immediately drain and cool under cold running water. Pat dry and set aside while you finish the salad.

Thoroughly wash the watercress. Remove the thicker stalks and discard any yellowing leaves. Dry and place in a mixing bowl.

Whisk together the sugar, soy sauce, rice vinegar and sesame oil. If a lighter flavour is preferred, substitute peanut oil for half the sesame oil.

Toss the watercress and spring onions in two-thirds of the dressing and arrange on 4 plates. Arrange some fish on each plate, then drizzle the remaining dressing over it. Garnish with lemon wedges and a small dab of wasabi horseradish paste.

ASPARAGUS

The arrival of the first English asparagus in May still sends a shiver of delight through many cooks, even although they can buy imported varieties throughout the year. Truly fresh asparagus has a superb flavour and is worth growing if you have a garden. Traditionally, Norfolk-grown asparagus was regarded as the best.

Asparagus is rarely sold by name but rather according to size or colour. The cheapest is the thin 'sparrowgrass' or 'sprue' asparagus, which some believe has the finest flavour. At the other end of the scale are the huge 'jumbo' asparagus. To my mind these are rather gross and not worth the extra cost when you can buy ordinary plump, succulent stalks. May also sees the arrival of white (blanched) asparagus, imported from Europe. This has a distinctive flavour that is worth trying, although many believe it to be an acquired taste.

Whichever type of asparagus you choose, select stems that have tight, dry, unfurled tips and supple stems. Avoid any with scars or slimy patches. A great mystique has developed around asparagus cooking. Cooks are usually advised to boil their trimmed asparagus, neatly tied in a bundle, in a tall, narrow asparagus pan, so that the tips can steam while the stalks are boiled. Not having such a pan, I have always cooked my asparagus loose in plenty of boiling, salted water – just like any other green vegetable – and have always found the results to be excellent. Cooking times vary according to the size of the asparagus, so add an extra stalk for testing.

ASPARAGUS WITH BUTTER

Buttered asparagus has been served since at least the eighteenth century.
Today the butter is either melted or served as a mousseline or a hollandaise sauce. Choose as many asparagus as you wish, depending on their
size and your generosity. (Serves 4)

| 24 asparagus spears | 115g/4oz butter |
| salt | |

Carefully wash the asparagus in cold water, as their heads sometimes
hide tiny granules of sand. Cut off the hard stalk ends and, using a
flexible potato peeler, lightly pare off the tough skin on the lower part of
the stems.

If you are serving a butter sauce, make it up now and keep it warm in a
Thermos flask while you cook the asparagus.

Choose a saucepan large enough to hold the asparagus comfortably on
their sides and fill it with water. Bring this to a rolling boil, then add salt
and the loose asparagus. If there is not enough room for all the asparagus,
cook them in two batches, for 5–7 minutes or until just tender. Carefully
drain, making sure they do not fall on their delicate heads, and allow
them to steam dry in the colander for a couple of minutes while you melt
the butter. There is nothing worse than finding a pool of asparagus water
on your plate.

Place on warm plates, pour the melted butter over the asparagus tips or
into small individual bowls, and serve immediately.

WHITE ASPARAGUS VINAIGRETTE

White asparagus has been considered a delicacy here since the early seventeenth century, although the fashion for serving asparagus cold is relatively recent in Britain. Eliza Acton observes in her *Modern Cookery* (1845) that 'abroad, boiled asparagus is very frequently served cold and eaten with oil and vinegar, or a sauce Mayonnaise'. (Serves 2)

12–14 white asparagus spears	6 tablespoons olive oil
½ tablespoon whole-grain mustard	pinch of caster sugar
2 tablespoons champagne or white wine vinegar	salt and freshly ground black pepper

Prepare and cook the asparagus as in the previous recipe. Drain and spread them out to cool on a large plate.

Meanwhile, whisk together the mustard and vinegar, before slowly adding the olive oil, sugar, salt and pepper.

The asparagus can be served once it is cold. Serve the dressing separately.

ASPARAGUS SOUP

Asparagus soup has been a British favourite for many years. It can be
served hot or cold. (Serves 4)

455g/1lb asparagus	285ml/½ pint asparagus
1 small onion, finely diced	water
1 clove garlic, crushed	285ml/½ pint chicken stock
15g/½oz butter	salt and freshly ground black
15g/½oz flour	pepper
	140ml/¼ pint double cream

Wash the asparagus and cut off the tips. Trim and roughly slice the
stalks. Bring a pan of water to the boil, and salt, and boil the tips for 4
minutes. Remove them with a slotted spoon and allow to cool. Return
the water to the boil, then add the asparagus stalks. Cook for 5 minutes
then drain, saving the water.

Gently soften the onion and garlic in the butter. Stir in the flour and
cook over a low heat for 5 minutes, stirring regularly. Then add the
reserved asparagus water and the chicken stock. Simmer gently for 15
minutes. Add the cooked stems to the soup and simmer for a further 5–10
minutes before removing from heat.

Liquidize and strain the soup. Adjust the seasoning and gently reheat.
Add the cream and the asparagus tips and serve.

ASPARAGUS TARTLETS

Tinned asparagus tips were once considered the height of luxury. They used to be served at office parties as nibbles, wrapped in white sliced bread, or on top of croûtons or in tartlets. Everybody loved them. Happily, the current superabundance of fresh, small asparagus has allowed them to become the delicacy they once were. (Serves 6)

225g/8oz shortcrust pastry (see page 327)
1 medium onion, finely diced
2 tablespoons vegetable oil
170g/6oz cooked asparagus
55g/2 oz freshly grated Parmesan cheese
1 large egg
1 egg yolk
200ml/7fl oz double cream
salt and freshly ground black pepper

Roll out the pastry on a lightly floured surface and line 6 small greased tart tins. Line with greaseproof paper, fill with rice or beans and chill for 30 minutes.

Preheat the oven to 200°C/400°F/gas 6 and bake the tartlets blind for 10–15 minutes, until the pastry begins to colour. Remove the paper and rice or beans and return to the oven to dry out for a further 5 minutes.

While the pastry cases are baking, gently fry the onion in the oil until soft and cut the cooked asparagus into small bite-size pieces.

Divide the onion between the tart cases. Place the asparagus pieces on top and generously sprinkle with Parmesan. Beat together the egg, egg yolk and cream. Season to taste and pour over the fillings. Return to the oven and cook for about 15–20 minutes or until just set and golden. For maximum asparagus flavour serve warm.

PASTA

Pasta is not new to Britain. The first English reference to it can be found in *Forme of Cury* (c.1390), where a recipe for 'macrows' strewn with butter and served with grated cheese is given. Until recently macaroni was the generic British name for pasta. In the eighteenth century many aristocrats on the Grand Tour became known as 'macaronis', due to their excessive passion for all things Italian, including pasta. But it was not until the nineteenth century that pasta became more accessible to the middle classes. Both Mrs Rundell (*Modern Domestic Cookery*) and Eliza Acton give full accounts of the different types of macaroni (pasta) available, along with detailed cooking instructions.

Today it is possible to purchase an enormous variety of both fresh and dried pasta. As a general guide, allow 85–115g/3–4oz dried pasta for a main course portion and cook it in plenty of boiling salted water (with a dash of oil) for around 12 minutes or until it is *al dente*, that is, tender but with a slight bite. Cooking times will vary with different pastas – fresh pasta only takes a few minutes.

BROAD BEAN AND BACON TAGLIATELLE

Broad beans are to many another incomprehensible British favourite. They must be cooked while still small and tender, otherwise they can be tough and mealy. However, if you have no choice and plenty of time, you can serve the tender inner beans, by blanching the shelled beans and removing their tough outer casing. (Serves 4)

salt	4 fat cloves garlic, crushed
225g/8oz shelled young	6 spring onions, thinly sliced
broad beans	1 teaspoon finely chopped
340g/12oz fresh tagliatelle	sage
½ tablespoon vegetable oil	170g/6oz soft goat's cheese,
225g/8oz smoked back	diced
bacon	freshly ground black pepper
6 tablespoons fruity olive oil	

Bring a small pan of salted water to the boil, add the beans, cover and simmer for 4–5 minutes until tender. Drain and set aside.

Cook the pasta in a large pan of boiling salted water to which the vegetable oil has been added. Fresh pasta will take only a few minutes to cook.

Trim the fat off the bacon slices and cut into neat lardons. Heat half the olive oil in a frying pan and fry the bacon until it is just beginning to turn crispy. Stir in the garlic and spring onions and quickly fry for another minute before adding the broad beans and remaining oil. When the beans are warm, toss the drained pasta into the mixture until it is evenly coated. Add the sage, cheese and seasoning. Mix thoroughly and serve immediately.

ROASTED PEPPER AND PASTA SALAD

Sweet, roasted peppers have become one of the signature ingredients of 'Mediterranean' cooking. Easy to prepare, roasting rids peppers of that unpleasant metallic after-taste. (Serves 4)

1 red pepper, quartered and seeded
1 yellow pepper, quartered and seeded
salt
1 dessertspoon vegetable oil
255g/9oz pasta swirls or rotelle
2 tablespoons roughly torn basil leaves
2 cloves garlic, crushed
2 tablespoons white wine vinegar
6 tablespoons olive oil
freshly ground black pepper
225g/8oz cherry tomatoes, halved
8 green olives, stoned and cut into thin strips

Preheat the grill to its highest setting. Arrange the peppers skin side up under the grill. As soon as their skin blisters, remove and place in a covered bowl. After 10 minutes, peel the peppers and cut into diamond shapes.

Bring a large pan of water to the boil, then add the salt, vegetable oil and pasta. Cook for 10 minutes or until the pasta is *al dente*, then drain well.

Meanwhile, whisk together the basil, garlic, vinegar, olive oil and seasoning to make the vinaigrette. Place in a large bowl. Add the cherry tomatoes, olives, roasted peppers and pasta as and when they are ready. Allow to cool. Adjust the seasoning and serve.

PAPPARDELLE WITH CEPS

Fresh ceps appear briefly in the shops for a few short weeks in spring and it is worth indulging in them if you are feeling extravagant. But this recipe is also very good made with shiitake, oyster and brown cap mushrooms – use a handful of each, as they will drastically reduce when cooked. (Serves 2)

3 tablespoons olive oil	¼ teaspoon finely chopped
2 shallots, finely diced	thyme
2 cloves garlic, crushed	½ tablespoon finely sliced
4–5 fat ceps	chives
6 tablespoons dry white	salt and freshly ground black
wine	pepper
1 tablespoon finely chopped	1 tablespoon vegetable oil
parsley	170g/6oz fresh pappardelle
pinch of finely chopped	or any form of tagliatelle
rosemary	55g/2oz butter

Place a large pan of water on to boil for the pasta.

Heat the olive oil over a moderate heat. Gently fry the shallots and garlic until soft and golden. Wipe the ceps clean with a damp cloth and trim their stems. Cut the mushrooms into medium slices and add to the shallots.

Once the mushrooms have turned golden and become soft, add the white wine, herbs and seasoning. Allow the mixture to bubble up and reduce a little.

Add the vegetable oil, salt and pasta to the boiling water and cook until *al dente*. Drain the pasta and swirl the butter into the mushrooms, so that it thickens their juices a little. Serve immediately.

DUCK

At last Jemima told him that she intended to begin to sit the next day – 'and I will bring a bag of corn with me, so that I need never leave my nest until the eggs are hatched. They might catch cold,' said the conscientious Jemima.

'Madam, I beg you not to trouble yourself with a bag; I will provide oats. But before you commence your tedious sitting, I intend to give you a treat. Let us have a dinner-party all to ourselves!

'May I ask you to bring up some herbs from the farm-garden to make a savoury omelette? Sage and thyme, and mint and two onions, and some parsley. I will provide lard for the stuff – lard for the omelette,' said the hospitable gentleman with sandy whiskers.

Jemima Puddle-Duck was a simpleton: not even the mention of sage and onions made her suspicious.

She went round the farm-garden, nibbling off snippets of all the different sorts of herbs that are used for stuffing roast duck. (*The Tale of Jemima Puddle-Duck* by Beatrix Potter)

Beatrix Potter's fox obviously had a discerning palate, since his roast duck was not going to have a plain sage and onion stuffing but would be filled with fragrant mint and parsley as well.

Traditionally, young ducks were roasted for Whitsun, stuffed with a simple breadcrumb sage and onion stuffing and served with young vegetables such as peas, new potatoes or glazed turnips. Lack of time (and possibly experience) has meant that many modern cooks prefer to cook duck breasts, rather than stuff a whole duck. Consequently our duck recipes are changing and classics such as roast duck are being altered to suit modern tastes.

DUCK BREAST WITH MINT PEAS

Peas cooked with mint and lettuce are a traditional accompaniment to duck. This recipe has been adapted for duck breasts so that it only takes a few minutes to cook. The juices of the peas act as a gravy to the duck. (Serves 4)

4 duck breasts	370g/13oz shelled peas
salt and freshly ground black pepper	2 little gem lettuces, roughly sliced
2 cloves garlic, crushed	285ml/½ pint chicken stock
2 tablespoons olive oil	30g/1oz butter
170g/6oz smoked back bacon, cut into lardons	1 tablespoon finely chopped mint
6 spring onions, sliced into pea-sized chunks	

Begin by preparing the duck breasts. Remove any nasty bloody veins or tough-looking sinews from the underside of the breast. Lightly score the duck skin into diamonds and rub all over with salt and half the garlic.

Place the duck breasts skin side down in a heavy-bottomed frying pan over a moderately low heat. The fat will gradually melt enough for you to increase the heat and turn the duck breasts over. Seal their underside and continue to fry gently on both sides until cooked to your liking.

Meanwhile, heat 2 tablespoons of olive oil in a saucepan and sauté the bacon until it begins to colour and no longer releases any water. Add the remaining garlic and all the spring onions and continue to fry gently for 2 minutes. Stir in the peas and lettuce along with 140ml/¼ pint of the chicken stock and simmer for a further 5 minutes.

Once the duck breasts are nicely browned but still rare and juicy, remove from the pan and keep warm. Pour off the excess duck fat and deglaze the pan with the remaining chicken stock. Reduce and stir into the peas.

Quickly stir the butter into the peas and remove from the heat. Add the mint and adjust the seasoning to taste. Serve immediately with the duck breasts.

MARINATED DUCK BREAST

One of the commonest complaints against duck breast is toughness. The following recipe eradicates this problem by tenderizing the meat. Try serving with honey mustard turnips or crispy fried potato cakes (page 286) and a green salad. (Serves 4)

4 duck breasts

Marinade
285ml/½ pint Beaumes de Venise
1 leek, roughly chopped
1 celery stick, roughly chopped
1 carrot, roughly chopped
1 small onion, roughly chopped
2 cloves garlic, roughly chopped

1 sprig parsley
1 bay leaf
1 sprig thyme

To serve
salt and freshly ground black pepper
2 cloves garlic, crushed
3 tablespoons olive oil
140ml/¼ pint Beaumes de Venise
2 tablespoons butter

The night before, pull away the skin from the duck breasts and remove any nasty bloody veins or tough-looking sinews from their underside. (You can make your own duck fat by cutting the fatty skin into small dice and placing it in a small heavy-bottomed pan over a low heat. All the fat will slowly melt and can then be strained and stored, covered, in the fridge. Wonderful for roasting potatoes.)

Place each duck breast between 2 sheets of clingfilm. Using a rolling pin, gently beat each breast until it spreads out into a thin steak. Place them in a china bowl with the marinade ingredients, cover and chill until needed.

Shortly before serving, remove the breasts from the marinade, pat dry, season and smear with a little crushed garlic. Strain the marinade juices, saving the vegetables at the same time.

Heat the olive oil in a large heavy frying pan. Sear the breasts over a high heat, allowing 2–3 minutes each side. Remove from the pan and keep warm while you make the sauce.

Lower the heat and add a further tablespoon of oil to the frying pan. Stir in the marinade vegetables and gently fry for 5 minutes. Pour in the marinade and loosen any sediment. Allow the mixture to reduce down by half, then strain into a small clean pan.

Add the remaining wine and bring to the boil. Reduce by half, then quickly swirl in the butter and transfer to a sauce-boat. Serve immediately with the duck breasts.

Note: If you wish to serve honey mustard turnips with the duck, boil 24 baby turnips until tender. Meanwhile, whisk together 1 tablespoon of runny honey, 1 tablespoon of Dijon mustard, 2 tablespoons of rice or white wine vinegar, 6 tablespoons of olive oil and 1 tablespoon of finely chopped chives. Toss the hot turnips in this dressing and season to taste. Chive flowers make a very pretty garnish.

SOY ROAST DUCK SALAD

An increasingly popular method of roasting duck is to steam it initially in the oven before roasting. Steaming makes the duck meltingly tender and has the added advantage of allowing the cook to half prepare the dish in advance. The final 50 minutes is quite labour-intensive but it is worth the effort. Incidentally, this technique can be adapted to plain roasts, where the duck is simply basted with honey and orange or just with olive oil. (Serves 4)

2.15kg/4lb 11oz oven-ready duck	6 tablespoons sake
½ tablespoon Sichuan peppercorns (optional)	*Salad*
½ teaspoon ground star anise	1 cucumber, peeled
1 teaspoon salt	salt
¼ teaspoon freshly ground black pepper	2 tablespoons caster sugar
	1 tablespoon rice vinegar
6 tablespoons soy sauce	1 fat cos lettuce, thickly sliced
6 tablespoons mirin	12 spring onions, finely sliced

Balance a cooling rack on 4 small soufflé dishes in your roasting tray. Half-fill the tray with water, but make sure that it does not come into contact with the rack. Preheat the oven to 190°C/375°F/gas 5.

Remove the duck's wing tips and pull out any pin feathers. Pull out any fatty deposits inside the vent. Prick the skin with a fork, particularly in any obviously fatty areas. Crush the Sichuan peppercorns under a rolling pin or in a pestle and mortar. Mix with the star anise, salt and black pepper. Season the duck's cavity with the pepper mixture and lightly rub all over its skin.

Place the duck, breast side up, on the cooling rack and carefully wrap a generous amount of foil over the bird, tucking it in around the rim of the roasting tray. You must ensure that the foil is as airtight as possible, so use as many sheets as necessary. As the duck cooks the foil will billow up with the steam, so it needs plenty of room in the oven to puff up.

Place in the preheated oven and steam for 1 hour. Then remove the duck. If you are not using it immediately, allow it to cool in a dry airy place then cover and chill. Otherwise continue as below.

Increase the oven temperature to 220°C/425°F/gas 7. Place the soy sauce, mirin and sake in a small saucepan and gently heat. Brush the duck liberally with some of this mixture and roast for 30 minutes, basting it with the sauce every 10 minutes.

Reduce the heat to 190°C/375°F/gas 5 and continue to cook the duck for a further 20 minutes, basting every 5 minutes. Remove from the oven and allow to rest for 5 minutes before carving.

Slice the cucumber in half lengthways and then cut into half-moon slices. Liberally season with salt and leave for 5 minutes, then mix in the sugar and vinegar. Heat the remaining glaze.

Neatly carve the duck so that it is easy to eat. Then mix together the lettuce leaves, spring onions and the cucumber along with its sweet juices and arrange on each plate. Top with the duck pieces, pour over the hot sauce and serve immediately.

Note: Ingredients such as ground star arise and mirin can now be found in some supermarkets as well as Asian shops.

HERBS

One subtle change in modern British cooking is the increasing use of fresh herbs. It is now possible to buy a large variety of herbs and edible flowers, ranging from lemon grass and garlic chives to the more mundane pot marigolds and parsley. A variety of salad flowers can be bought in pillow packets, including pot marigolds, pansies (which taste of lettuce) and tiny borage flowers. The quality of even the most ordinary herb has been radically improved with the recent introduction by the supermarkets of disposable herb pots. These can be left on a sunny window-sill to grow and be picked as needed. Even garden centres have expanded their range, to include old-fashioned herbs such as salad burnet, lemon balm, flavoured mints and tansy, to name but a few. Consequently it is hard to find a savoury recipe that does not use herbs – even puddings are beginning to use them.

ENGLISH HERBAL SALAD

Herbal salads have long been a traditional part of English cooking, dating back in written form to the late fourteenth century with a book called *Forme of Cury*. They are altered to taste throughout the year so that the cook gathers only the tenderest salads. In 1699 John Evelyn wrote *Acetaria*, which was devoted to the growing and cooking of vegetables, including salads. His sensible advice with regard to salad-making is still apposite: '. . . every Plant should come in to bear its art, without being over-power'd by some Herb of a stronger Taste, so as to endanger the native Sapor and Vertue of the rest; but fall into their places, like the Notes on Music, in which there should be nothing harsh or grating.' (Serves 4)

2 tablespoons rice or champagne vinegar	3 tablespoons roughly sliced chives
6 tablespoons olive oil	3 tablespoons picked flat-leaf parsley leaves
salt and freshly ground black pepper	30g/1oz tender young sorrel leaves, roughly torn
1 small garlic clove, crushed (optional)	large bunch of chervil
2 little gem lettuces	3 pot marigold heads or other edible flowers
55g/2oz rocket	

Whisk together the vinegar and oil and season to taste. You can add a touch of garlic if you wish.

Gently wash and trim all the lettuces and herbs as necessary.

Place in a large mixing bowl. When you are ready to serve, quickly toss in the dressing and sprinkle with the marigold or other flower petals. Serve immediately.

Note: I have suggested rice or champagne vinegars because they have a fine light flavour, but you can use any favourite light vinegar.

LEMON BALM PISTACHIO SAUCE

Lemon balm grows rampantly in most British gardens, but still has to be ordered from greengrocers.

This delicate-flavoured sauce is a modern British adaptation of pesto. Sally Clarke used to make many herb and nut variations of pesto sauce in her restaurant, Clarke's, adding cheese only when it enhanced the taste of the purée. This particular variation is good served with white fish or tossed in shellfish salads. (Serves 4)

55g/2oz lemon balm leaves, stripped from their stalks	30g/1oz shelled pistachio nuts
4 tablespoons parsley leaves	1 lemon, finely grated (optional)
1 tablespoon lemon thyme leaves	3–4 tablespoons olive oil

Ideally this sauce should be made in a food processor, but otherwise use elbow power and a pestle and mortar. Place all the herb leaves in the bowl and process until finely chopped. Add the nuts and briefly grind. Any type of nut can easily be overworked, which will make it unpleasantly oily and will split the sauce.

Add the lemon zest only if your herbs do not have a fragrant lemony flavour. Quickly pour in the olive oil while the machine is running, so that it becomes amalgamated. Remove and season to taste. Add more oil if you wish for a thinner sauce.

TARRAGON CHICKEN SALAD

Certain foods are traditionally partnered with a particular herb, and tarragon and chicken are just such a modern marriage. (Serves 4)

1 lemon, cut in half
1.4kg/3lb oven-ready
   corn-fed chicken
4 large sprigs tarragon
3 tablespoons olive oil
salt and freshly ground black
   pepper

Tarragon mayonnaise
2 egg yolks
salt
1–2 tablespoons picked
   tarragon leaves

2 tablespoons white wine
   vinegar
2 teaspoons Dijon mustard
140ml/¼ pint sunflower oil
140ml/¼ pint olive oil

Salad
455g/1lb grapes, halved and
   seeded
455g/1lb tomatoes, peeled,
   seeded and cut into strips
4 spring onions, finely sliced
1 crisp lettuce

Preheat the oven to 230°C/450°F/gas 8.

Roughly squeeze some of the lemon juice over the chicken, then stuff the lemon halves into its cavity along with the tarragon. Rub the whole bird with olive oil, liberally season, and place in a roasting tray.

Roast in the preheated oven for 15 minutes, then reduce the temperature to 190°C/375°F/gas 5 and continue to cook for a further 35 minutes, basting occasionally with olive oil. Test to see if the bird is cooked by inserting a skewer in between its thigh and breast. If the juices run clear, the chicken is cooked. Once the bird is cooked, remove and allow to cool as quickly as possible.

Meanwhile, make the tarragon mayonnaise by placing the egg yolks, a pinch of salt, the tarragon leaves, vinegar and mustard in a food processor. Whizz until pale and frothy and the tarragon is finely chopped. Then slowly add the 2 oils while still processing, until you have a thick, pale mayonnaise. Chill until needed. Prepare the grapes, tomatoes and spring onions.

Peel off the chicken skin and gently prise its flesh away from the carcass. Dice or cut into strips, according to your taste.

Mix together the chicken, grape halves, tomato strips and sliced spring onions. Liberally coat in the tarragon mayonnaise and season to taste. When ready to serve, arrange some of the lettuce leaves in a large bowl and spoon in the salad.

CHERRIES AND APRICOTS

The arrival of the first cherries in the shops signifies to me the beginning of summer. Just to sit munching a bag of cherries on a warm sunny day is sheer bliss. Virtually all our cherries and apricots are imported, which given our weather is not surprising, although both are still grown in Britain. The last of our cherry orchards are in Kent, while apricots can only be found in private gardens and both fruit later in the year. Our cherry orchards were first introduced by the Romans, while the first apricot trees were planted in 1542 by Jean Le Loup, Henry VIII's gardener.

Modern tastes demand that much of our food, especially puddings, is quick and easy to prepare. The arrival of summer acts as an excuse for many people (including myself) to restrict themselves to making fruit salads drenched in Grand Marnier and the odd summer pudding or ice-cream. But our weather is very variable and it is nice to have warm as well as cold puddings.

WARM CHERRY SALAD

Warm summer fruit salads may seem very modern, but were mentioned in Dorothy Hartley's *Food in England* (1954). They are an excellent way of using slightly underripe fruit, such as the early imported peaches. (Serves 4)

1 lemon, finely pared and juiced	140ml/¼ pint water
1 split vanilla pod	200g/7oz blueberries
115g/4oz granulated sugar	225g/8oz fat, juicy cherries
140ml/¼ pint dry white wine	4 peaches

Place the lemon peel in a non-corrosive pan with the vanilla pod, sugar, white wine and water. Dissolve the sugar and simmer gently for 10 minutes.

Put the lemon juice and blueberries in a heat resistant bowl. Stem and stone the cherries and mix with the blueberries. Peel and stone the peaches. If they do not peel easily, cut a small cross in the base and cover with boiling water for a minute – just like tomatoes. Cut each peach into 8 or 12 segments, depending on their size. Add these to the cherries.

Reheat the sugar syrup and once it comes up to the boil pour over the fruit. Remove the lemon peel and vanilla pod. Serve immediately, with lots of crème fraîche.

FLAMBÉED CHERRIES

Cherries can be cooked in batters, pies, tarts and creams, but this simple pudding is perfectly suited to our modern sweet, juicy cherries and takes only a few minutes to make. (Serves 2)

30g/1oz butter	55g/2oz caster sugar or to
1 tablespoon lemon juice	taste
1 tablespoon orange juice	340g/12oz fat, juicy cherries
	3–4 tablespoons Cointreau

Melt the butter, lemon and orange juice over a low heat in a large heavy-bottomed frying pan. Add the sugar and stir until it melts.

Wash and stem the cherries. Cut each cherry in half and remove the stone. Try to save the juice as you do this. Reheat the citrus juices and add the cherries. (Cherries discolour quite quickly, so it is advisable to have everything ready before you start stoning them.) Fry over a high heat for 3 minutes then pour in the Cointreau. Set a match to it and shake the pan to allow the alcohol to burn evenly. Serve hot with lots of thick double cream or crème fraîche.

APRICOT ROSEWATER PIE

This is an adaptation of a English recipe written by Antoine Carême in his book *Le Cuisinier Parisien* of 1828 (although I came across it in Jane Grigson's *English Food*). Carême was at one time employed by the Prince Regent for the incredible salary of £2,000 per annum – so valued were his culinary skills. In this adaptation, I have added rosewater to the apricots as it imbues the pie with a wonderful fragrance. (Serves 4)

225g/8oz rough puff or puff
   pastry (see pages 328–9)
680g/1½lb ripe apricots
55g/2oz butter
2 tablespoons water

225g/8oz caster sugar or to
   taste
3 teaspoons rosewater
1 egg white, beaten
1 tablespoon granulated
   sugar

Preheat the oven to 220°C/425°F/gas 7.

Roll out the pastry on a lightly floured surface to roughly the same shape as your pie dish only larger. Cut a ribbon from the edge of your dough and press it firmly on to the rim of your pie dish.

Wash, halve and stone the apricots. Melt the butter and water over a low heat in a large, heavy-bottomed frying pan. Add the sugar and stir until it melts (adding a little more water if necessary). As soon as the sugar has melted, but not before, add the apricots and rosewater and thoroughly coat in the buttery sugar. Immediately tip the fruit into the pie dish, packing it in neatly.

Brush the pastry rim with some of the beaten egg white. Then loosely roll the pastry on to the rolling pin and lift on to the pie dish. Using a fork or spoon, firmly press around the rim so that the 2 pastries are glued together in a pretty manner. Cut off the excess pastry. Prick the lid with a knife and paint with some more egg white before sprinkling with granulated sugar.

Place the pie in the centre of the preheated oven and bake for 20 minutes, then reduce the temperature to 180°C/350°F/gas 4 and bake for a further 10–15 minutes or until the pastry has puffed up and turned golden.

SUMMER DRINKS

The arrival of summer heralds the beginning of the summer party season, where long cooling drinks are essential. These drinks literally taste of summer, flavoured with cucumber peel, borage flowers and lemon. They are still mixed in the traditional method by the host of the party and poured from large glass jugs.

PIMM'S

Pimm's was created in the 1880s by James Pimm, who devised an unusual gin sling that was served in his restaurant. He very sensibly put it into commercial production, so beginning the delectable British custom of drinking Pimm's by the pint throughout the summer. No summer in Oxford would be complete without sitting by the river sipping pints of Pimm's and feeling the day slip dreamily away.

Pimm's No. 1 (gin-based)	sliced lemon
chilled lemonade	mint sprigs and/or borage
cucumber rounds (or just	flowers
the peel)	

Pimm's is a drink that has to be mixed to taste in a large jug. Some people believe it is sacrilege to add lemon, while others add orange slices as well. It is best to experiment, but make sure you add lots of ice and preferably serve it in glass pint pots.

WHITE WINE CUP

Another refreshing alcoholic cup. (Serves 12–16)

2 bottles Riesling wine	cucumber peel
2 wineglasses Grand	borage flowers
Marnier	1 bottle (425ml/¾ pint) soda
1 tablespoon caster sugar	water
sliced orange	
strawberries	

Mix together and chill the first 6 ingredients for 1–2 hours. Add the borage flowers, soda water and lots of ice just before serving.

JUNE

CHILLED SOUPS
Cucumber soup
Minted pea soup
Gazpacho

SOUFFLÉS
Apricot soufflé
Cheese and tomato soufflé
Green herb lobster soufflé

SUMMER ROASTS
Roast veal with anchovy cream sauce
Lemon roast chicken
Spiced roast pork with apple sorrel sauce
Roast beef with cucumber horseradish sauce

SUMMER VEGETABLES
Steamed Norfolk samphire
Spinach with mint and crème fraîche
Summer vegetable ragout

GOOSEBERRIES
Gooseberry sauce
Gooseberry elderflower fool
Lady Llanover's gooseberry and rhubarb jam

SUMMER TEA
Elderflower cordial
Crab and cress sandwiches
Fairy cakes

The classic simplicity of British cooking has in part been shaped by the quality and abundance of produce that began to be produced in the eighteenth century. The advent of both the agricultural and industrial revolutions at this time not only vastly improved the quality, variety and availability of many foods, but also introduced better kitchens and cooking utensils. As a result, the over-complicated recipes of the seventeenth century were set aside in favour of an elegant, new simplicity. Modern British food still retains elements of this classical approach. Delicate summer soups, lightly cooked vegetables, simple roasts and fragrant fools all reflect their eighteenth-century heritage.

The abundance of wonderful ingredients in June still invites cooks to prepare their food simply, combining the now fashionable Mediterranean influences with more traditional recipes to produce delicacies such as lemon-and-garlic-infused roast veal, or a lobster soufflé flavoured with chervil, tarragon and chives. The sweet, fresh flavour of young vegetables still tempts British cooks to serve them in a manner that enhances their fragrance – thus peas are still puréed with mint to make an elegant soup.

Soufflés have drifted out of fashion with the domestic cook in recent years, as they still suffer from the false stigma of being difficult to prepare. Complicated dishes have slipped from fashion on dinner party menus. Yet despite these vacillations, they remain a popular choice on many restaurant menus, so I have decided to include a few examples as they are, contrary to popular belief, very easy to make.

Summer roasts such as lemon roast chicken or beef fillet adapt perfectly to the unpredictable June weather and can be served hot or cold accordingly, without the fuss of all the usual trimmings. They need only a simple sauce and a few summer vegetables or salad. Originally, roast meats could be served with any one of a large number of complementary sauces – for example, roast pork might be eaten with a tart gooseberry sauce, apple sauce or apple and sorrel sauce. Many of these sauces have lapsed from common usage, but I have included some of them as I feel that they are still very much to the modern taste.

The quintessential British fruit for June has to be strawberries, but since they are so widely written about and I have limited space I have taken the radical step of not dedicating a section to them. Instead I have chosen the much maligned but totally delicious gooseberry. This peculiar fruit used to be very difficult to obtain if you were unfortunate enough not to have a garden, but happily even the supermarkets now sell both the sour, hard, green fruit and the large, sweet dessert varieties. Like rhubarb, gooseberries have suffered at the hands of school cooks, who somehow managed to turn them into a peculiarly nasty stewed fruit. As a result some people are instilled with a revulsion for them which is difficult to cure. Perhaps the only answer is to serve them initially as an exquisite gooseberry and elderflower fool.

The arrival of summer also marks the beginning of eating outside, and tea is the easiest meal to transfer to the garden, being only one step removed from a picnic. The tradition of serving a dainty meal of afternoon tea originated as recently as the 1840s, when it seems that society ladies began to suffer pangs of hunger between a light one o'clock lunch and an increasingly late dinner. Its popularity was soon to spread down the classes, as each adapted it to fit in with its own life. The working classes always ate their dinner on their return home from work – hence the two meals merged to create high tea. Curiously, our taste has changed little since its invention, although ice-creams are perhaps rarely served today. But our penchant for lightly whisked cakes is unabated, as is our love of delicate sweet and savoury sandwiches and fancy biscuits.

CHILLED SOUPS

Cold soups have always received a mixed reception in Britain. Some people consider a chilled consommé or thin cream soup such as vichyssoise to be heavenly, others élitist, while the remainder toy nervously with their soup spoon if presented with such an unnaturally cold bowl of fluid. Even today it is wise to know your guests' tastes before proffering them any iced soup. Despite this national reticence, chilled soups have their fans and their own fashions.

Cold fruit soups such as melon or wild cherry were originally served as appetizers in the eighteenth century but fell from favour with the Victorians, who preferred the more ostentatious chilled consommé. One of the few cold cream soups enjoyed in the nineteenth century was watercress. It became fashionable because it was such a novelty to buy fresh watercress free from water fluke. They had just built watercress beds with running water, thereby ridding it of this nasty creature.

The combined introduction of the refrigerator and new American recipes for chilled foods (written as a result of several Anglo-American society marriages) helped to reinstate cold soups in between the wars. Vichyssoise has remained popular since its creation in 1926. Since then chilled avocado soup, carrot and orange soup, gazpacho, and mint, cucumber and yoghurt soup have all had their day. Many cold soups are currently being refined, so that hearty gazpachos have transcended their Spanish roots and become delicate British interpretations, finely puréed and filled with tiny diced vegetables. Summer vegetables are lightly cooked and puréed to produce pastel coloured soups flecked with herbs or a simple garnish.

CUCUMBER SOUP

Recipes for warm cucumber soup can be found from the mid-nineteenth century onwards but this delicious recipe, which I have adapted from Katie Stewart's *The Times Cookery Book* (1972), was the first one I came across which recommended chilling the soup. It is a classic summer recipe, with a delicate flavour and velvety texture. (Serves 4)

285ml/½ pint milk
1 small onion, stuck with 2 cloves
1 small bay leaf
2 black peppercorns
salt
3 large cucumbers, peeled and seeded

30g/1oz butter
freshly ground black pepper
pinch of sugar
30g/1oz plain flour
285ml/½ pint chicken stock
285ml/½ pint double cream

Place the milk, onion, bay leaf and peppercorns in a small saucepan and scald. Remove from the heat, cover, and leave to infuse for 30 minutes.

Bring a large pan of salted water to the boil. Peel and halve the cucumbers before seeding them with a teaspoon. Then slice thickly and add to the boiling water. As soon as the water returns to the boil, drain the cucumber.

Melt the butter in a large heavy-bottomed saucepan over a moderately low heat. Add the cucumber and season generously with the black pepper and sugar. Gently stew until the cucumber becomes soft.

Sprinkle the flour over this and mix in with a wooden spoon. Cook for a further 3 minutes. Meanwhile, strain the milk. Once the flour has cooked through, slowly begin to add the milk, stirring all the time. As the mixture thickens add more milk, followed by the chicken stock. Leave the soup to simmer gently for 20 minutes, then liquidize.

Add the cream, adjust the seasoning to taste and chill until needed.

MINTED PEA SOUP

Pea soup has been made since at least the eighteenth century, although the varieties of peas have changed over the centuries. This version makes a beautiful cold soup. (Serves 4)

2 bunches of spring onions, finely sliced
3 cloves garlic, crushed
3 tablespoons olive oil
795g/1¾lb (shelled weight) peas
small bunch of mint
850ml/1½ pints hot chicken stock

salt and freshly ground black pepper
285ml/½ pint single cream

Croûtons
2 slices bread, crusted
3–4 tablespoons olive oil
2 cloves garlic, peeled and left whole

Take a medium-sized saucepan and gently fry the spring onions and garlic in the olive oil until soft. Add the peas, mint and chicken stock and season to taste. Bring to the boil, then simmer gently for 20 minutes or until the peas are soft.

Remove the mint, liquidize the soup, strain and add the cream. Chill until needed.

Cut the bread into small evenly sized cubes. Heat the olive oil in a frying pan with the garlic cloves. Fry the bread, turning it constantly until it turns golden. Drain on kitchen paper, season with salt and scatter on to the soup just before serving.

GAZPACHO

Traditionally, gazpacho is thickened with bread. This modern variation is thickened only by puréed fresh tomatoes. It is best made in advance so that it can release lots of aromatic juices. (Serves 4)

795g/1¾lb ripe tomatoes	2 tablespoons white wine
½ cucumber	vinegar
½ red or orange pepper,	1 teaspoon finely chopped
seeded and finely diced	basil
4 spring onions, finely diced	salt and freshly ground black
2 cloves garlic, crushed	pepper
4 tablespoons olive oil	¼ teaspoon caster sugar
2 small courgettes, trimmed	(optional)
and finely diced	

Cut a small cross on the base of each tomato and deftly cut out the little white core to which the stalk is usually attached. Plunge into boiling water – then as soon as the skin begins to peel, transfer to cold water. Peel and cut into quarters. Place half the tomatoes in a food processor. (Do not purée yet.) Remove the seeds from the remaining tomatoes and add the seeds to the food processor. Neatly dice the remaining flesh and place in a large mixing bowl.

Peel the cucumber and cut in half lengthways. Using a teaspoon, scoop out the seeds and add these to the food processor. Finely dice the cucumber flesh and add to the mixing bowl.

Process the tomatoes and cucumber seeds until they form a purée. Pour into a sieve over the mixing bowl and – using a soup ladle – push through as much liquid as possible on to the diced tomatoes.

Add the diced pepper, spring onions and garlic to the soup.

Heat 2 tablespoons of olive oil in a frying pan over a moderately high heat and quickly fry the courgette for 1 minute until it is just beginning to soften. Remove and add, oil and all, to the tomatoes.

Stir in the remaining olive oil, the vinegar and the basil. Season to taste, adding a pinch of sugar if necessary. Cover and chill until needed.

SOUFFLÉS

The perfect soufflé used to be every debutante's culinary ambition: a deadly weapon to enslave her man and make every female guest green with envy. They became very popular between the wars, fishy soufflés being served as an appetizer, while vegetable soufflés such as spinach were served as a separate vegetable course. Cheese soufflés were eaten as a savoury at the end of the meal.

Soufflés are very easy to make provided you follow a few simple guidelines. They all need a well-flavoured and stable base sauce. Savoury soufflés usually begin with a simple béchamel, while sweet soufflés tend to use a crème patissière or a thick fruit purée (chocolate is an exception to these rules). In either case, remember that the flavour will become diluted with the addition of eggs.

Ideally the soufflé should billow up above the rim of its dish as it cooks. To encourage this, liberally grease the side of the soufflé dish(es) with butter or oil. Lightly coat with either breadcrumbs, flour or cheese (for savoury soufflés) or caster sugar (for sweet soufflés) to give added grip.

Always ensure that your foundation sauce is cool before adding the beaten egg whites – otherwise they will collapse. It helps to 'slacken' the foundation sauce with a couple of spoonfuls of whisked egg white, so that it is easy to gently fold in the remaining whites. Use a metal spoon to cut through the mixture and draw the heavier sauce up over the egg whites as you quickly fold them under. Turn the bowl as you do this. Never stir or beat, as this deflates all the air suspended in the egg whites and will give you a sad, flat soufflé.

Lastly, the oven should always be preheated to a high setting around 200°C/400°F/gas 6, but as soon as your soufflé is in the oven you should reduce the temperature to 180°C/350°F/gas 4. A perfect soufflé is supposed to have a well-mushroomed top, with a light crust and a very soft centre. Some people dislike this 'sauce from the inside' and prefer to eat it drier, in which case extend the cooking time by 5 minutes for a large soufflé and 2 minutes for the individual ones.

APRICOT SOUFFLÉ

This recipe can easily be adapted to other fruits such as apples, peaches or plums. (Serves 6)

340g/12oz stoned, ripe apricots	1 teaspoon arrowroot
115g/4oz sugar	55g/2oz butter, melted
55ml/2fl oz water	caster sugar to dust dishes
1 small split vanilla pod	6 egg whites

Roughly chop the stoned apricots and place them in a non-corrosive pan with the sugar, water and vanilla pod. Bring to the boil, then simmer gently for 30 minutes. Leave to infuse for 10 minutes.

Remove the vanilla pod and purée the fruit mixture. Dilute the arrowroot in a little water and stir into the apricot purée. Reheat the apricots and boil for 2 minutes until the mixture thickens. Remove and cool.

Preheat the oven and baking sheet to 220°C/425°F/gas 7. Brush 6 individual soufflé dishes with the melted butter, coat with sugar and set aside.

Whisk the egg whites until they become fluffy, add a pinch of caster sugar and continue to whisk until stiff. Loosen the apricots with one-third of the whipped whites and then gently fold in the remainder.

Carefully fill the soufflé dishes. Smooth the top and run a knife around the rim. Place on the hot baking sheet and cook in the preheated oven for 8 minutes. Serve immediately.

CHEESE AND TOMATO SOUFFLÉ

Modern chefs have taken to adding an intensely flavoured layer of finely diced ingredients in the centre of their soufflés – here is a modern adaptation of a traditional cheese soufflé. (Serves 6)

butter and 1 tablespoon
   grated Parmesan cheese
   to coat the dishes
285ml/½ pint milk
55g/2oz butter
55g/2oz plain flour
85g/3oz Gruyère cheese,
   grated
85g/3oz Parmesan cheese,
   finely grated

pinch of cayenne pepper
pinch of dry English mustard
salt and freshly ground black
   pepper
5 eggs, separated
3 ripe tomatoes
1 tablespoon finely chopped
   basil

Preheat the oven to 200°C/400°F/gas 6. Butter 6 soufflé dishes and dust with finely grated Parmesan. Arrange on a baking sheet.

Scald the milk. Melt the butter and add the flour in a heavy-bottomed pan. Cook for 2–3 minutes and then slowly beat in the hot milk, stirring all the time to prevent lumps. Simmer gently for 3 minutes, stirring frequently to prevent the sauce from catching. Beat in the Gruyère, Parmesan, cayenne pepper, mustard powder and seasoning. Allow to cool a little, then beat in the egg yolks, one at a time.

Peel, seed and dice the tomatoes and toss with the finely chopped basil. Season to taste.

Whisk the egg whites with a pinch of salt until stiff but not dry. Slacken the cheese mixture with one-third of the egg whites, then carefully fold in the rest.

Layer half the mixture into the dishes, spoon in the tomato dice and top with the remaining mixture. Smooth the surface and run a knife around the rim. Place in the centre of the preheated oven and immediately lower the temperature to 180°C/350°F/gas 4. Bake for 10 minutes. (If you are making just 1 large soufflé, bake for 40 minutes, until well puffed up with a golden crust but soft inside – if too wobbly allow a further 5–10 minutes.)

GREEN HERB LOBSTER SOUFFLÉ

Do not be discouraged by the length of this recipe, it is well worth the effort. If you are entertaining, prepare the base and dishes in advance and whisk your egg whites at the last minute. (Serves 6 as a starter)

butter and finely grated
    Parmesan cheese to coat
    the dishes
2 tablespoons finely
    chopped chervil, stems
    reserved
2 tablespoons finely
    chopped tarragon, stems
    reserved
285ml/½ pint milk
455g/1lb cooked lobster,
    shelled

5–6 tablespoons finely
    chopped chives
30g/1oz butter
30g/1oz plain flour
85g/3oz Gruyère cheese,
    roughly grated
cayenne pepper
salt and freshly ground black
    pepper
4 egg yolks
5 egg whites

Preheat the oven to 200°C/400°F/gas 6. Butter 6 soufflé dishes and dust with finely grated Parmesan. Arrange on a baking sheet.

Place the chervil and tarragon stems in a small pan with the milk. Bring to the boil, remove from the heat and leave to infuse for 10 minutes.

Remove the lobster meat from its shell and dice one-third. Place the remaining lobster meat in the food processor with the finely chopped chervil, tarragon and chives, and quickly blend.

Melt the butter in a heavy-bottomed pan and add the flour. Cook for 2–3 minutes and then slowly beat in the hot (strained) milk, stirring all the time to prevent any lumps forming. Simmer gently for 5 minutes, stirring frequently to prevent the sauce from catching. Remove from the heat and add the cheese. Stir until it has melted. Season with the cayenne pepper, salt and pepper. Allow to cool a little before beating in the egg yolks. Add the sauce to the lobster and herb mixture and quickly blend. Transfer to a mixing bowl and stir in the diced lobster.

Whisk the egg whites with a pinch of salt until stiff but not dry. Slacken the lobster mixture with one-third of the egg whites before carefully folding in the remainder.

Spoon into the dishes and give each one a sharp rap. Smooth the surface and run a knife around the rim. Place in the centre of the preheated oven and immediately lower the temperature to 180°C/350°F/ gas 4. Bake for 10 minutes.

Note: If you are making just 1 large soufflé, bake it for 30 minutes, until well puffed up with a golden crust but soft inside – if too wobbly allow a further 5–10 minutes.

SUMMER ROASTS

Britain has produced excellent meat since the agricultural revolution in the eighteenth century. So good was our beef and mutton that we had little need to extend or flavour it in complicated sauces and stews. Instead large joints were plainly cooked and served with piquant sauces. This tradition has continued into the twentieth century and, for simple, summer roasts, admirably suits the modern cook. Naturally a few Mediterranean influences have been incorporated into our recipes, such as stuffing and flavouring a chicken with lemon or infusing roast veal with garlic, but the principles behind the cooking remain the same.

Many of these sauces can be found in *British Cookery*, edited by Lizzie Boyd. They contain many surprises, such as cranberry and apple sauce for goose and Lord Welby's sauce of grated parsnip and double cream for roast beef. The following sauces have been taken and in some cases adapted from this useful book.

ROAST VEAL WITH ANCHOVY CREAM SAUCE

Veal enjoyed some popularity in the nineteenth century, when employing a French chef and eating French food became very fashionable. Since then it has had a chequered history, with concern for calves' welfare in the last two decades making it a meat to boycott. It is important that you buy only veal that has been reared in Britain, since these animals are free-range, just like lambs. If you are concerned, look at the colour of the meat, which should be a rosy pink rather than an anaemic pale pink.

The partnership of veal and anchovies may seem very Italian, but salted anchovies have been used in British cooking since at least the seventeenth century. This sauce was traditionally served with roast beef, but it brings out the inherent sweetness of roast veal. (Serves 4)

1.1kg/2½lb rolled loin of veal	285ml/½ pint water
2 cloves garlic, roughly sliced	30g/1oz butter, diced
3 tablespoons olive oil	*Anchovy cream sauce*
1 heaped tablespoon thyme or lemon thyme leaves	6 salted anchovy fillets, finely chopped
1 lemon, grated and juiced	2 hard-boiled egg yolks
salt and freshly ground black pepper	3 tablespoons meat juices (from the roast)
140ml/¼ pint vermouth	140ml/¼ pint double cream

Using a small sharp knife, cut small incisions all over the meat and insert the garlic strips. Place the veal in a china bowl and rub the olive oil, thyme leaves and lemon zest into it. Season with the pepper, cover, and leave in the fridge for 8–24 hours, turning occasionally.

Preheat the oven to 170°F/325°F/gas 3.

Rub the veal with the lemon juice and season with salt before placing it on a roasting tray. Add the marinade and roast in the preheated oven for 1 hour 10 minutes, basting regularly.

Mash together the anchovies and egg yolks until they form a paste. Mix in 3 tablespoons of the roasting juices (not fat) before stirring in the cream. This will thicken as it is added. Add a little pepper and serve in the same way as horseradish sauce.

Allow the veal to rest for 10 minutes in a warm place while you deglaze the pan with the vermouth and water. Scrape and dissolve all the crusty bits as the liquid reduces. As soon as it has a good flavour, strain it into a clean pan and whisk in the butter. Season to taste and serve in a warm gravy-boat.

The veal and anchovy sauce are equally good eaten cold.

LEMON ROAST CHICKEN

This dish can be served hot or cold. If you wish to eat it hot, make a light gravy from the juices, otherwise omit the butter, substitute another tablespoon of olive oil when cooking, and chill as quickly as possible. Serve cold with lemon mayonnaise. (Serves 4)

1 lemon, cut in half	2 tablespoons olive oil
1.4kg/3lb oven-ready	salt and freshly ground black
corn-fed chicken	pepper
4 large sprigs rosemary,	30g/1oz butter, diced
thyme or tarragon	

Preheat the oven to 230°C/450°F/gas 8.

Roughly squeeze some of the lemon juice over the chicken, then stuff the lemon halves into its cavity along with your chosen herb. Rub the whole bird with olive oil, liberally season and place in a roasting tray. Dot the butter on the chicken's breast.

Roast in the preheated oven for 15 minutes, then reduce the temperature to 190°C/375°F/gas 5 and continue to cook for a further 35 minutes, basting occasionally. Test to see if the bird is cooked by inserting a skewer in between its thigh and breast. If the juices run clear, the chicken is cooked.

Once the bird is cooked, remove it from the oven and either allow it to rest while you prepare the gravy or cool rapidly.

SPICED ROAST PORK WITH APPLE SORREL SAUCE

Although suckling pigs have been eaten in Britain for centuries, fresh pork meat was not commonly roasted until the latter part of the nineteenth century. Until then, pigs, with their large proportion of fat, were good for bacon but otherwise were considered food for the poor due to their cheap, if unsavoury, eating habits. However, the demand for variety, coupled with new breeds of leaner pig, led to the rising popularity of roast pork.

All manner of sorrel sauces have become very fashionable recently, usually as an accompaniment to salmon or chicken. This traditional combination of apple and sorrel is wonderful with pork and goose. (Serves 4–6)

905g/2lb chined loin pork (with fat for crackling)	*Apple sorrel sauce*
	225g/8oz dessert apples
salt and freshly ground black pepper	140ml/¼ pint white wine vinegar
4 tablespoons soft brown sugar	55g/2oz sugar
1 teaspoon powdered cloves	115g/4oz sorrel leaves, washed
	30g/1oz butter (optional)

Preheat the oven to 150°C/300°F/gas 2.

If the skin has already been removed from the joint, ask your butcher for it so that you can make crackling. Otherwise remove it yourself by carefully cutting underneath the skin so that you can lift it from the loin, leaving a thin layer of fat still attached to baste the pork. Score the skin into diamonds, liberally rub with salt, and place on a separate roasting tray.

Season the pork and place in the preheated oven, along with the salted skin (which should go on the top shelf). Baste the pork regularly and roast for 1¼ hours.

Mix together the sugar and spice. Remove the pork and coat with the spiced sugar. Increase the oven temperature to 230°C/450°F/gas 8 and return the pork to the oven for a further 15 minutes. Remove from the oven and allow to rest if you are serving it hot.

While the pork is cooking prepare the sauce. Peel, core and dice the apples and place in a non-corrosive saucepan with the vinegar and sugar. Simmer gently until very soft. Add the sorrel and cook for 5 minutes, then purée and beat in the butter. Serve warm or cold with the pork and crackling.

ROAST BEEF WITH CUCUMBER HORSERADISH SAUCE

Beef *aficionados* will explain that rib of beef or even sirloin are much the best cuts of beef to roast, because they have a finer flavour from being cooked on the bone or from their natural larding of tiny ripples of fat through the meat. However, cooking in summer can be uncomfortable, so to avoid working in a hot kitchen choose a quick-cooking cut such as beef fillet. It also makes an excellent addition to salads, dressed with a garlic horseradish vinaigrette and tossed with young French beans, blanched cauliflower florets, olives and tomatoes. (Serves 8)

2.3kg/5lb fillet of beef,
   stripped of fat
Worcestershire sauce
freshly ground black pepper
3 tablespoons olive oil or
   beef dripping

Cucumber horseradish sauce
170g/6oz peeled, seeded
   and finely diced
   cucumber

2 tablespoons white wine
   vinegar
salt and freshly ground black
   pepper
1 heaped tablespoon grated
   horseradish
285ml/½ pint lightly
   whipped double cream

Preheat the oven to 220°C/425°F/gas 7.

Rub the beef with Worcestershire sauce and season with freshly ground pepper. Tuck the narrow tail end under the fillet, so that the entire piece of beef is of the same thickness. Heat the olive oil or dripping in a roasting tray and quickly colour the beef on all sides before placing in the centre of the preheated oven.

Allow 8 minutes per lb for rare meat, 14 minutes per lb for medium rare beef and 22 minutes per lb for a well done roast. Once cooked, if you are serving it hot, allow to rest for 5–10 minutes before carving.

Meanwhile, prepare the sauce. Place the cucumber and vinegar in a bowl and season generously with salt and freshly ground black pepper. Leave for 15 minutes, then strain. Mix together the cucumber and grated fresh horseradish, before folding in the cream. Adjust the seasoning to taste.

SUMMER VEGETABLES

A British summer brings with it a superabundance of sweet-tasting vegetables, every one of which is good enough to eat on its own. Despite the debates that have raged over the last few years, it seems to me that each year sees an improvement in the flavour and variety of vegetables that we can buy. A young British carrot may not have the flavour of a garden-grown carrot, but it certainly tastes much better than those anaemic Dutch specimens we used to be sold.

Vegetables, perhaps more than any other food, are subjected to the whim of fashion. In the eighteenth century the cookery writer Hannah Glasse bewailed of the British, 'Most people spoil garden things by over boiling them. All things that are green should have a little crispness, for if they are overboil'd they neither have sweetness or beauty,' in much the same way as more recent writers. Currently, restaurants are on the rebound from the ultra-crispy vegetable, but there are many home cooks who still over-cook their vegetables fearfully.

STEAMED NORFOLK SAMPHIRE

Samphire has been rediscovered over the last few years by London's chic. Every smart fishmonger now sells it, and fashionable restaurants serve it in warm salads or as a subtle garnish to fish. Traditionally it was washed and picked over before being tied in bundles and quickly cooked in boiling water. It was then served with lots of melted butter and eaten like asparagus, the diner nibbling the tender tips and discarding the tougher, lower stems. (Serves 2)

> 225g/8oz samphire
> 30g/1oz butter

Fill a large bowl with cold water and add the samphire. Rinse it several times with fresh water to remove any mud. Then sort through the samphire, removing any slimy stems or tough woody stalks. Keep cool until ready to cook.

Bring a pan of water to the boil (no salt is necessary, as samphire tastes salty). When you are ready, add the samphire and cook for 1 minute. Drain, toss in butter and serve.

SPINACH WITH MINT AND CRÈME FRAÎCHE

Fresh spinach should always be used, as it has a much sweeter taste and better texture then frozen. This method of blanching the spinach ahead allows you to get rid of any excess water and helps prevent over-cooking. (Serves 2)

200g/7oz cleaned young spinach	1 tablespoon crème fraîche
salt	1 tablespoon finely chopped mint
1 tablespoon olive oil	
2 spring onions, finely sliced	freshly ground black pepper

Bring a large pan of water to the boil and add the spinach and a pinch of salt. Wait until the spinach changes colour, then immediately drain and cool under cold running water. Squeeze out as much water as you can and roughly reshape into leaves. Set aside until needed.

When you are ready to eat, heat the olive oil in a saucepan and gently fry the spring onions for 30 seconds. As soon as they have softened, add the blanched spinach and warm it through, stirring gently. Mix in the crème fraîche with the mint over a low heat and adjust the seasoning to taste. Serve as soon as it is hot.

SUMMER VEGETABLE RAGOUT

Any tender young vegetable such as carrots or turnips can be added to this fragrant recipe, so adapt it according to your mood. (Serves 6)

55g/2oz butter	115g/4oz shelled broad
5 salad or spring onions,	beans
quartered	salt and freshly ground black
1 clove garlic, crushed	pepper
115g/4oz asparagus, cut	2 little gem lettuces,
into short lengths	quartered
115g/4oz shelled peas	1 teaspoon finely chopped
	tarragon

Melt half the butter in a saucepan and gently fry the onions and garlic until soft.

Add the asparagus, peas and broad beans, along with enough water just to moisten the vegetables. Season to taste and bring up to the boil, then reduce the heat and simmer gently for 3 minutes.

At this stage add the lettuce and continue to cook for another 3 minutes. Then stir in the remaining butter along with the tarragon. Serve immediately.

GOOSEBERRIES

Gooseberries, like rhubarb, are either adored or abhorred by the British. They grow throughout the British Isles, even in the Orkneys, and as a general rule begin to fruit in May. They can be neatly divided into two categories – small, tart cooking berries and large, sweet dessert varieties. The latter appear later in the summer, some as late as August, and are unsuitable for cooking. They range in colour from pale gold to ruby red and have a fragrant, almost grape-like flavour. The former make wonderful sauces, fools, pies and tarts.

But one of the most magical and distinctive ways the British cook gooseberries is with elderflowers, which imbues them with the flavour of Muscat wine. The gooseberries usually begin to fruit just as the elders are nearing the end of flowering. This combination can be found in recipes for fools, ice-creams, sorbets, jellies, pies, curds and jams.

GOOSEBERRY SAUCE

Gooseberry sauce is traditionally served with roast pork and grilled mackerel. It was commonly made by thickening the gooseberries with flour or folding them into a white sauce. This lighter version is more in keeping with modern taste. (Serves 4)

455g/1lb gooseberries, topped and tailed	30g/1oz granulated sugar or to taste
30g/1oz butter	salt
	freshly grated nutmeg

Put the gooseberries in a non-corrosive pan and cook then with a tablespoon of water until very soft. Purée and strain.

Reheat to serve, then beat in the butter, sugar and seasoning to taste.

GOOSEBERRY ELDERFLOWER FOOL

Elderflowers can be found everywhere – from country lanes to city car-parks. However, it is best to pick them from a lead-free area. It is worth noting that the flower heads freeze very well, if you want to preserve that peculiarly summer taste. (Serves 4)

455g/1lb gooseberries, topped and tailed	caster sugar, to taste
2–3 elderflower heads	285ml/½ pint double cream

Place the gooseberries in a heavy-bottomed non-corrosive saucepan. Wash the elderflowers very gently in a bowl of cold water, as they often harbour tiny insects, then tuck them into the gooseberries. Add 2 table-spoons of sugar and 2 tablespoons of water and cover. Cook gently over a low heat until the gooseberries are tender. You do not want to turn them into a slush by over-cooking. Adjust their sweetness to taste and cool.

Once the fruit is cold, remove the cooked elderflowers and lightly crush the gooseberries with a fork, so that they exude their juices but do not totally lose their shape. Whip the cream until it holds soft floppy peaks and gently fold in the gooseberries and their juice, so that they swirl through the cream.

LADY LLANOVER'S GOOSEBERRY AND RHUBARB JAM

Lady Llanover wrote *The First Principles of Good Cookery* (published 1867) in order to 'preserve or restore all the good old habits of my country, and utterly repudiate all immoral introductions which ruin the health as well as imperil the soul'. Happily, this meant that she made a careful record of the cooking of South Wales. This recipe originated from a Mrs Faulkener of Tenby, aged ninety-three, so it probably dates back to the turn of the century. (Makes 5.4kg/12lb jam)

1.8kg/4lb rhubarb	2.7kg/6lb granulated sugar
1.8kg/4lb gooseberries,	6 elderflower heads, rinsed
topped and tailed	in a bowl of water

Wash and trim the rhubarb before cutting it into small chunks. Place in a jam pan with the gooseberries and sugar and barely cover with water. Clip a thermometer (see note below) on to the side of the pan and bring up to the boil.

Boil rapidly until the mixture reaches setting point (106°C/220°F on the thermometer). Just before it reaches this point, add the elderflowers but continue to boil until setting point is reached. Remove the pan from the heat and leave to sit for 10 minutes.

Remove the elderflowers and pour the jam into warm, sterilized jam-jars. Seal as usual.

Note: If you do not have a thermometer, place a saucer in the fridge and test the setting of the jam by dropping a blob on the saucer after it has been boiling for about 20 minutes. If it wrinkles the jam is ready.

SUMMER TEA

The trouble with tea is that originally it was quite a good drink.

So a group of the most eminent British scientists put their heads together, and made complicated biological experiments to find a way of spoiling it.

To the eternal glory of British science their labour bore fruit. They suggested that if you do not drink it clear, or with lemon or rum and sugar, but pour a few drops of cold milk into it, and no sugar at all, the desired object is achieved. Once this refreshing, aromatic, oriental beverage was successfully transformed into colourless and tasteless gargling-water, it suddenly became the national drink of Great Britain and Ireland – still retaining, indeed usurping, the high-sounding title of tea.

So thought George Mikes in *How to be an Alien*. In all seriousness, summer tea still has a certain modern romance about it, associated as it is with sitting on smooth lawns, under shady trees, enjoying an elegant feast of sandwiches, cakes and fragrant tea – with lemon or otherwise.

Winter or summer, tea is still an indulgent meal for both adult and child, eaten only on special occasions in some homes, enjoyed every day in others. Summer teas are designed to tempt the appetite, whereas winter teas are made to comfort, serving such delights as butter-soaked crumpets, anchovy toasts and sticky ginger bread. A summer tea usually has delicate sandwiches, filled according to taste with eggs and cress, cucumber or even fresh strawberries. These are normally followed by, or sometimes replaced by, cake and (bought) biscuits. There are hundreds of cake recipes, ranging from walnut cakes to tiny fairy cakes, which is not surprising as cake-making is virtually classed as a hobby among the British.

ELDERFLOWER CORDIAL

Large jugs of cooling cordials such as elderflower water or lemon barley water are still served at tea to children and hot adults alike. The commercial production of elderflower cordial has returned it to fashion, although it never lost its popularity in the country. This is my mother's recipe. Wonderful served chilled with water or soda and lots of ice.

12 large or 24 small	565ml/1 pint water
elderflower heads	1 lemon, finely pared and
225g/8oz sugar	juiced

Pick the elderflower heads, dip them in a bowl of cold water to remove any insects and then gently shake. Set aside.

Place the sugar, water and lemon peel in a non-corrosive saucepan. Dissolve the sugar over a low heat, then bring to the boil. Add the flowers, return to the boil, and immediately remove the saucepan from the heat. Cover and leave to cool.

Once cold, add the lemon juice to the syrup. Strain through muslin and bottle in a sterilized bottle or jam jar. Store in the fridge or freeze.

CRAB AND CRESS SANDWICHES

Ever since the sandwich was invented at the gambling table by the Earl of Sandwich, it has gone from strength to strength, adapting to the needs of each century. The modern sandwich encompasses everything from hearty hunks of wholemeal bread filled with every conceivable goodie to scented rose petals, sandwiched between thin slices of crustless white bread. (Makes 2 rounds)

2 tablespoons white crab meat	4 slices brown bread
1 tablespoon mayonnaise	watercress leaves, picked from their stems
lemon juice, to taste	1 little gem lettuce heart
pinch of cayenne pepper	
salt and freshly ground black pepper	

Pick through the crab meat to ensure that there are no tiny shell fragments, then mix in the mayonnaise, lemon juice, cayenne pepper and seasoning to taste.

Spread the crab mixture over 2 of the bread slices. Cover with watercress and one layer of lettuce leaves. Lightly spread the remaining 2 slices with a little extra mayonnaise and lay on top of the lettuce. Press together and cut each sandwich into 4.

FAIRY CAKES

These are cakes of childhood, baked in little paper cases, temptingly flavoured and coated with prettily coloured icing, topped with Smarties, silver beads or hundreds and thousands. They should be eaten within two days of baking. (Makes 12)

85g/3oz softened butter
85g/3oz caster sugar
1 lemon (or orange), finely
   grated and juiced
1 large egg
140g/5oz self-raising flour
pinch of salt

Icing
icing sugar diluted with
   lemon or orange juice

Garnish
1 packet Smarties or
   hundreds and thousands
   or silver beads or
   crystallized flower petals

Preheat the oven to 200°C/400°F/gas 6.

Beat the butter and sugar until pale and fluffy, then beat in the lemon (or orange) zest, followed by the egg.

Sift the flour and salt into a bowl. Measure out a tablespoon of lemon (or orange) juice. Quickly and lightly fold the flour into the butter mixture, along with the citrus juice.

Put 12 paper cake cups on a baking tray and spoon in the sponge mix. Place in the centre of the preheated oven and bake for 15 minutes or until they are well-risen and golden. Test for readiness by lightly pressing the cakes with your fingertips – the sponge should bounce back.

Leave to cool on a wire rack. Mix some lemon (or orange) juice into the icing sugar until it forms a thick paste. Spread over the cold cakes and decorate.

Note: Butterfly cakes are made in exactly the same way except that the top of each cake is sliced off and cut in 2 before each cake is thickly coated in butter cream. The 2 sponge butterfly wings are then pressed into the icing and dusted with icing sugar. Make the butter cream by beating together 55g/2oz softened butter with 85g/3oz icing sugar and the finely grated zest of a lemon (or orange). Add some lemon (or orange) juice to taste.

JULY

APPETIZERS
Red onion and tomato pizza
Grilled pigeon salad
Roasted aubergine pepper salad

BARBECUES
Squid with spicy peanut butter
Brill with English green sauce
Lemon veal sausages

LETTUCES
Wallop salad
Rocket pasta salad
Watercress relish

SUMMER PUDDINGS
Summer pudding
Peach blueberry cobbler
Summer trifle
Raspberry strawberry fool

EDIBLE FLOWERS
Sweet scented geranium champagne sorbet
Marigold scrambled eggs
Nasturtium salad

CORDIALS AND RATAFIAS
Raspberry ratafia
Strawberry cordial
Lemon barley water

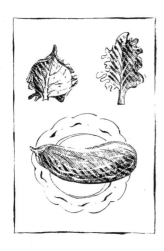

Warm weather does curious things to the British – they become more gregarious and relaxed. Curiously, it seems to have the same effect on their cooking, as the British shamelessly draw on Mediterranean and Californian influences to produce deliciously distinctive dishes during the hot summer months.

July is one of those glorious months when there is an extraordinary variety of food. Wonderful vegetables, salads and herbs as well as the best of summer fruit: red, white and black currants, raspberries, strawberries, blueberries and gooseberries, not to mention all the peaches, apricots and nectarines. But whereas in the past these foods would have been converted into conventional dishes and relegated to a formal lunch or dinner, modern cooks are allowed a far freer hand to be creative. There are no unspoken rules regarding dining for the majority of people. Eating at home has become completely informal, even when entertaining. You no longer have to worry about pre-set orders and combinations of dishes for meals. Instead, cooks are allowed to convert main courses into appetizers and appetizers into main courses. The more flexible the recipe, the better it is liked.

The arrival of the barbecue has allowed summer food to become even more informal. Initially, barbecues were used only for special occasions, but they proved to be such fun that they rapidly became a summer essential. Even flat-dwellers can buy tiny disposable 2-portion barbecues for their balconies. Consequently, British cooks are beginning to explore new recipes – after all, even sausages can become dull. Cookery columns are full of helpful advice on how and what to grill. Simple marinades, piquant salsas and spicy butters have become the latest rage. Their use of chillies, coriander, limes, lemons and olive oils is a direct imitation of Californian cooking. This is hardly surprising, since the Americans, char-grillers *par excellence*, have, just like the British, been assimilating Mediter-ranean and Oriental recipes into their own cooking.

Food fashions regularly sweep the world and have a subtle effect on the indigenous cooking of each country that they visit. Nouvelle Cuisine, for example, fundamentally altered the way the British regarded food – allowing them to experiment with new combinations of flavour and break away from their more classical (French-influenced) past. Its demise marked the beginning of a gradual movement to re-examine and in some cases reinterpret recipes from the past. This in turn has led to a resurgence in all sorts of unexpected areas. Old-fashioned (additive-free) drinks such as home-made lemonade are back in fashion, while many almost forgotten varieties of fruit and vegetables have been rediscovered and commercial-ized. Modern cooks can now buy whitecurrants, alongside eighteenth-century wallop lettuces and peppery nasturtium flowers. Naturally, this sudden influx of rediscovered ingredients has prompted many cooks to explore both traditional and modern recipes.

Summer puddings are just one area that has blossomed as a result of these new-found interests. Delicate champagne ices are now infused with sweet-scented geranium leaves, while peaches are flavoured with a vanilla pod to make fragrant pies and cobblers. Even the ubiquitous trifle has been reinterpreted in a manner much closer to its elegant ancestors. Macerated summer fruit and a light home-made custard are sprinkled with tiny cubes of sugared sponge and topped with softly whipped cream.

APPETIZERS

Almost any form of savoury food could, in theory, be served as an appetizer today, as modern meals become increasingly individualistic. The art is all in the presentation. A simple pizza can be served as a starter, a main course or even a cocktail nibble, provided it is made suitably appetizing.

For the fashion-conscious, appetizers appear to be following two trends – Mediterranean Italian and 'new' British. The former are more popular and tend to be vegetarian, often including some element of roasted or sun-dried vegetables, and encompass pasta, pizza, risotto and polenta; the latter usually contain some native produce, such as smoked salmon, either served in a salad, as with grilled pigeon salad, or incorporated into a refined version of a more traditional recipe.

GRILLED PIGEON SALAD

The grilled pigeon breasts have to be marinated for 24 hours before serving, so this is a good way of using the hot charcoal on a barbecue for a further meal. Otherwise use a cast-iron griddle plate or pan-fry the pigeon breasts over a high heat. (Serves 4)

Vinaigrette	*Salad*
½ shallot, finely diced	4 pigeon breasts, skinned
1 tablespoon finely chopped mint	1 tablespoon vegetable oil
1 tablespoon finely chopped parsley	2 ripe pears
1 tablespoon runny honey	1 tablespoon lemon juice
2 tablespoons white wine vinegar	200g/7oz mixed lettuce leaves
6 tablespoons walnut oil	15g/½oz broken walnut halves
salt and freshly ground black pepper	

Whisk together all the vinaigrette ingredients. Season to taste and set aside while you cook the pigeon.

Season the pigeon breasts and rub with oil. Sear over a high heat, browning the outside but leaving the inside very pink. Immediately place them in a clean bowl and pour over half the vinaigrette. Mix thoroughly and cover. Once cool, refrigerate and leave to marinate for 24 hours.

When ready to serve, peel the pears. Quarter and core them before cutting into further segments, then toss in the lemon juice.

Thinly slice the pigeon breasts at a slight angle. Place in a large bowl with the lettuce leaves, walnuts and pears and dress with the remaining vinaigrette. Arrange prettily on individual plates.

RED ONION AND TOMATO PIZZA

Since the opening of the first Pizza Express in 1965, pizza has become part of the national diet. It is too recent an arrival for large numbers of home cooks to make the dough at home, although with the ready availability of easy-blend dried yeast, it is only a matter of time before they become more confident. (Serves 4)

Pizza dough
225g/8oz plain flour
½ teaspoon salt
¼ teaspoon sugar
1 teaspoon easy-blend
   dried yeast
85ml/3fl oz milk
85ml/3fl oz warm water
1 tablespoon olive oil

Topping
2 cloves garlic, crushed

4 tablespoons olive oil
2 small red onions, finely
   sliced
salt and freshly ground black
   pepper
4 ripe tomatoes, sliced
large pinch of dried chilli
   flakes
1 Mozzarella cheese, sliced
4 tablespoons finely grated
   Parmesan cheese

Sift the flour, salt and sugar into a bowl and stir in the yeast. Pour in the milk and water and mix together, adding a little more warm water if necessary, until the dough is soft and pliant.

Turn the dough out and knead for 5 minutes on a lightly floured surface until it feels silky smooth and elastic. Roughly flatten it and make a few deep indentations with your fingertips. Pour on 1 tablespoon of olive oil and fold the dough over it, carefully kneading until the oil is absorbed. It will be very squelchy initially.

Shape into a ball, lightly oil, and return it to a large warm bowl. Cover with clingfilm and leave in a warm place for 1 hour or until the dough has doubled in size.

Place the heaviest baking sheet you have in the oven and preheat to its highest setting. I use a 30cm/12 inch diameter cast-iron round baking sheet.

Meanwhile, prepare the ingredients for the topping. Mix together the garlic, olive oil, onions and seasoning. Slice the tomatoes, season lightly, and if possible leave to drain.

Lightly flour your work surface and roll the dough in a 30cm/12 inch wide circle. (If wished you can roll out 4 discs instead.) Transfer the dough on to the very hot, greased baking sheet and cover it with the olive oil onion mixture, working as quickly as you can. Scatter with the sliced tomatoes, chilli flakes and Mozzarella slices. Season once again and sprinkle with grated Parmesan. Season and bake in the preheated oven for 15–20 minutes, or until the cheese has melted and the crust looks crisp and golden. Slice and serve.

Note: Rather than waste the rest of the sachet of yeast, multiply the quantities above for the dough by 3 and freeze 2 portions. Thaw as needed and treat like fresh dough. Vary the toppings according to your taste.

ROASTED AUBERGINE PEPPER SALAD

Another Italian-influenced salad. The aubergine and peppers can be prepared in advance and left to marinate until needed. (Serves 4)

1 clove garlic, crushed	1 aubergine
2 tablespoons balsamic vinegar	1 oak leaf or lollo rosso lettuce
6 tablespoons olive oil	handful of rocket leaves
salt and freshly ground black pepper	2 Mozzarella cheeses, sliced
1 red pepper, quartered and seeded	2 tablespoons basil leaves

Preheat the grill to high or use your barbecue. Make the dressing by whisking together the garlic, vinegar and olive oil. Season to taste.

Place the pepper quarters skin side up under the grill and cook until they begin to blister. Remove and place in a covered bowl to steam for 5 minutes.

Meanwhile, trim the top of the aubergine and cut into thick slices. Brush with olive oil, season and place under the grill. As soon as they begin to colour turn them over and continue to cook until just soft. Remove and soak in half the vinaigrette.

Peel the peppers and slice into thick strips. Add to the grilled aubergine.

Trim, wash and dry the salad leaves. Toss in the remaining dressing and arrange on individual plates, along with the marinated aubergine and peppers. Lightly season the Mozzarella slices and neatly weave them into the aubergine mixture. Garnish with the basil leaves and serve immediately.

BARBECUES

The arrival of the barbecue has introduced the British to a new and enjoyable form of summer cooking. A few years ago it was the centre of afternoon garden parties, where long-suffering guests were usually fed lunch at around four or five in the afternoon. Curiously, it has been the preserve of men, the women of the household or guests being relegated to salad- or pudding-making.

In order to barbecue successfully it is worth investing in good-quality charcoal. The best charcoals (Mexican mesquite and Australian Heat Beads) burn very hot and never spit unpleasant gritty cinders. The high heat will quickly seal the food, giving it a tasty caramelized crust while allowing it to remain moist inside. Wipe the grid with vegetable oil and allow it to heat through before you begin cooking; the charcoal is ready when it glows red and white with heat. The maximum time a barbecue should take to reach the right temperature is an hour, although some take as little as 30 minutes. It depends on the design of the barbecue and the type of charcoal used.

SQUID WITH SPICY PEANUT BUTTER

This recipe is typical of the modern British (East meets West) Californian-influenced grilled dish – despite which it still tastes delicious. (Serves 4)

Spicy peanut butter
5 heaped tablespoons
    chunky peanut butter
55g/2oz softened butter
1 lime, finely grated and
    juiced
1 small red or green chilli,
    seeded and finely
    chopped

2 tablespoons finely
    chopped coriander
salt and freshly ground black
    pepper

Squid
1 clove garlic, crushed
2 tablespoons olive oil
680g/1½lb squid, cleaned
2 limes, cut into wedges

Beat together all the ingredients for the spicy butter. Adjust any one of the ingredients to taste. Make sure the butter is at room temperature before serving.

Mix together the garlic and oil. Rinse the cleaned squid and cut into 2 if large. Using a sharp knife, neatly score a diamond pattern on the outside of each squid. If you are cooking the tentacles, carefully scrape off their suckers as many people find these off-putting.

Brush the prepared squid with some garlic olive oil and season. Place on a very hot barbecue and quickly cook both sides, until the squid are flecked with gold and no longer look translucent. Just before removing them from the grill, brush with some of the peanut butter and serve with extra butter and the lime wedges.

BRILL WITH ENGLISH GREEN SAUCE

Piquant green herb sauces can be traced back to medieval cooking and are an early English interpretation of a salsa verde. Traditionally served with roast beef, they work well with grilled fish. Alter the herbs to your taste. (Serves 4)

Fish
4 medium brill fillets,
   skinned
1 tablespoon olive oil
salt and freshly ground
   pepper
1 lemon

Sauce
3 tablespoons finely
   chopped parsley
4 tablespoons finely
   chopped chives

1 tablespoon finely
   chopped mint
2 tablespoons finely
   chopped tarragon
2 tablespoons finely
   chopped chervil
2 cloves garlic, crushed
6 tablespoons olive oil
2 tablespoons champagne
   or white wine vinegar
salt and freshly ground black
   pepper

Trim the brill fillets if necessary and cut each fillet in half. Loosely cover and chill until needed.

Mix together all the ingredients for the sauce and season to taste.

Lightly brush each fillet with oil, then season before placing them on a very hot barbecue – best side down first. Cook for about 2–3 minutes on each side, depending on the thickness of the fillets. Squeeze some lemon juice over the fish and serve with the sauce.

LEMON VEAL SAUSAGES

Home-made sausages or meat patties are an excellent way of using minced meat. But do not think that these sausages are finely minced and stuffed into casings – few cooks at home have the time or inclination to make such delicacies. Rather, these are typical of the new school of British cooking, where Eastern ingredients such as chillies and coriander are used to bring out the fine flavour of the meat. If you are concerned about using veal, just use minced pork instead. However, British-reared veal is supposed to be farmed humanely. (Makes 8 sausages)

1 small onion, finely diced	2 lemons, finely grated
2 cloves garlic, crushed	1 tablespoon finely chopped
1 chilli, seeded and finely	coriander
diced	salt and freshly ground black
2 tablespoons olive oil	pepper
455g/1lb minced veal	1 tablespoon vegetable oil

Gently fry the onion, garlic and chilli in the olive oil until soft. Mix into the minced veal along with the lemon zest, coriander, salt and pepper. Fry a small patty to check the seasoning and adjust to taste. Shape the meat into 8 sausages and chill, covered, until needed.

When ready to grill, brush the sausages with oil and season. Turn regularly until they develop a delicious golden crust but are still moist inside. This will take around 5 minutes. Serve with a spicy roast pepper salsa and lots of hot buttered new potatoes.

LETTUCES

One of the joys of British supermarkets is the enormous variety of lettuces and salad greens that you can now buy. Gone are the days of cos lettuce in summer and round lettuce in winter. Instead you can either choose from countless bags of ready mixed delicate greens or select your own choice. Pot-grown peppery rocket or red and green oak leafs. Lollo rosso, lamb's lettuce, escaroles, little gems or wallops . . . to name but a few. It seems that the current marketing adage that greater variety means increased sales is changing the shape of our vegetable counters. Even Japanese and Chinese salad greens are being introduced.

Naturally, it will take time for our recipes to evolve around these new introductions, despite the fact that many of these salad greens were grown in Britain in the seventeenth and eighteenth centuries. However, there is already a fashion for sensitive dressing of salads. No longer is it a question of chucking over the same old vinaigrette; these days cooks must know their olive oils and vinegars and be sympathetic to the different flavours and textures of salad leaves. The delicate leaves of lamb's lettuce will quickly wilt under a heavy balsamic vinaigrette, while the delicious heat of rocket can be emphasized with the inclusion of whole-grain mustard in the dressing.

Nor are lettuces automatically thrown into a plain salad. The current fashion for composite salads means that careful consideration has to be given to which leaf might be appropriate to the remaining ingredients. Lettuces are returning to their older role of herb, salad and vegetable. Rocket is puréed into pesto, while watercress is turned into a relish. Young spinach and herb leaves are tossed into pasta salads while cos is stir-fried as a vegetable.

WALLOP SALAD

This is a typical example of a plain modern salad – simplicity itself – made with a good crisp lettuce and dressed with a slightly sweetened piquant vinaigrette. The wallop is an eighteenth-century relation of the cos lettuce. Rediscovered by supermarket growers, it has a sweeter flavour and a slightly more rounded shape than the cos. You can use cos, romaine or little gems instead. (Serves 4)

2 wallop lettuces	*Dressing*
1 bunch (or packet) radishes	½ teaspoon good Dijon mustard (for example, Grey Poupon)
½ cucumber, peeled and sliced	pinch of caster sugar
8 spring onions, cut into thick rings (optional)	1 clove garlic, crushed
	2 tablespoons rice or white wine vinegar
	6 tablespoons good olive oil
	salt and freshly ground black pepper

Prepare the lettuce by cutting away the base and discarding the tough outer leaves. Break the inner leaves apart and wash in cold water. Dry and roughly tear the larger leaves before placing in a large salad bowl. Wash, trim and halve the radishes.

Add the cucumber, spring onions and radishes to the lettuces.

Mix together the mustard, sugar and garlic. Whisk in the vinegar, followed by the olive oil and season to taste. Dress the salad at the moment you wish to eat it.

ROCKET PASTA SALAD

This recipe makes an excellent appetizer and the salad leaves and herbs can be varied to taste. Young sorrel leaves make a pleasant alternative to rocket. (Serves 4)

225g/8oz fettucine
salt
1 tablespoon vegetable oil

Vinaigrette
1 shallot, finely diced
2 tablespoons sherry
  vinegar
6 tablespoons olive oil
salt and freshly ground black
  pepper

Salad
3 tablespoons roughly sliced
  chives
3 tablespoons flat-leaf
  parsley leaves
1 tablespoon tarragon
  leaves
85g/3oz rocket leaves
140g/5oz baby spinach
  leaves
55g/2oz crumbled Feta
  cheese

Cook the pasta until *al dente* in a large pan of salted boiling water with the vegetable oil. Drain thoroughly.

While it is cooking, whisk together the shallot, sherry vinegar and olive oil. Season to taste and toss over the warm pasta.

Prepare the remaining ingredients and mix thoroughly into the pasta once it is cool. Add a little more olive oil if necessary and serve immediately.

WATERCRESS RELISH

Originating from Japan, this recipe is a cross between a relish and a salad. Serve it cold with grilled chicken or fish. Only a small quantity is necessary, as it has an intense flavour. (Serves 2)

1 pillow packet prepared
   watercress (see note
   below)
1 tablespoon white sesame
   seeds
1 clove garlic, crushed

½ tablespoon soy sauce
1 tablespoon mirin (or 1
   teaspoon sugar mixed
   with 1 tablespoon sake)
1 tablespoon sesame oil

Bring a large pan of water to the boil and add the watercress. Leave for 30 seconds, in which time it will change colour, then immediately drain and cool under cold running water. Gently squeeze out as much water as you can and carefully stretch the leaves back into shape. Set aside until needed.

Put the sesame seeds in a small dry frying pan and place over a low heat. Gently move them around the pan until they turn a pale gold and release a lovely smell. Remove and roughly grind (with a rolling pin if you do not have a pestle and mortar). Place in a small bowl.

Whisk the garlic, soy sauce, mirin and sesame oil into the sesame seeds. When you are ready to eat, coat the watercress in the dressing and serve.

Note: If you have bought a bunch of watercress instead, roughly trim and wash thoroughly in several changes of water.

SUMMER PUDDINGS

The British are notorious for their sweet tooth. Their love of sugar was, so to speak, at first taste in around 1100, but they were unable to indulge it properly until the sixteenth century, when the Portuguese and Spanish began to export sugar from their West Indian plantations. It was so widely eaten by the Elizabethan aristocracy that they became famed for their black and rotting teeth. But our predilection for sugar led us to spend the next three hundred years creating the most exquisite puddings, from simple fools to health-imbued summer puddings.

Many of these recipes have remained with us, if somewhat adapted to modern tastes, and are commonly served in the summer months. Summer pudding and fruit fools are frequently served for family meals, while fruit pies and cobblers make a welcome change if the weather is uncertain. Only trifles have been neglected, since they have become firmly associated with Christmas. However, before the invention of custard powder, trifles were a delicate light pudding, closely interlinked with fools and syllabubs. Originally they contained little biscuits such as ratafias, soaked in alcohol before being topped in syllabub and strewn with coloured comfits. But the term came to include such variations as fruit purées layered with custard and whipped cream. Syllabubs were in turn made with fruit syrups or alcohol, while fruit fools could be made with crushed or puréed fruit folded into a custard or whipped cream. But modern tastes have begun to reinstate the trifle to its original, elegant nature.

SUMMER PUDDING

This was created in the eighteenth century for patients who were not allowed the incredibly rich pastry puddings then fashionable, and consequently it also acquired the name hydropathic pudding! You can use any variation of fruit you like, but it is best served with lashings of extra thick double cream. (Serves 6)

225g/8oz redcurrants, washed and stripped from their stalks

225g/8oz small strawberries, washed and hulled

225g/8oz blueberries, washed

170g/6oz vanilla caster sugar

3 tablespoons crème de cassis

225g/8oz raspberries

8–10 medium slices good white bread

Prepare all the fruit, then take a large non-corrosive pan and mix together the redcurrants, strawberries and blueberries with the sugar and crème de cassis. Cover and place over a low heat for 5 minutes, until the sugar has dissolved and the fruit is releasing plenty of juice. Stir in the raspberries and continue to simmer covered for a further 2 minutes. Remove and leave to cool. The fruit should continue to release lots of juice as it cools.

Lightly oil a 850ml/1½ pint pudding basin. Remove the crusts from the bread and neatly line the pudding basin. Cut a circle and place in the bottom of the bowl. Slice the bread into neat triangles or wedges and line the sides, making sure that you have no gaps, otherwise the turned-out pudding will leak and collapse. Set aside one large slice of bread to cover the top.

Tightly pack the fruit into the lined basin. Seal the fruit in by turning over the bottom of the bread wedges and cover with the last circle of bread. Cover with a saucer. Save the spare fruit and juice. Place the basin in a dish (to catch any juices) and place a heavy weight on the saucer. Leave for a minimum of 8 hours in the fridge.

Before serving, gently loosen the bread around the basin's rim and invert on to a plate – giving it a good shake. Pour over the reserved juices so that it looks deliciously glossy, and serve with thick cream. Blackcurrant leaves also make a very pretty garnish.

PEACH BLUEBERRY COBBLER

Cobblers are fruit baked with a scone topping. Eaten with summer fruit and lashings of cream, they are reminiscent of summer scones dripping with clotted cream and home-made jam. (Serves 4)

6 peaches, skinned and
   stoned
225g/8oz blueberries
1 split vanilla pod
sugar, to taste

Scone topping
225g/8oz self-raising flour

salt
85g/3oz cold butter, diced
55g/2oz caster sugar
1 egg
4 tablespoons milk
1 tablespoon granulated
   sugar

Preheat the oven to 200°C/400°F/gas 6.

Cut the peaches into large chunks and mix with the blueberries, vanilla pod and sugar. Place in a pie dish with 3 tablespoons of water.

Sift the flour and salt into a bowl and rub in the butter until it forms fine crumbs. Stir in the sugar. Beat the egg and place in a measuring jug. Add enough milk to reach 140ml/¼ pint. Then pour into the flour and roughly mix with a fork until it forms a lumpy dough.

Transfer to a floured surface and lightly knead until it becomes smooth. Quickly roll out to 1cm/½ inch depth, then stamp out about 9 scones using a floured pastry cutter. Arrange these in neatly overlapping circles on top of the fruit. Brush with milk and scatter with sugar.

Place in the centre of the preheated oven and bake for 15 minutes. Then reduce the temperature to 190°C/375°F/gas 5 and bake for a further 10–15 minutes. It is best served warm, although very good both hot and cold.

SUMMER TRIFLE

This is essentially a modern dish – simplified and lightened, yet exquisitely beautiful. I have adapted the method from a dish we used to make in Sally Clarke's restaurant. Don't be put off by the length of the recipe – the sponge and custard can be made the day before, so that it takes only a few minutes to assemble on the day. (Serves 6)

Sponge
2 eggs
55g/2oz caster sugar
55g/2oz plain flour, sifted
pinch of salt

Custard
425ml/¾ pint milk
1 split vanilla pod
115g/4oz caster sugar
6 egg yolks

Fruit base
115g/4oz sugar
140ml/¼ pint water

1 small lemon, juiced
3–4 tablespoons Grand
   Marnier
115g/4oz redcurrants
225g/8oz strawberries
225g/8oz raspberries

Topping
285ml/½ pint double cream,
   softly whipped
extra caster sugar
sugared rose petals or 2
   tablespoons roughly
   chopped pistachio nuts

Preheat the oven to 190°C/375°F/gas 5, and butter and flour a shallow baking tray.

Whisk together the eggs and sugar until they become pale and very thick. Once the mixture leaves a slight trail, quickly fold in the sifted flour and salt and as soon as it is mixed pour on to the baking tray.

Bake for 20 minutes or until the sponge is golden and springy to touch. Remove, turn out and cool on a cake rack. Shortly before you need the sponge, trim off the edges and cut into neat diamonds.

Meanwhile, make the custard by scalding the milk, vanilla pod and half the sugar. Remove from the heat and stir to ensure that all the sugar has dissolved. Leave to infuse for 5 minutes.

Beat the egg yolks with the remaining sugar until they leave a trail. Slowly pour the hot milk into the egg yolks, whisking all the time to prevent them from curdling. Immediately return the mixture to the saucepan and continue to stir vigorously. Place the pan over a low heat and continue to stir until the custard is as thick as runny double cream. Do not let the custard boil or it will split. Strain into a cold bowl and sit in a large bowl of very cold water – keep stirring until the custard has cooled. Cover and chill until needed.

An hour or so before you need it, prepare the fruit base. Dissolve the sugar in the water over a low heat, then pour into a bowl and add the lemon juice and Grand Marnier.

While the syrup is cooling, prepare the fruit. Wash and strip the currants from their stalks and add to the syrup. Wash and hull the strawberries, then slice into halves or quarters – depending on how big they are – and add to the currants. Add the raspberries at the last moment.

Take 6 shallow soup bowls and arrange the fruit salad around the outer part of the bowls. Pour the custard into the centre and then sprinkle the whole with the cake diamonds. Sift some caster sugar over these and then place a soft dollop of whipped cream in the middle. Liberally scatter with sugared rose petals or chopped pistachios.

Note: Use this recipe for custard if you need it as an accompaniment. Just gently heat when needed.

RASPBERRY STRAWBERRY FOOL

This recipe used to be cooked by my mother during the short period when you could pick both strawberries and raspberries, now no longer a problem with late fruiting varieties. She cannot remember where it comes from, but it follows the old tradition of thickening cream by boiling it. The orange flower water is an essential flavouring. (Serves 4)

425ml/¾ pint double cream	115g/4oz icing sugar or to
680g/1½lb strawberries	taste
340g/12oz raspberries	1 tablespoon orange flower
	water

Pour the cream into a saucepan, bring to the boil and then simmer gently until it has thickened and reduced by one third. Transfer to a bowl and chill.

Wash the strawberries, then hull and place in a food processor with the raspberries. (Alternatively, crush the fruit with a potato masher.) Reduce to a purée and push through a fine sieve.

Stir the cold cream into the puréed fruit. Sweeten to taste and add the orange flower water – again to taste. Serve with sponge biscuits.

EDIBLE FLOWERS

Edible flowers have enjoyed a quiet resurgence over the last few years, with several supermarkets selling small mixed packets of edible leaves and blossoms. Despite the odd joke about rabbit food, flowers have traditionally been regarded as a useful component of British cooking since time immemorial. But, since many plants or some of their parts can be poisonous, it is essential that you make doubly sure that what you pick is edible and free from chemical sprays.

Both pot marigolds (*Calendula*) and nasturtiums are often included in supermarket packs, but they are very easy to grow at home. Marigold petals have been used as a common or garden flavouring for centuries. They were infused into cheeses, savoury custards and mutton broths, as well as tossed into salads, hence their name 'pot' marigolds. When heated they release a delicate saffron-like flavour. Nasturtiums are a more recent seventeenth-century introduction. Their flowers were used mainly as an edible garnish, while their peppery hot leaves were added to salads and their buds were pickled as mock capers in rural England.

Scented geraniums are really pelargoniums (*P. radula*) and should not be confused with ordinary geraniums or pelargoniums. It is difficult to know where to place them, since it is their leaves rather than their flowers that contain any scent. These can smell of orange, mint, lemon, rose or even cinnamon, and are used to flavour custards and sugar syrups in much the same way as blackcurrant leaves. Elizabeth David recommends cooking them with blackberries for a thick summer jelly. They have to be bought from garden centres, but are well worth it, since they release the most delicious aroma on even the smallest of sunny window sills.

SWEET SCENTED GERANIUM CHAMPAGNE SORBET

A taste of summer. (Serves 4)

115g/4oz granulated sugar	425ml/¾ pint dry
285ml/½ pint water	champagne
10 lemon-scented	
geranium leaves, washed	

Dissolve the sugar in the water and bring to the boil. Add the geranium leaves and simmer for 10 minutes. Leave to infuse until cold, then strain the mixture. Add the champagne and chill. Once cold, place in the ice-cream maker and churn, or see page 62.

Leave for a couple of hours in the freezer to set more firmly, as the large quantity of alcohol in this recipe gives it a softer consistency than an ordinary sorbet.

MARIGOLD SCRAMBLED EGGS

A beautiful dish for brunch. (Serves 4)

12 pot marigold heads	2 tablespoons double
3 tablespoons finely	cream
chopped chives	salt and freshly ground black
55g/2oz softened butter	pepper
8 eggs	115g/4oz grated Cheshire
	cheese

Pull the petals off the marigold heads and discard their centres. Place in a bowl with the finely chopped chives and softened butter. Gently mash until well mixed. Leave for 10 minutes to allow the flavours to infuse into the butter.

Beat the eggs with the double cream and season to taste.

Melt the marigold butter over a low heat. As soon as it begins to sizzle add the egg mixture and stir with a wooden spoon. Once the eggs begin to scramble add the grated cheese and cook to desired consistency. Serve with hot toast or crusty bread.

NASTURTIUM SALAD

A latter-day nasturtium salad. The peppery mustard-like heat of the nasturtiums acts as a lovely foil to the delicately flavoured chicken and tart tomatoes. (Serves 4)

4 skinned chicken breasts,
  thinly sliced
9 tablespoons olive oil
2 cloves garlic, crushed
salt and freshly ground black
  pepper

2 tablespoons rice or sherry
  vinegar
2 punnets cherry tomatoes
1 tablespoon roughly sliced
  chives
20 nasturtium leaves
20 nasturtium flowers

Mix the sliced chicken breast with 3 tablespoons of olive oil, half the garlic, salt and pepper. Leave for 15 minutes.

Whisk together the remaining olive oil and garlic with the vinegar in a large bowl. Season to taste.

Wash and stalk the cherry tomatoes before cutting in half and adding to the vinaigrette. Mix in the chives.

Heat a non-stick frying pan until very hot, then quickly sear the marinated chicken slices – you will not need any extra oil. As soon as they are cooked, add to the tomato salad.

When you are ready to serve the salad, mix in the nasturtium leaves. Adjust the seasoning to taste and carefully fold in the flowers.

CORDIALS AND RATAFIAS

I have included cordials and ratafias because I suspect that they are going to enjoy a revival over the next few years. They have a long history of being made in the still rooms of the great homes and the kitchens of many country houses, but with the renewed interest in additive-free drinks and the increasingly widespread availability of top-quality fruit, they may well enjoy a resurgence in popularity.

RASPBERRY RATAFIA

You can use any red fruit or a selection of red fruits for this recipe, but they ought to be at their best – not overripe.

905g/2lb raspberries
brandy
115g/4oz granulated sugar
    to each 565ml/1 pint
    liquid

1 long strip lemon peel
    without any pith attached

Place the raspberries in a large china bowl and roughly bruise with a potato masher. Cover and leave in the fridge for 3 days.

Pour the mixture through a fine sieve and measure the juice. Add an equal quantity of brandy. Add the sugar, allowing 115g/4oz sugar to each pint of liquid.

Sterilize a bottle either in the dishwasher or by thoroughly washing in warm soapy water, rinsing, then drying in a low oven. Pour in the sweetened liquid and add the lemon peel. Leave in a cool dark place for 2 months before drinking.

STRAWBERRY CORDIAL

Fruit cordials taste glorious and should be served diluted with soda water or water and lots of ice. They also make excellent milk shakes and sauces. This recipe can be adapted to other soft fruits such as loganberries, raspberries, redcurrants, blackcurrants and blackberries, although the latter two will need to be simmered in 285ml/½ pint water to every 455g/ 1lb of fruit. (Makes approx. 710ml/1¼ pints)

> 1.35kg/2¾lb strawberries
> 340g/12oz granulated sugar

Put the fruit in a non-corrosive pan and crush with a potato masher. Place over a gentle heat and wait until the fruit exudes lots of juice – about 12 minutes. Then increase the heat and bring rapidly to the boil. Boil for 1 minute.

Strain through a scalded jelly bag and leave to drip overnight. The next morning measure the strawberry juice and pour into a clean non-corrosive pan.

Allow 340g/12oz granulated sugar to every 565ml/1 pint strawberry juice. Stir the sugar into the juice over a low heat until it is dissolved – do not let it boil or it will form a jam-like scum. Pour into a sterilized bottle (see previous recipe) and refrigerate.

Note: If you wish, 225g/8oz redcurrants can be added to the strawberries for a more tart syrup. Just adjust the sugar quantity to keep in proportion with the extra liquid.

LEMON BARLEY WATER

Barley water was originally made to nourish the sick. Mrs Glasse suggested the following recipe in 1747: 'put a quarter of a pound of Pearl-Barley into two Quarts of Water, let it boil, and skim it very clean, boil half away, and strain it off. Sweeten to your Palate, but not too sweet, and put in two Spoonfuls of White wine; drink it luke-warm.' But lemon barley water was so well liked that it is now served as a cool refreshing summer drink. (Makes 565ml/1 pint)

55g/2oz pearl barley	1 lemon, finely pared and
55g/2oz caster sugar	juiced
	565ml/1 pint boiling water

This simple and refreshing drink is made by placing the barley, sugar, lemon peel and juice in a bowl. Pour in the boiling water and stir until the sugar has dissolved. Cover and leave to cool. Once cold, strain the barley water and serve well chilled.

AUGUST

MORE SUMMER SALADS
Lime-dressed melon
Denhay ham, fig and rocket salad
Artichoke and green bean salad
Noodle salad

PICNICS
Chicken sandwiches
Salmon and dill tart
Nectarines in Sauterne

TOMATOES
Tomato gratin
Prawn and tomato fettucine
Spiced tomato and courgette salad

SUMMER FISH
Cockles, winkles and whelks
Grilled langoustine with chilli lime butter
Sea bass with samphire vinaigrette
Cold sea trout

ICE-CREAM
Blackcurrant ice-cream
Peach and ratafia ice-cream
Raspberry ripple

JAM-MAKING
Greengage jam
Raspberry redcurrant jam
Yorkshire blueberry jam

August is the last month in the year when summer food can truly be enjoyed, as a profusion of ingredients floods the shops, from artichokes to greengages. Traditionally this was a month when cooks worked hard to preserve food for the winter, but these days August means holiday picnics, lazy meals, ice-creams and sultry jam-making for most.

Modern British food is shaped by its extraordinary flexibility. Modern life may be filled with creature comforts, but each household has to fit cooking in with countless other occupations and meals have to be adaptable. August is a period when many British cooks prefer to spend a minimum amount of time in the kitchen and consequently they need good produce to make simple, fast meals appetizing. No one culinary style dominates – but simplicity is applauded. The days of egg mousse and aspic-coated cold salmon have gone.

A simplicity of preparation means that the quality of many of our ingredients is open to comparison with those available on the continent. Since this is a favourite holiday destination during the summer months, the comparisons are rarely in our favour. Tomatoes eaten on a sun-drenched picnic in the Ardennes are sure to taste sweeter than those eaten on a wet afternoon at home. Not surprisingly, over the last ten years both the supermarkets and many farmers have tried to improve many of our foods, ranging from new varieties of tomatoes to air-dried hams.

These changes have coincided with a movement to rediscover good native produce, which developed in collaboration with a renaissance in British cooking. Smart restaurants now serve the British interpretation of a *plateau de fruits de mer* with Welsh cockles, Essex winkles, Cornish spider crab and Scottish langoustines. Fresh Norfolk marsh samphire has begun to reappear in fishmongers, while blueberry plants (slightly larger than our native bilberries) are being sold in garden centres. Although commonly thought of as being American, bilberries are widely used in traditional British cooking. Yorkshire in particular was famed for its bilberry dishes, which they often flavoured with mint. Naturally, these fashions are beginning to filter down to the ordinary domestic cook, who may well buy fresh samphire to serve with Cornish sea bass or splash out on some langoustines to grill on a summer barbecue.

The current vogue for ice-cream can really be enjoyed during August, when a wide variety of summer fruits can be mashed and folded into double cream or a velvety custard before being churned in an ice-cream machine. As always, such fashions are regarded as new, despite the fact that the British have been enjoying ice-creams for well over a century. But with the aid of modern technology even raspberry ripples are easy to make.

Jams, on the other hand, have slipped from fashion in the sense that many cooks do not feel they have the time, the space or even the knowledge to make them. In the past they were an essential if you wanted a concentrated jar of fruit rather than pulpy coloured sugar. But the pleasure of opening a pot of home-made raspberry or currant jam in the middle of winter cannot be under-estimated, especially when added to puddings, cakes and pastries. Not to mention that delicious feeling of satisfaction of having converted beautiful summer fruit so easily into a glorious preserve.

MORE SUMMER SALADS

Inevitably, the heat of summer encourages cooks to replace warm summer dishes with cool salads. It has become perfectly acceptable to serve a composite salad such as spiced noodles as a light main course or to replace a dish of hot vegetables with a tart salad of cold vegetables.

Such is the choice of ingredients that modern cooks are freer than ever before to mix and match culinary influences with their ingredients. Modern British air-dried hams can be served in the Italian manner with figs and rocket, while melon can be dressed Indian-style with lime and pepper.

LIME-DRESSED MELON

The simplest of appetizers – this can be made with any ripe, scented melon. (Serves 2)

1 ripe charentais, cantaloupe or ogen melon	salt and freshly ground black pepper
1 lime, juiced	lime wedges or mint sprigs

Peel the melon by cutting off its top and bottom. Sit it cut side up on your chopping board, then remove its skin by cutting off the rind in strips from top to bottom.

Cut the melon in half and scrape out its seeds. Cut each half into neat segments and toss in the lime juice. Season with the salt and pepper and arrange on 2 plates. Garnish with lime wedges or a couple of mint sprigs.

Note: Select your melon by picking it up and sniffing around its stem. Ripe melons exude a sweet fragrance and are usually slightly soft around their stems. Avoid any that are too soft, scarred or have moist patches on their skin.

DENHAY HAM, FIG AND ROCKET SALAD

Denhay farm soaks their hams in a traditional Dorset marinade of apple juice and spices, before curing and smoking them in a Continental manner. The result is delicious. If you cannot buy any Denhay ham, use an equivalent air-dried ham such as Parma. (Serves 4)

1 dessertspoon lemon juice	4 ripe figs
3 dessertspoons olive oil	12 paper-thin slices Denhay ham
salt and freshly ground black pepper	115g/4oz rocket

Whisk together the lemon juice and olive oil before seasoning to taste. Trim the fig stalks and neatly quarter each fig. Trim, wash and dry the rocket.

Divide the figs between 4 plates, weaving the ham slices around them. Dress the rocket with the lemon dressing and arrange in piles on each plate. Serve immediately.

ARTICHOKE AND GREEN BEAN SALAD

The custom of cooking vegetables for salads dates back to medieval times, when it was considered dangerous to eat raw vegetables. This belief was later dismissed but the habit remained. Eliza Acton gives a recipe for 'An excellent salad of young vegetables' that includes artichoke hearts, new potatoes, carrots, French beans or asparagus points and cauliflower florets. However, modern recipes favour fewer ingredients and lighter dressings. (Serves 4)

3 globe artichokes	½ teaspoon Dijon mustard
2 tablespoons lemon juice	2 tablespoons white wine
or vinegar to 1 litre/1¾	vinegar
pints water	6 tablespoons olive oil
salt	freshly ground black pepper
2 cloves garlic, crushed	455g/1lb French beans

Cut off the artichoke stems and wash in plenty of cold water. Add the lemon juice to the boiling salted water (it prevents discoloration) and cook the artichokes for 30–40 minutes.

Whisk together the garlic, mustard, vinegar and olive oil. Season to taste.

Top and tail the beans and cut into easy-to-eat lengths. Bring a separate pan of water to the boil, add the salt, and boil the beans briefly until they are tender. Drain thoroughly and toss while warm in the vinaigrette.

Test the artichokes by pulling away one of the bottom leaves of the fattest artichoke. If the leaf comes away easily and the flesh at the base of the leaf is tender, they are ready. Transfer the artichokes (upside down) to a colander and leave to drain and cool. Once cold, pull away all their leaves. These can be nibbled as a crudité or you can scrape out the fleshy part of the leaves to make a puréed dip with olive oil, garlic and lemon juice.

Using a teaspoon or small sharp knife, cut away the fuzzy choke from each heart and discard. Carefully cut away any tough fibres running underneath each heart and trim the edges. Slice into strips and toss with the vinaigrette-coated beans.

NOODLE SALAD

Eastern influences are slowly being assimilated into modern British food as the British palate becomes increasingly partial to Chinese, Thai and Japanese flavours. (Serves 4)

1 teaspoon vegetable oil	340g/12oz beansprouts
225g/8oz Chinese egg noodles	2 tablespoons coriander leaves
2 medium aubergines	3 cloves garlic, crushed
4 tablespoons sesame oil	2 tablespoons rice or wine vinegar
salt and freshly ground black pepper	4 tablespoons mirin
1 red pepper, seeded and quartered	4 tablespoons soy sauce
1 bunch spring onions	2 tablespoons vegetable oil

Preheat the grill to its highest setting.

Bring a large pan of salted water to the boil and add the vegetable oil and noodles. Cook according to the manufacturer's instructions or until the noodles retain a slight bite. Drain, then cool under cold running water. Drain again.

Slice the aubergine lengthways into 5mm/¼ inch thick strips. Brush the slices with 2 tablespoons sesame oil, lightly season and place under the grill. As soon as they begin to colour, turn them over and cook them for a further 2 minutes. Set aside to cool.

Cut the pepper, spring onions and aubergines into fine strips. Place in a mixing bowl with the noodles, beansprouts and coriander leaves.

Whisk together the garlic, vinegar, mirin, soy sauce, vegetable oil and remaining sesame oil. Pour over the salad ingredients, mix and serve.

PICNICS

The picnic has an ancient tradition in Britain, stretching back to at least
the sixteenth century when Elizabeth I among others enjoyed an outdoor
meal before hunting:

> That doone: he spreades his cloth, upon the grassye banke,
> And sets to shewe his deintie drinkes, to winne his Princes thanke.
> Then commes the captain Cooke, with many a warlike wight,
> Which armor bring and weapons both, with hunger for to fight . . .
> For whiles colde loynes of Veale, cold Capon, Beefe and Goose,
> With Pygeon pyes, and Mutton colde, are set on hunger loose . . .
> First Neates tongs poudred well, and Gambones of the Hogge,
> The Saulsages and savery knackes, to set mens myndes on
>   gogge . . .
> Then King or comely Queene, then Lorde and Lady looke,
> To see which side will bear the bell, the Butler or the Cooke.
> At last the Cooke takes flight, the Butlers still abyde,
> And sound their Drummes and make retreate, with bottles by their
>   syde.

The comestibles may have changed through the centuries, dictated by
fashion, family custom and convenience, but the British still love picnick-
ing, even if it is tucked up in a car on a rainy windswept day.

Modern picnics are designed around convenience. Gone are the days of
slavishly making cold pork pies filled with home-made veal stock. Most
modern cooks consider any preparation the night before to be fairly
excessive, although it does allow for a relaxed start to the day. Fortunately, it is becoming increasingly easy to buy excellent breads, specialist
meats, cheeses, olives and fruit. One simply needs to remember to pack
the knives, plates and napkins, along with the essential liquid refreshments
such as ginger beer and iced coffee.

CHICKEN SANDWICHES

Sandwiches have become a movable feast in recent years, with hundreds of different combinations being created to service office workers. Chicken must still rate as a favourite filling. Here is an instant recipe that is guaranteed to make an impression. (Serves 2)

2 chicken breasts, skinned
3 tablespoons olive oil
1 lemon, finely grated and
    juiced
1 clove garlic, crushed
pinch of roughly chopped
    thyme leaves (optional)

salt and freshly ground black
    pepper
1 large French stick
4 tablespoons mayonnaise
3 spring onions, finely sliced
¼ cucumber, peeled and
    thinly sliced
1 little gem lettuce

Remove the fillet from each chicken breast. Slice (at an angle) each breast into 4 thin pieces and place with the fillets in the olive oil, with the lemon zest and juice, garlic and thyme. Season and set aside for a minute.

Divide the French stick into 4 pieces, cut open and spread with mayonnaise. Then layer each quarter with the spring onions and seasoned cucumber slices.

Place a non-stick frying pan over a high heat. When it is extremely hot, add the chicken pieces with their juices and sear. Once they have become flecked with gold, turn them over and continue to cook for another minute.

Stuff the sandwiches with the chicken and lettuce leaves before squashing down the top of each roll and quickly wrapping (while warm) in clingfilm. As the chicken cools it will release delicious juices into the bread. Take napkins!

SALMON AND DILL TART

Cold savoury tarts make excellent additions to picnics. This wonderfully rich tart comes from Jane Grigson's *Fish Cookery*. (Serves 4)

225g/8oz puff pastry (see page 329)	1 heaped tablespoon roughly grated Gruyère cheese
225g/8oz cooked, flaked salmon	2 eggs
1 heaped teaspoon finely chopped dill	2 egg yolks
1 heaped tablespoon finely grated Parmesan cheese	285ml/½ pint double cream
	salt, cayenne and black pepper

Preheat the oven to 220°C/425°F/gas 7.

Roll out the pastry on a lightly floured surface and line a 23cm/9 inch tart dish. Line the base with greaseproof paper and fill with old beans or rice. Chill for 30 minutes. Place in the centre of the preheated oven and bake for 15 minutes, then remove the paper and return the dish to the oven for a further 5 minutes. Remove and allow to cool.

Mix the salmon with the dill. Scatter over the pastry base and sprinkle with the two cheeses. Beat the egg and egg yolks with the cream and season to taste with salt, cayenne and black pepper. Pour over the fish. Place in the centre of the oven, reduce the temperature to 200°C/400°F/gas 6 and bake for 30 minutes.

NECTARINES IN SAUTERNE

Picnics are best eaten with the fingers, as there is nothing more wearisome than having to drag extra bowls, spoons and so on with all the food. (Serves 4)

4 ripe nectarines	1 small bottle Sauterne, chilled

Pack the nectarines with the wine, a corkscrew and a small sharp knife. Serve by pouring out the Sauterne into picnic cups and then allow each guest to slice up and dip their fruit into their glass before eating it and sipping the wine.

Note: If you normally take cheese and fresh fruit on your picnics, it is worth sweetening lots of fromage frais with caster sugar at home and then serving it with your peaches, nectarines, grapes or even raspberries.

TOMATOES

Tomatoes have become an essential part of modern British cookery, which is extraordinary when one considers that even as late as 1840 many people still believed that raw tomatoes were poisonous. There is a romantic tale about a certain Colonel Robert Gibbon, who defied death by publicly eating a raw tomato on the steps of the courthouse in Salem, New Jersey, to prove that they were safe.

The tomato belongs to the Solanaceae family, which includes deadly nightshade and black henbane as its members as well as potatoes and aubergines. The Spanish discovered it in South America in 1519 and brought it back to Europe. By the eighteenth century tomatoes were widely used in Italian cooking, although the British preferred to eat them safely cooked to a sterilized pulp in ketchup. By 1845, Eliza Acton gives a number of appetizing 'tomata' recipes in her *Modern Cookery for Private Families*. She gently stews, stuffs and purées her tomatoes as well as briefly roasting them as an accompaniment to the roast joint.

But the poor British tomato became a victim of our post-war farming policies, which encouraged quantity in favour of quality. This provoked a long campaign by many foodwriters to encourage growers and retailers to produce better fruit. Amazingly, they did. The modern cook can now buy an increasingly wide range – from tiny cherry tomatoes to vine-ripened plum tomatoes. New breeds with that distinctly British acidic sweetness can be bought alongside old-fashioned varieties like 'Ailsa Craig'.

TOMATO GRATIN

A classic modern British dish with minimum effort and maximum effect.
(Serves 4)

285ml/½ pint double cream
2 sprigs tarragon
3 beef tomatoes

salt and freshly ground black
pepper
2 tablespoons finely grated
fresh Parmesan cheese

Preheat the oven to 220°C/425°F/gas 7 and lightly butter a shallow gratin
dish.

Place the cream and tarragon in a saucepan and bring to the boil.
Lower the heat and simmer until the cream has thickened and reduced by
half, then strain.

Neatly cut out the tough white core beneath the stem of each tomato
and cut a small cross on the bottom. Cover with boiling water for a few
seconds, then quickly cool and peel. Slice into 1cm/½ inch thick rounds.

Layer and generously season the tomato slices in the gratin dish. Pour
over the reduced cream, sprinkle with the cheese and place in the
preheated oven. Bake for 15 minutes and serve.

PRAWN AND TOMATO FETTUCINE

Recipes are in a constant state of development. Many of our early tomato
pastas were careful copies of Italian recipes. But with better-tasting
tomatoes, cooks began to discard the supposedly better-flavoured tinned
tomatoes for simple fresh tomato dressings. The tomato vinaigrette
evolved from these. (Serves 4 as a starter or 2 as a main course)

4 large well-flavoured
tomatoes, peeled
3 tablespoons white wine
vinegar
9 tablespoons olive oil
2 cloves garlic, crushed
½ tablespoon finely sliced
basil leaves
1 tablespoon finely sliced
chives

salt and freshly ground
black pepper
225g/8oz raw peeled prawn
or scampi tails (see note
below)
225g/8oz fettucine or
tagliarini
4 tablespoons vegetable oil

Cut the tomatoes into quarters. Carefully remove the seeds, placing them in a strainer over a bowl as you clean the tomatoes. Strain as much juice as possible from them and discard the pips. Cut the tomato flesh into neat dice and set aside.

Whisk the vinegar and olive oil into the tomato juice and once emulsified add the tomato dice, garlic, herbs and seasoning. Set aside.

Before cooking the prawns check that the black digestive cord has been removed from the length of the back. If it has not, cut a tiny slit down the backs of the prawns and pull it out, then rinse them under a tap. Pat dry and season.

Cook the pasta in boiling salted water with a tablespoon of vegetable oil. Drain thoroughly and keep warm while you cook the prawns.

Heat the remaining 3 tablespoons of vegetable oil in a non-stick frying pan. When it is very hot, add the prawns and stir-fry until they turn pink. Toss the tomato vinaigrette and prawns into the pasta and serve hot or cold.

Note: Cooked prawns can be substituted, but they must be heated very gently so that they do not toughen. .

SPICED TOMATO AND COURGETTE SALAD

This recipe reflects the current vogue for Middle Eastern flavourings. French beans are also very good cooked in this manner. (Serves 4)

3 tablespoons olive oil	6 courgettes, cut into
1 small onion, finely diced	rounds
2 cloves garlic, crushed	sugar, salt and freshly
large pinch of chilli powder	ground black pepper
½ broken stick cinnamon	1 tablespoon finely chopped
1 teaspoon ground cumin	parsley
6 ripe tomatoes, peeled and	
diced	

Heat the olive oil in a large frying pan and gently fry the onion and garlic for 3 minutes. Add the spices and continue to cook until the onion is very soft.

Increase the heat and add the tomatoes. Keep stirring until they reduce down to a thick mush. Add the courgettes and adjust the seasoning to taste. Continue to stir the courgettes until they are well coloured and tender. Remove from the heat, transfer to a bowl and allow to cool.

Remove the cinnamon stick, stir in the parsley and serve cold with crusty bread and seasoned Greek yoghurt.

SUMMER FISH

Fish, just like other foods, are regularly subjected to the whim of fashion. At one time, no seaside holiday would have been complete without sampling the local cockles, winkles and whelks, while up to the fifties, it was virtually impossible to buy any British-caught langoustines, as the majority of fishermen would toss them back into the sea as worthless. The advent of the frozen scampi market reversed this trend, creating a massive demand for Scottish langoustines, while the lowly cockles et al went out of fashion. Today, the renewed interest in native British produce is showing signs of reinstating these strange creatures to our tables. Ironically, many of our native shellfish were mainly eaten by the poor as a free source of food. In her autobiography, *A London Girl of the Eighties*, Molly Hughes gives an account of gathering cockles in the 1880s while on a holiday visit to her impoverished future mother-in-law (Mrs Hughes):

> We consulted the old Aberdovey salts, who waved their hands towards the Borth shore, and told us that there were plenty of cockles to be had over there at low tide.
>
> 'How do you catch cockles?' said I, having no notion of what they even looked like.
>
> 'Oh, quite easy,' said Alfred, 'you just pick them up and stow them in a bag, or pail, but they jump about like anything.'
>
> So while the boys went to hire a boat Mrs Hughes looked out a kitchen pail, a canvas bag, and a fishing-basket, and as soon as the tide was about right we started across to the further side of the river, stranded the boat, and strayed apart from one another with our receptacles in the grand pursuit of trying to get the biggest amount. The cockles certainly jumped astounding distances, by what internal mechanism I couldn't make out.

Sea bass and sea trout (salmon trout) have also become fashionable summer fish. This is hardly surprising, since both have a fine flavour and moist flesh which benefits from the current mode of plain cooking. They are also equally good eaten hot or cold.

COCKLES, WINKLES AND WHELKS

Although these are often grouped together, they are very different. Cockles are relatively stationary bivalves which feed by filtering the water around them, in much the same way as a clam or oyster. They live in the sandy mud of the middle shore and can be gathered by hand (usually with the help of a blunt rake) or dredged. Winkles (periwinkles) look like tiny dark grey sea snails and live on the rocks and weeds in the middle shore, feeding on other molluscs and algae. Whelks have a similar diet to winkles but live offshore and have to be caught in baited pots. They are much larger than winkles and have long pointed spiral shells.

All three are usually sold ready cooked, but some seaside shops still sell them alive. If this is the case they are very simple to prepare – all you need is a little patience, as you have to rid them of any grit they may be harbouring. Soak them in salted water for about 12 hours until they stop releasing any sand. Keep changing the water until it remains free of any grit. They are now ready to cook. Bring a large pan of salted water (or court bouillon) to the boil. Cockles should be carefully inspected to check that they are alive. Lightly tap any open shells and discard any that do not close, then cook until they open, which usually takes about 5 minutes. Keep a watch over them, as overcooked cockles are very tough. Winkles and whelks are simmered for 10 minutes, before being drained and cooled. The RSPCA recommend that in each case you cook them in small batches, so that the water temperature is maintained and the shellfish die within seconds.

Once you have your cooked shellfish you can settle down to the therapeutic task of 'winkling' them out of their shells. Using a long pin (stuck in a cork), twist out the body from inside the winkle or whelk. Cut off the small hard disc at the mouth of their shell – which allows them to shut themselves in – and only eat the plump 'foot'. Cockles, on the other hand, need only to be removed from their shells like mussels.

Traditionally, all three are eaten with a light seasoning of vinegar, salt and pepper, preferably as an accompaniment to a Sunday beer. They make a delicious addition to seafood salads, flavoured with a tarragon parsley vinaigrette, or they can be tossed in garlic butter and served with crusty bread and a glass of chilled kir.

GRILLED LANGOUSTINES WITH CHILLI LIME BUTTER

Langoustines often cause confusion because they are also known as Dublin Bay prawns, Norway lobsters and scampi. As 'scampi' they have become an essential item on many pub menus – while as 'langoustines' they are part of the recherché restaurant world, drizzled with a divine saffron sauce or served with a tart mayonnaise. Technically, they belong to the lobster family and are worth buying if freshly caught. (Serves 4)

1 small red or green chilli, seeded and finely chopped

1 clove garlic, crushed

2 limes, finely grated, 1 juiced

2 tablespoons finely chopped coriander

115g/4oz softened butter

salt and freshly ground black pepper

20 peeled (raw) langoustine tails

These should either be grilled on a very hot barbecue or seared on an oven-top cast-iron ribbed grill.

Beat together the chilli, garlic, lime zest, coriander and butter. Add the juice of one lime along with some salt and pepper and adjust the flavourings to taste.

Clean the langoustine tails and thread on to the skewers. Lightly brush with a little of the flavoured butter. Cook for about 3 minutes on each side. Liberally coat with more butter and serve with a crisp salad and a simple risotto.

Note: Wooden skewers should be soaked in water for 3 hours before grilling to prevent them from burning.

SEA BASS WITH SAMPHIRE VINAIGRETTE

Freshly picked Norfolk samphire has at last become more widely available. Although often sold pickled, fresh samphire is excellent lightly cooked and dressed in a simple vinaigrette. Ask your fishmonger to scale and fillet the sea bass. Sea bass barbecues very well, but if you wish to cook inside it is best to pan-fry it in a little olive oil, in which case only season lightly with the sea salt. (Serves 4)

140g/5oz fresh samphire	6 tablespoons olive oil
3 tomatoes, peeled	salt and freshly ground black
1 small clove garlic, crushed	pepper
2 tablespoons white wine	1.4kg/3lb sea bass, scaled
vinegar	and filleted
	sea salt and extra olive oil

Wash the samphire and pick off any slimy or woody pieces. Bring a pan of water to the boil and immerse the samphire in it for about 3 seconds before quickly draining. Cool under cold running water and leave to drain.

Cut the tomatoes into quarters and remove the seeds, placing them in a sieve above a bowl. Press the juice from the seeds and discard the pips. Whisk the garlic, vinegar and olive oil into the tomato juice. Cut the tomato flesh into strips and add to the vinaigrette with the cold samphire. Season to taste.

Cut each fish fillet into 2 and lightly brush with olive oil. Rub the sea salt into its skin and place over a hot grill, skin side down. Once this begins to blister and turn golden, flip the bass over and continue to cook for another 5 minutes. Serve with lots of samphire vinaigrette.

COLD SEA TROUT

Sea trout or salmon trout are also known as sewin in Wales. They are brown river trout that have taken to the sea and can vary in size from 680g/1½lb to 1.8kg/4lb. To my mind sea trout is far superior to salmon, as it combines the fine texture of a trout with a salmon-like flavour. Our cooking methods have varied little over the centuries, as this fish benefits from plain cooking. (Serves 6)

1.4kg/3lb sea trout, cleaned	sea salt and freshly ground
olive oil	black pepper

Preheat the oven to 150°C/300°F/gas 2.

Rub the fish inside and out with olive oil, salt and pepper before wrapping in a large piece of well-oiled foil. Make a baggy parcel, twisting the edges tightly together. Lay it over 2 foil straps so as to support the fish as you lift the package.

Bake in the preheated oven for 50 minutes. Then remove the sea trout – still in its foil – and allow to cool a little in the coolest place you can find. If it is a hot day, place the fish in a dish and float this in a large roasting pan filled with iced water. As soon as possible transfer the foil-wrapped fish to the fridge.

Once cold, unwrap the fish. Peel off its skin along with the brown fat directly underneath. Then slip a knife along the side of the fish, working your way around, until you are able to lift up the top fillet. Pull the backbone away from the remaining fillet and discard. Replace the top fillet. If you have problems you can divide the top fillet by running your knife down the length of the backbone and splitting the top fillet into 2 lengths.

To prevent its flesh from drying out, neatly cover with clingfilm until you are ready. Serve prettily garnished with a bunch of fresh herbs, lemon wedges and either mayonnaise (see page 105) or a home-made horseradish sauce (see page 305) which you have thinned with extra cream.

Note: Salmon can be cooked in the same manner.

ICE-CREAM

Ice-creams were food for the rich until the latter part of the nineteenth century. But with the influx of Italian refugees, some skilled in the manufacture of ice-creams, they began to enjoy a widespread popularity (not to say notoriety) as penny licks and small paper-wrapped brickets, which were sold on the streets and at seaside resorts. These often spread disease, due to the insanitary conditions in which they were manufactured and the unpleasant practice of reusing 'licked' containers. But the great British public had developed a taste for ice-creams which they were never to lose.

The earliest eighteenth-century English ice-creams were made from cream that had been flavoured with sweetened fruit purées. But by the latter part of the century a new custard-based ice-cream was introduced. By the nineteenth century, ice-creams had become so popular that they were frequently served turned out of elaborate moulds as a spectacular dessert. Their tendency to melt and collapse was a constant worry to any aspiring hostess. The majority of these early domestic concoctions were still made with a plain flavoured cream, but as the recipes became more complicated so custards became more popular.

Modern recipes have remained very attached to the custard, as it allows the cook to make a wide variety of flavoured ice-creams such as coffee, praline or chocolate nut chip. But with the current concern over using fresh egg yolks in custards it is worth remembering that the old-fashioned cream and fruit recipes do still work, whether they are made by hand or in an ice-cream machine. They have a deliciously fresh flavour and can be mixed within minutes.

BLACKCURRANT ICE-CREAM

Blackcurrants tend to be made into sorbets, but they also make luxurious ice-cream. (Serves 4)

225g/8oz blackcurrants	255ml/9 fl oz thick double
140ml/¼ pint whipping	cream
cream	4 tablespoons crème de
2 large egg yolks	cassis
4 tablespoons caster sugar	

Wash the blackcurrants and strip from their stems. Place in a non-corrosive saucepan with a couple of spoonfuls of water and simmer for 5 minutes or until they are soft and mushy. Push them through a fine sieve.

Gently heat the whipping cream to just below boiling point. Whisk together the egg yolks and sugar in a bowl until pale. Gradually whisk in the hot cream. Do not add too quickly, or the egg yolks will curdle. Return the mixture to the saucepan and stir continuously over a low heat until the custard thickens to the consistency of runny double cream. Immediately pour through a sieve into the currants. Stir in the cold double cream and crème de cassis. Adjust the sweetness to taste and chill.

Churn in your ice-cream machine or see page 62.

PEACH AND RATAFIA ICE-CREAM

A fragrant, fresh-tasting pink ice-cream that is made with double cream rather than custard. Bitter almonds were a popular flavouring for ice-creams in the early part of the nineteenth century. (Serves 4)

3 tablespoons Cointreau or	4–6 tablespoons caster sugar
Grand Marnier	9 ratafia biscuits
2 tablespoons lemon juice	285ml/½ pint thick double
3 large ripe peaches	cream

Pour the liqueur and lemon juice into a mixing bowl. Peel, quarter and stone the peaches, tossing them in the liqueur as you do so. Vigorously mash by hand to a finely textured purée and taste. Add sugar if necessary and leave to chill for an hour.

Roughly crush the ratafias with a rolling pin, so that they retain small chunks. Fold them into the cream. Gradually stir the peach purée into the cream. Add extra sugar or lemon juice to taste and freeze according to your ice-cream machine instructions or see page 62.

RASPBERRY RIPPLE

The British have fond memories of childhood ice-creams ranging from Cornish hedgehogs to raspberry ripples. This recipe can be adapted to any tart fruit, such as loganberries or redcurrants. (Serves 4)

Vanilla ice-cream	55g/2oz caster sugar
425ml/¾ pint double	
cream	*Ripple*
140ml/¼ pint milk	225g/8oz raspberries
1 split vanilla pod	55g/2oz caster sugar
4 egg yolks	

Place the cream, milk and vanilla pod in a saucepan and scald. Remove from the heat, cover and leave to infuse for 30 minutes.

Beat together the egg yolks and sugar until pale and creamy, then reheat the cream to scalding point and gradually stir into the egg yolks. Transfer back to the saucepan and return to a low heat. Stir continuously until the custard thickens enough to leave a slight trail. Immediately pour through a strainer into a clean bowl and keep stirring until tepid. Cover and chill.

Meanwhile, make the raspberry purée. Place the raspberries in a non-corrosive saucepan with the sugar and 4 tablespoons of water. Dissolve the sugar, then cover and simmer for 5 minutes. Purée and push through a fine sieve. Cover and chill.

When you are ready to churn your vanilla ice-cream, place the raspberry purée in the freezer along with a mixing bowl. Ideally, it should be very cold, almost frozen, when the custard is ready, although this is not essential.

Churn the custard according to your ice-cream machine instructions or see page 62. As soon as it reaches the consistency of softly whipped cream, place half in the chilled bowl. Cover this with one half of the raspberry purée. Cover with the remaining ice-cream and top with the remaining purée.

Using a metal spoon, softly fold the mixture in on itself, just like making a cake – but only make about 2 or 3 folds, so that the purée ripples through the vanilla. Cover and freeze for a minimum of 1 hour or until ready to serve.

Note: For an adult ripple, add 3 tablespoons of raspberry liqueur to the purée in place of the water.

JAM-MAKING

Jam-making is a British institution in the Counties and is an area of cooking that can arouse deep-seated passion. Every keen jam-maker has favourite combinations of ingredients, ranging from gooseberry elder-flower jam to marrow and ginger jam, and will have their own theory as to which sugar is best and whether or not commercial pectin should be added. Even the different methods of bottling can generate strong emotions. So I will immediately admit that I am not a practised jam-maker, although I love making jam. I hope, though, that the following tips will help new jam-makers.

An ordinary jam is made of fruit, water and sugar. The fruit is always initially cooked with water but without the sugar, as sugar has the effect of hardening fruit. As soon as the fruit is soft and has released plenty of juice, the sugar can be added. Normally, the sugar is warmed in advance, so as to allow the jam to be cooked in the shortest possible time, thereby retaining a fresh flavour. Once the sugar has been dissolved (usually off the heat), the jam is boiled vigorously until the mixture can set.

Three factors cause jam to set – sugar, pectin and acid. All fruit contains pectin and acid, but in varying degrees. Pectin is released from cells in the fruit as it breaks down with cooking. The pectin then reacts with the sugar and forms a gel. Acid speeds the release of the pectin. Thus fruits which contain high levels of pectin and acid, such as cooking apples, gooseberries and currants, make excellent jams. Fruits which contain little acid or pectin, for example melons or strawberries, are harder to set. Many cooks will add another acidic ingredient, such as lemon or redcurrant juice to help setting, while others resort to commercial pectin. If using lemon juice, allow 2 tablespoons of juice to each 1.8kg/ 4lb fruit.

PECTIN LEVELS IN FRUIT

high	medium	low
cooking apples	dessert apples	cherries
damsons	apricots	elderberries
gooseberries	blackberries	figs
lemons	greengages	melons
limes	loganberries	peaches
Seville oranges	plums	pineapple
plums (some)	raspberries	rhubarb
currants	sweet oranges	strawberries

Supermarkets sell preserving sugar alongside granulated and caster. The difference between these sugars is purely the time they take to dissolve, although there is a marked difference in cost. Preserving sugar is supposed to dissolve more slowly and give a clearer jam. Preserving sugar does not contain any pectin.

Another important factor in jam-making is your saucepan. Jam has to be rapidly boiled to a high temperature. If your saucepan is too small it will boil over, but if you increase the heat too slowly the jam will taste of boiled sweets. If you enjoy making marmalades, jams and chutneys (which also need plenty of room for the excess liquid to evaporate) then it is worth investing in a good jam pan, provided you can find the room to store it.

Once the sugar has been added, it is only a matter of time before the jam reaches setting point. The easiest method is to use a thermometer, otherwise chill a couple of saucers in the fridge and keep dropping tiny spoonfuls of liquid on to them. As it cools a skin will form. If this wrinkles when gently pushed, the setting point has been reached. Some fruits will be ready within 3 minutes, whereas others can take as long as 20 minutes.

Lastly, it is important to sterilize your jam jars. Wash them in plenty of hot soapy water before rinsing in very hot water. Place them in a cool oven to dry. Fill with the warm jam, then cover with a disc of waxed paper (wax side down) and push out any air bubbles. Carefully wipe clean the rim with a clean damp cloth before tightly covering with damp cellophane discs. These will contract as they dry, forming an airtight cover. If bottling in preserving jars, just clip down the glass lid instead of covering with cellophane when the jam is cool. Label, date and store in a dark, cool place.

GREENGAGE JAM

(Makes about 2.3kg/5lb)

1.8kg/4lb greengages	1.4kg/3lb granulated or
425ml/¾ pint water	preserving sugar

Wash and halve the greengages. Tie the stones in a clean square of muslin. Put the fruit, water and muslin bag of stones in a jam pan. Clip a thermometer on to the rim and place over a low heat.

Preheat the oven to low and warm the sugar along with the washed jam jars.

Gently simmer the fruit until it collapses to a pulp. Remove from the heat and stir in the warm sugar until it has dissolved. Return to a high heat and boil rapidly until the thermometer registers 106°C/220°F – jam setting point. This will take between 15 and 20 minutes.

Remove from the heat and allow to rest for 15 minutes. Using a slotted spoon, skim off any scum, remove the muslin bag and then pot in the warm dry jars.

RASPBERRY REDCURRANT JAM

This is a very popular summer jam, as the redcurrants not only add an intense flavour but they also help the raspberries to set. (Makes about 2.3kg/5lb)

1.4kg/3lb granulated or	680g/1½lb raspberries
preserving sugar	565ml/1 pint water
680g/1½lb redcurrants	

Preheat the oven to low and warm the sugar along with the washed jam jars.

Wash the redcurrants and strip from their stems. Place in a jam pan along with the raspberries and water. Clip a thermometer on to the side of the saucepan and gently simmer over a low heat until the fruit collapses.

Remove from the heat and stir in the warm sugar until it has dissolved. Return to a high heat and boil rapidly until the thermometer registers 106°C/220°F – jam setting point. This will take about 7 minutes.

Remove from the heat and allow to rest for 15 minutes. Using a slotted spoon, skim off any scum and pour into the warm dry jars.

YORKSHIRE BLUEBERRY JAM

Blueberries are also called bilberries, blaeberries, whortleberries and even blackberries depending on where you live in Britain. They can be found growing wild on acidic heaths and moors, but their American cousins are becoming popular garden plants. (Makes about 2.3kg/5lb)

1.4kg/3lb granulated or preserving sugar	6 large sprigs mint, tied together with string
1.4kg/3lb bilberries or blueberries	1 tablespoon water
	1 lemon, juiced

Preheat the oven to low and warm the sugar along with the washed jam jars.

Wash the fruit. Place in a jam pan along with the mint sprigs, water and lemon juice. Clip a thermometer on to the side of the saucepan and gently simmer over a low heat until the fruit collapses.

Remove from the heat and stir in the warm sugar until it has dissolved. Return to a high heat and boil rapidly until the thermometer registers 106°C/220°F – jam setting point. This will take about 10 minutes.

Remove from the heat and allow to rest for 15 minutes. Using a slotted spoon, skim off any scum. Remove the mint leaves and pour into the warm dry jars.

SEPTEMBER

HEARTY SOUPS
Scallop chowder
Minestrone
Mushroom and barley soup

FRITTERS
Oyster fritters with tomato salsa
Pakoras with coriander chutney
Apple cinnamon fritters
Banana fritters

SPICED FOOD
Chicken spinach curry
Potato cauliflower curry
Spiced red kidney beans

FRUIT PIES, CRUSTS AND CRUMBLES
Apple and raspberry Jonathan
Damson pie
Greengage almond crumble

BREAD AND CHEESE
Walnut bread
Oat cakes
Welsh rarebit

WILD FOOD
Blackberry roly poly
Elderberry jelly
Sloe gin

British cooking can almost be divided into two categories – cold weather comfort food and light summery food. When the first frost falls and the nights draw in, the British begin to crave heavier, warming dishes. But whereas in the past most cooks were concerned with fighting the cold with plain hearty food, modern cooks have to be sensitive to the complicated demands of modern life. After all, an ideal meal today is expected to be healthy, interesting and attractive as well as quick to prepare.

Modern hearty soups appear at first glance to owe more to foreign influences than to national traditions. Minestrones and chowders are more likely to be made these days than oxtail soup or cock-a-leekie. Perhaps this is due partly to the time it takes to simmer oxtail or a whole boiling fowl with stewing steak, prunes and leeks, since the former requires a good 4–5 hours and the latter 3–4 hours! But I suspect that the British have also come to prefer the livelier flavours of minestrone or chowder.

Elizabeth David suggests in *Spices, Salt and Aromatics in the English Kitchen* that the British, as a northern race, have a natural taste for highly seasoned food. Certainly, the onset of cold weather often provokes the desire for spicy food. Although not commonly regarded as part of British food, curries and spicy chutneys have been cooked in the home for at least two hundred and fifty years. Hannah Glasse gives a couple of recipes in *The Art of Cookery Made Plain and Easy* (1747) where she even roasts some of her spices in a traditional Indian manner. By 1845, Indian dishes were rife, partly due to the pervasive atmosphere of an India about to become the British Raj. 'The great superiority of the oriental curries over those generally prepared in England is not, we believe, altogether the result of a want of skill or of experience on the part of our cooks, but is attributable in some measure, to many of the ingredients, which in a *fresh and green state* add so much to their excellence, being here beyond our reach,' states Eliza Acton at the beginning of her section on curries in *Modern Cookery* (1845). She then follows with a recipe for home-made curry powder, before continuing with anglicized recipes for curries of every description, ranging from oysters to eggs.

The desire for different foods at this time of the year often provokes the cook into indulging personal whims. Fritters definitely fall into the category of whimsical food, since they are rarely cooked routinely at home, despite the fact that most people love them. They are a treat that takes only a few minutes to make and they vanish just as quickly. In much the same way, many cooks suddenly get the romantic urge to gather wild blackberries or even sloes. There is something strangely satisfying about picking wild fruits on a beautiful autumn walk and transforming them into fragrant puddings, delicate jellies and liqueurs.

September has always been a wonderful month for baking fruit puddings, from pies to sponge toppings. There is an abundance of traditional fruits such as plums, damsons, greengages, apples and blackberries along with the end-of-season peaches, nectarines and raspberries. But for the modern cook it has been further improved by more late cropping fruit varieties such as strawberries. These were developed by British farmers, who were keen to erode the Spanish imports by extending their own season to as late as October when the weather is fine. As many of these fruits complement each other, the cook can create endless exquisite combinations such as peach and strawberry cobbler or raspberry and apple sponge, not to mention the ubiquitous blackberry and apple crumble.

HEARTY SOUPS

Soups and stews developed simultaneously from cooking the household meal in a single cauldron. In medieval Britain everyone from peasant to lord ate a soup-like dish called pottage. This was made from a thickened pot broth and filled with pappy vegetables, pulses or grains and herbs, along with meat or fish for the wealthy. Gradually pottage was refined by the rich into separate dishes of soup and stews, and served in a manner described in the fourteenth-century poem *Sir Gawain and the Green Knight:*

> In a trice on fine trestles a table was put up,
> Then covered with a cloth shining clean and white,
> And set with silver spoons, salt-cellars and overlays.
> The worthy knight washed willingly and went to his meat,
> In seemly enough style servants brought him
> Several fine soups, seasoned lavishly
> Twice-fold, as is fitting, and fish of all kinds –
> Some baked in bread, some browned on coals,
> Some seethed, some stewed and savoured with spice,
> But always subtly sauced, and so the man liked it.

But for the poor, pot broths such as barley broth were to remain their staple dish for centuries. Ironically, modern chunky peasant soups such as minestrone or chowder are considered fashionable today for the very same reason, that they still provide a satisfying yet easy meal.

SCALLOP CHOWDER

Fish chowders have been served in Britain since at least the turn of the century. Although famed as American, it is commonly believed that they were initially introduced to the New World by the Breton fishermen, who cooked fish, salt pork and biscuits in their chaudron (caldron) while fishing off Iceland and Newfoundland. (Serves 4)

55g/2oz butter	285ml/½ pint double cream
1 large onion, finely diced	565ml/1 pint milk
4 inner celery stalks, diced	½ small bay leaf
225g/8oz smoked back	salt and freshly ground black
bacon, diced small	pepper
2 potatoes, finely diced	8 large scallops or 225g/8oz
4 large heads sweetcorn	Queen scallops, cleaned
3 tablespoons plain flour	2 tablespoons finely
285ml/½ pint dry white	chopped parsley
wine	½ lemon, juiced (optional)

Melt the butter in a large, heavy-bottomed saucepan and gently fry the onion, celery and bacon until soft.

Add the diced potato to the onions and stir regularly to prevent it from sticking. Strip the corn cobs of their leaves and fine hairs. Slice off the kernels by cutting down each cob. Mix into the potatoes and cook for about 2 minutes.

Stir in the flour and cook for 3 minutes. Increase the heat a little and gradually stir in the wine, followed by the cream and milk. Add the bay leaf and season to taste. Bring to the boil, then simmer gently for 20 minutes or until the potato is soft.

While the soup is cooking, prepare the scallops. Check their girths to see if they have a thin black intestinal thread and a small tough white muscle. Remove these by pulling them away with your fingers. Then rinse the scallops and pat dry. If they have corals, pull them off and cut in half. Cut the scallops neatly into large dice.

Remove the bay leaf from the soup and add the scallops and parsley. Simmer gently until the scallops are just cooked. Stir in the lemon juice and serve.

MINESTRONE

Minestrones can be made from a wide selection of ingredients, but they usually include a pulse of some kind along with some form of pasta. Curiously, the concept behind minestrone is very close to the old British soup of hotch-potch, otherwise known as hodge-podge, hodge-pot and hotch-pot. This strange soup was made up of a whole 'hotch-potch' of ingredients that were changed according to mood and availability. (Serves 4)

3 tablespoons olive oil
2 leeks, cut into thin rounds
2 cloves garlic, crushed
225g/8oz tomatoes, peeled and chopped
1 mixed tablespoon finely chopped basil, parsley and chives
1 carrot, finely diced
2 celery sticks, diced
1 litre/1¾ pints vegetable or chicken stock
30g/1oz stelline or other small pasta shapes
200g/7oz tinned cannellini beans, drained and rinsed
salt and freshly ground black pepper
115g/4oz green cabbage, roughly chopped
1 large handful prepared spinach
2 tablespoons freshly grated Parmesan cheese
1 tablespoon finely chopped parsley

Heat the olive oil in a large saucepan and gently fry the leeks and garlic until soft. Stir in the tomatoes and herbs and simmer until they form a thick sauce.

Add the diced carrot and celery. Cook for a few minutes before adding the stock. Return to the boil, then add the pasta and beans and season to taste. Simmer briskly for 10 minutes.

Once the pasta is cooked, stir in the cabbage and spinach and cook for a further 5 minutes. Stir 2 tablespoons of Parmesan and the parsley into the broth before serving it piping hot with lots of extra Parmesan.

MUSHROOM AND BARLEY SOUP

Barley is supposed to be the next fashionable grain, following in the footsteps of arborio rice and polenta. Modern chefs are serving it in risottos, soups and stews. This is a fast recipe that is lighter than the traditional mutton barley broth, but very good nonetheless. (Serves 4)

225g/8oz shiitake mushrooms
225g/8oz oyster mushrooms
225g/8oz brown cap mushrooms
4 tablespoons olive oil
3 cloves garlic, crushed
1 onion, finely sliced
285ml/½ pint dry white wine

565ml/1 pint chicken stock
1 sprig parsley tied with 1 sprig thyme and 1 strip lemon peel
55g/2oz barley
salt and freshly ground black pepper
55g/2oz butter
1 tablespoon mixed finely chopped parsley, thyme and chervil

Wipe the mushrooms with a damp cloth. Discard the shiitake stalks and tear their heads into smallish pieces. Cut off the tougher stem ends of the oyster mushrooms and pull apart in a similar manner. Trim and thickly slice the brown caps.

Heat the olive oil in a heavy-bottomed saucepan and gently fry the garlic and onion until soft and golden. Add the mushrooms, adding a little more oil if necessary, and continue to fry until they begin to soften. Add the white wine, stock and herb bundle before bringing to the boil.

Stir in the barley and season to taste. Leave to simmer for 20 minutes or until the barley is tender.

When ready to serve, remove the herbs, adjust the seasoning to taste and stir in the butter and freshly chopped herbs.

Note: A richer version of this soup can be made by replacing the butter at the end with 3 tablespoons of double cream.

FRITTERS

Delicate golden fritters are much loved by the British but rarely cooked at home these days. They have a long history of being served at aristocratic tables. In the fifteenth century both root vegetables and apple fritters were eaten at the end of a meal, while by the eighteenth century the number of fritter recipes had dramatically increased to include vine leaves, curds, herbs and chicken – all liberally strewn with sugar. Modern restaurant fritters are more likely to be savoury and dipped in a tempura or spicy gram batter than served as a delicate dessert. Even apple fritters are served as a savoury garnish to game or pork. Nevertheless fritters are so good and simple to make that it seems a shame not to enjoy the odd banana fritter for supper.

OYSTER FRITTERS WITH TOMATO SALSA

It is often forgotten that oysters were so cheap and plentiful in the past that the Victorians transformed them into stews, stuffings and sausages as well as deep-frying them as fritters. They are delicious cooked in this manner. Here is a modern interpretation with a piquant relish. (Serve 4)

285g/10oz plain flour	*Tomato salsa*
pinch of salt	455g/1lb ripe tomatoes
2 small eggs, roughly beaten	2 cloves garlic, crushed
285ml/½ pint lager	1 red or green chilli, seeded
1 tablespoon olive oil	and finely diced
vegetable oil (for deep-	1 tablespoon finely chopped
frying)	coriander
2 dozen oysters, removed	2 tablespoons wine vinegar
from their shells	6 tablespoons olive oil
	salt and freshly ground black
	pepper

Sift the flour and salt into a mixing bowl and make a hollow in the centre. Add the eggs and begin to beat them into the flour, before gradually beating in the lager. Keep stirring until the batter is smooth and has the consistency of double cream. Mix in the olive oil and leave to rest for 30 minutes.

Peel the tomatoes, cut into quarters and seed. Press the seeds through a strainer and save the juice. Neatly dice the tomato flesh and add to the juice, along with the garlic, chilli and coriander. Whisk together the vinegar and olive oil and mix into the tomatoes. Season to taste and set aside until ready to serve.

Heat the vegetable oil to 190°C/375°F.

Drain the shelled oysters. Save their juice to add to a fish sauce or soup. Pat the oysters dry and dip into the batter. Fry them in small batches until they become golden and crisp. Quickly drain on kitchen paper, sprinkle with salt and serve immediately with the salsa.

Note: If you are worried about opening oysters, ask the fishmonger to open them. However, make sure that you keep them chilled and serve them the same day.

PAKORAS WITH CORIANDER CHUTNEY

The British love of spice has meant that pakoras and onion bhajees have become increasingly popular in recent years. Since they are very easy to make, I have included the former in this section. The key to success is to deep-fry the pakoras twice, so prepare them in advance and then quickly deep-fry before serving. They are also excellent eaten cold. Gram flour can be bought from some supermarkets and any Asian grocery shop. (Makes 20–30 pakoras)

3 small potatoes, sliced	frying)
1 onion, sliced into rings	
175g/6oz cauliflower, cut	*Batter*
into thin florets	170g/6oz gram flour
1½ teaspoons salt	1 teaspoon garam masala
½ teaspoon garam masala	2 teaspoons salt
½ teaspoon chilli powder	½ teaspoon ground turmeric
vegetable oil (for deep	½ teaspoon chilli powder

Prepare the vegetables, patting them dry if necessary, and place in a bowl. Liberally season with the salt and spices.

Heat the oil in a deep fat fryer or chip pan to 190°C/375°F.

Sift all the batter ingredients into a mixing bowl and slowly beat in 200ml/7fl oz water until you have a smooth thick batter.

Carefully dip the potato slices so that they are evenly coated with the batter and fry in batches over a medium heat until golden brown. Drain on kitchen paper and set aside to cool. Repeat until you have fried all the potatoes, followed by the onion rings and the cauliflower florets.

When ready to serve, reheat the oil to 190°C/375°F and re-fry the pakoras. Traditionally, they are eaten with tomato ketchup, tamarind sauce or mint or coriander chutney.

CORIANDER CHUTNEY

This spicy sauce will keep several days in the fridge. (Serves 6)

6 tablespoons finely	2 spring onions, finely
chopped coriander leaves	chopped
1–2 tablespoons lime juice	1 teaspoon salt
1 green chilli, seeded and	1 teaspoon sugar
finely chopped	½ teaspoon garam masala

Combine all the ingredients and serve with the pakoras.

APPLE CINNAMON FRITTERS

Choose any well-flavoured eating apple such as Spartan or Worcester
Pearmain. By October there will be many more varieties to choose from –
Cox's Orange Pippin or Charles Ross, for example. (Serves 4)

140g/5oz plain flour
1 egg, separated
140ml/¼ pint dry cider
small pinch of salt
vegetable oil (for deep-
    frying)

4 medium dessert apples
caster sugar, to taste
ground cinnamon, to taste

Sift the flour into a large mixing bowl and make a hollow in the centre.
Roughly beat the egg yolk with a little of the cider. Pour into the flour
well and gradually beat into the flour, before slowly adding the remaining
cider. Beat until the batter is smooth and thick. Leave to rest for 30
minutes.

When ready to cook, whisk the egg white with a pinch of salt until it
forms soft peaks. Fold into the batter. Heat the oil to 190°C/375°F.

Quickly peel, quarter and core the apples. Cut into medium slices and
coat in the batter before frying in batches for 3–4 minutes. Drain on
kitchen paper and serve immediately, dusted with plenty of sugar and
cinnamon.

BANANA FRITTERS

The recipe above can be adapted to use with bananas. Replace the cider
with milk. If feeling extravagant you can flavour the milk with rum. Peel
8 small or 4 large bananas and cut into large chunks. Dip in the batter
and fry as above.

SPICED FOOD

Indian food has been woven into British cooking for centuries, with dishes such as mulligatawny soup or kedgeree being created by British cooks reinterpreting Indian recipes. But the rapid expansion of Indian restaurants around the country is having a far greater impact on modern British cooking. The British palate is slowly but surely becoming addicted to spices, to such a degree that a recent survey showed that the majority of children, if given a choice, prefer to eat spicy food. Classic Indian dishes such as tandoori chicken are being anglicized by food manufacturers to produce tandoori chicken sandwiches or even tandoori chicken pasta.

But the true test of assimilation is whether such dishes are regularly cooked at home. Aside from the ever-increasing variety of Indian spices and ingredients available in the supermarkets, curry cooking has become almost a hobby in many British households. Inevitably, this rising popularity will in time lead to the development of new spicy British dishes.

CHICKEN SPINACH CURRY

One of the advantages of anglicizing food is that traditional rules can be broken. The majority of meat curries are simmered over long periods, whereas this recipe can be made very quickly, so that the chicken is deliciously tender. Crème fraîche is added instead of the traditional cream or milk whey. (Serves 4)

1 small onion, finely diced	6 tomatoes, peeled and chopped
2 cloves garlic, crushed	4 chicken breasts, skinned and boned
1 small chilli, seeded and diced	salt and freshly ground black pepper
3 tablespoons vegetable oil	200g/7oz prepared baby spinach
1 dessertspoon ground cumin	2 tablespoons crème fraîche
1 dessertspoon ground coriander	pinch of garam masala
1 dessertspoon ground turmeric	

Gently fry the onion, garlic and chilli in the oil until they are soft. Stir in the spices and continue to fry for a further minute before adding the tomatoes. Allow to reduce to a thick paste.

Cut the chicken into large chunks. Once the tomato purée looks as though it is releasing oil, stir in the chicken and colour. Season generously and add the spinach. As soon as it has reduced down, stir in the crème fraîche and continue to simmer gently for a further 5 minutes. Stir in the garam masala and cook for a further 2 minutes.

If wished the chicken can be made in advance and chilled until needed, in which case gently reheat when needed.

Note: Chilli seeds are especially hot, so if you wish for added heat, finely dice your chilli, seeds and all.

POTATO CAULIFLOWER CURRY

Domestic Indian cooking tends to be less complicated than many restaurant dishes. This is a traditional Punjabi 'dry' vegetable curry that can be served very simply with other vegetable curries, such as spiced kidney beans, and a simple raita. Kashmiri cumin seeds are more pungent than ordinary cumin seeds, but are not essential if you cannot find them in your local Asian grocery shop. (Serves 6)

6 small potatoes	1–2 green chillies
1 cauliflower	¼ teaspoon (Kashmiri)
3 tablespoons vegetable oil	cumin seeds
or clarified butter (ghee)	1½ teaspoons ground
(see page 107)	turmeric
2 cloves garlic, crushed	1 teaspoon garam masala
½ teaspoon finely diced root	2 teaspoons salt
ginger	

As the vegetables are going to be fried from raw, it is important to cut them in a manner that will allow them to cook through quickly. It is also a good idea to retain some water on them, as the steam will help them cook.

Scrape the potatoes and cut into quarters. Leave in cold water until ready to use. Wash the cauliflower, turn it upside down and cut away its stem. Break the florets apart, retaining a small stem on each, and cut in half if too fat.

Heat the oil in a wide non-stick saucepan. As soon as it is sizzling hot add the garlic, ginger, whole chillies and spices. Stir and fry for a minute, then add the cauliflower and potatoes with the salt. Quickly coat them in the spices and fry over a moderately high heat for 5 minutes. Cover and turn the heat to low, stirring occasionally to prevent the vegetables from sticking. Cook for 25 minutes or until the vegetables are meltingly tender.

SPICED RED KIDNEY BEANS

A quick glance along the supermarket shelves will show a wide range of dried pulses, which seems to increase each year as they gain in popularity. These come into their own in the winter months, when added to soups, stews and hearty salads. But one of the nicest ways to serve such vegetables is stewed, as an accompaniment to other dishes. Lightly spiced in the Indian manner, stewed kidney beans subtly complement both grilled meats and hearty casseroles. (Serves 4)

140g/5oz dried red kidney
  beans
2 cloves garlic, crushed
1 teaspoon ground turmeric
½ teaspoon chilli powder
3 tablespoons vegetable oil
  or butter or ghee (see
  page 107)

1 small onion, finely sliced
1 teaspoon garam masala
salt and freshly ground
  black pepper
2 tablespoons roughly
  chopped coriander leaves

Soak the kidney beans in plenty of cold water for 12 hours. Drain and place in a saucepan. Cover with cold water and bring to the boil. Remove any scum and continue to boil for 15 minutes before reducing the heat to a simmer. Add the garlic, turmeric and chilli powder. Gently cook for 2½ hours, adding extra water as needed, until the beans are meltingly soft in a thick sauce.

Heat the butter in a small pan and fry the onion slices. As soon as they are soft, add the garam masala and fry for 20 seconds before scraping the contents of the pan into the beans. Stir and season to taste. Serve whenever you wish, sprinkled with fresh coriander.

FRUIT PIES, CRUSTS AND CRUMBLES

Over the centuries the British have devised more and more recipes for fruit – baked in pies, covered in sponge or fine crumbs of sweetened buttery flour. The toppings and fillings have become interchangeable and are often served throughout the year. Many of the fruits that we commonly eat today, such as apples, pears, damsons, plums and cherries, have been cultivated since Roman times, while wild raspberries, strawberries, blackberries and elderberries have been eaten for even longer. Pastry also has a long history and by the Middle Ages spiced apple, pear and quince coffers (pies) were commonplace at the tables of the rich. Modern recipes are much simpler than their predecessors, the emphasis being on retaining the fresh flavour of the fruit, rather than masking it with spices or enriching it with a custard (poured into the crust).

APPLE AND RASPBERRY JONATHAN

Apples baked with a sponge topping are usually called Eve's Pudding, presumably because they taste so tempting. However, in my home, it went under the name of apple Jonathan although no one can remember why. So I have kept the name for this adaptation. Sponge toppings work well with many other fruits and are equally good eaten cold. (Serves 4)

2 cooking apples, peeled, cored and cubed	*Topping*
	55g/2oz butter
225g/8oz raspberries	55g/2oz caster sugar
sugar, to taste	1 egg
	2 tablespoons milk
	115g/4oz self-raising flour, sifted

Preheat the oven to 180°C/350°F/gas 4.

Gently mix together the apples, raspberries and sugar and place in a pie dish. Warm through in the oven for 10 minutes.

Beat the butter and sugar until pale and thick, then beat in the egg followed by the milk. Quickly fold in the flour, trying to keep the mixture as light as possible.

Spoon the topping evenly over the fruit and bake in the preheated oven for 25 minutes until golden and crusty.

DAMSON PIE

Damsons have an intense plum flavour that is gorgeous eaten with spoonfuls of thick double cream. If you are short of time, mix together 455g/1lb of plums and 225g/8oz damsons to lessen the number of fruit needing to be stoned. (Serves 4)

680g/1½lb ripe damsons
225g/8oz caster sugar or to
   taste
pinch of ground allspice or
   star anise (optional)
3 tablespoons water

225g/8oz rough puff pastry
   (see page 328)
2 tablespoons milk
1 tablespoon granulated
   sugar for topping
   (optional)

Preheat the oven to 220°C/425°F/gas 7.

Wash and stone the damsons (and plums if using). Place in a deep pie dish and coat with the sugar and spice (to taste) before adding the water.

Roll out the pastry on a lightly floured surface in roughly the same shape as your pie dish only larger. Cut a ribbon from the edge of the dough and press it firmly on to the rim of the pie dish. Brush this with some milk. Loosely roll the pastry on to the rolling pin and lift on to the pie dish. Using a fork, firmly press around the rim so that the 2 pastries are glued together. Cut off the excess pastry. Prick the lid with a fork. Then lightly brush it with some milk before liberally sprinkling with sugar.

Place in the centre of the preheated oven and bake for 35 minutes or until the pastry has puffed up and become golden. Eat hot, warm or cold with cream, crème fraîche or home-made custard.

GREENGAGE ALMOND CRUMBLE

The crumble has a very obscure beginning: according to Marguerite Patten, no recipes appear for it until the Second World War. She speculates in *Classic British Dishes* that it was created at that time to cope with the heavy flours and scarcity of butter. Modern crumble mixtures can be varied with ground almonds, hazelnuts or walnuts depending on your taste. Greengages are favourite fruit for crumbles, as they exude plenty of juice. (Serves 4)

905g/2lb juicy greengages	*Crumble topping*
3 tablespoons water	170g/6oz plain flour
sugar to taste	115g/4oz cold butter, diced
	55g/2oz ground almonds
	55g/2oz caster sugar

Preheat the oven to 200°C/400°F/gas 6.

Wash and halve the greengages, removing the stones as you do so. Place in a pie dish, adding the water and sugar to taste.

Sift the flour into a mixing bowl and add the diced butter. Using your fingertips, rub the butter into the flour until it forms coarse crumbs. Then, using a metal spoon, stir in the ground almonds and sugar until evenly mixed.

Cover the fruit with the crumble mixture and lightly press down. Place in the centre of the preheated oven and bake for 15 minutes before reducing the temperature to 190°C/375°F/gas 5. Continue to bake for a further 15 minutes. Best served hot or warm.

Note: For a plain crumble topping, rub 85g/3oz cold butter into 170g/6oz plain flour before stirring in 55g/2oz caster sugar. Try combining different fruits such as nectarines with loganberries or peaches with strawberries. Bake as above.

BREAD AND CHEESE

I go then to the cupboard, and take the damp bags of rich sultanas; I lift the heavy flour on to the clean scrubbed kitchen table. I knead; I stretch; I pull, plunging my hands in the warm inwards of the dough. I let the cold water stream fanwise through my fingers. The fire roars; the flies buzz in a circle. All my currants and rices, the silver bags and the blue bags, are locked again in the cupboard. The meat is stood in the oven; the bread rises in a soft dome under the clean towel.

That was Susan's description of making bread in *The Waves* by Virginia Woolf. According to Louie Mayer, her cook at Rodmell in Sussex, Virginia Woolf excelled at making cottage loaves.

Kneading and baking bread is one of the most satisfying tasks a cook can embark upon, yet over the years bread has developed the reputation of being too difficult to bother about. Perhaps this was true when cooks were dependent on the delicate nature of live yeast or, worse still, the idiosyncrasies of some dried yeasts. But the arrival of *easy-mix* packet yeasts has abolished these old problems and simplified the whole procedure. It is merely a question of mixing the dried yeast granules with the flour and adding liquid before enjoying the pleasure of kneading soft, supple dough.

Bread, like all staple foods, is subject to fashions, both in the home, restaurant and shop. Italian breads, for example, have enjoyed a sudden popularity in the supermarkets with the arrival of olive-oil-flavoured ciabattas and focaccias. These in turn may be superseded by the growing fashion for traditional British breads such as cottage loaves, soda breads or mixed grain breads. At the same time many committed home bakers have begun to support organic mills, buying their flours either direct or from health food shops. This support, in conjunction with a select group of bakers, is generating a new interest in reviving some of our older cereal crops. However, it is still too early to see whether these rediscovered grains will ultimately influence modern breads.

It seems appropriate to mention cheese in the same section as bread, despite the immensity of both topics. The reputation of British cheeses has suffered from the appalling processed specimens that have filled our shops. To many people it is still an alien concept that Britain actually produces several hundred different, but all exceptionally good, regional cheeses. Many of these cheeses come from small farms and many still supply only local markets. But with the foundation of the Specialist Cheesemakers' Association in 1989 they have already begun to be more widely marketed.

It is worth seeking out specialist British cheeses, as they are of the same quality as the French cheeses so widely admired in Britain. In just the same way they can be divided into cow's, sheep's and goat's milk categories; hard, soft and unpressed; blue-veined and, of course, soft curds. The impact of serving a creamy Cashel Blue or a sharp goat's milk Mendip with a home-made loaf of bread can be as great as spending hours over a cassoulet or complicated pudding.

WALNUT BREAD

Walnut bread became a trendy restaurant-made bread in the eighties. Aside from tasting divine spread with butter and lots of thick honey, it makes an excellent accompaniment to creamy cheeses or smoked fish. (Makes two 455g/1lb loaves)

340g/12oz strong plain flour	2 tablespoons walnut oil, plus
340g/12oz wholemeal flour	extra for oiling
2 teaspoons salt	425ml/¾ pint tepid water
1 sachet (6 or 7g/¼oz)	90g/3½oz walnut halves,
easy-blend dried yeast	roughly broken

Mix together the 2 flours, salt and dried yeast in a large bowl. Stir in the walnut oil and water and thoroughly mix until it forms a pliable dough. Turn the dough out and knead for 5 minutes or until it feels like satin. It should spring back if touched.

Spread out the dough and cover with some of the walnuts. Press these in and fold over the dough. Repeat until all the walnuts are incorporated into the dough. Gently knead the bread to distribute them evenly. Place the dough in a large mixing bowl and lightly oil with some extra walnut oil. Cover and leave to rise in a warm place for an hour or until it has doubled its size.

Lightly oil 2 bread tins (if using) or oil a heavy baking sheet. Divide the dough in half. Either knead into a suitable shape for the bread tins or shape into 2 round loaves and place on the baking sheet. Brush with walnut oil and loosely cover with clingfilm. Leave for 60–90 minutes or until the dough is well risen.

Preheat the oven to 230°C/450°F/gas 8.

When the bread is ready remove the clingfilm and bake in the centre of the preheated oven for 25–30 minutes. The bread will turn light brown and rise a little. Tap the base of the loaves as you turn them out – if they sound hollow the bread is cooked, if not, quickly return to the oven for a further 5 minutes. Cool on a rack.

Note: Bread is very amenable – if your kitchen is cold, just allow it more time to rise. It can even be kneaded in the morning and left in the fridge for the day, so that it rises slowly. Then continue as normal.

OAT CAKES

Although commonly regarded as Scottish, oat cakes were widely eaten for centuries in many parts of the British Isles in place of bread. This was because oats were one of our staple cereal crops, along with rye and barley. This recipe has been adapted from my battered 1946 copy of *The Scottish Women's Rural Institutes Cookery Book* but it still works well. Modern oat cakes are usually served as a cheese biscuit. (Makes 18 biscuits)

225g/8oz medium oatmeal
1 tablespoon plain flour
¼ teaspoon salt
½ teaspoon bicarbonate of
   soda

½ tablespoon melted butter
   or lard
warm water, to mix

Preheat the oven to 190°C/375°F/gas 5 and oil 2 heavy baking sheets.

Mix together the dry ingredients and stir in the fat. Add enough water to make a moderately stiff dough. Knead this a little to help bind the mixture together.

Sprinkle the work surface with some flour and roll the dough out as thinly as possible, squishing it together with your fingers if it breaks apart, before cutting it into small circles or triangles. Rework the trimmings until all the dough has been cut into biscuits. Place these on the baking sheets and bake in the centre of the preheated oven for about 10–15 minutes. They will colour slightly and turn crisp. Cool and serve.

WELSH RAREBIT

Rarebits (also known as rabbits) have been eaten in Wales as far back as the fourteenth century. They became a common savoury in Victorian times, eaten at the end of the meal before the desserts and sweet wines. Today they have been hijacked as a fast food and are often eaten as a snack, although they are still served as a savoury on High Table at Oxford and in certain London clubs. (Serves 4)

15g/½oz butter	1 teaspoon English mustard
70ml/2.5fl oz ale	(ready-made)
225g/8oz grated Caerphilly	salt and freshly ground black
cheese	pepper, to taste
	4 slices hot buttered toast

Preheat the grill to a moderately high setting.

Melt the butter in a small pan over a low heat. Add the ale and cheese and stir until the latter has melted. Finally, add the mustard and seasoning to taste.

Quickly spread the mixture on to the slices of hot buttered toast and place under the grill until flecked golden brown and bubbling.

WILD FOOD

Blackberries, elderberries and sloes are perhaps some of the most familiar wild fruits in Britain. Blackberries are so popular that certain strains have been cultivated to produce larger fruit. Both blackberries and elders are easily found in both urban and country areas, whereas sloes have to be sought out.

All three fruits have been eaten for centuries (even Neolithic Britons were very partial to both sloes and blackberries, it seems) and there have been countless recipes to preserve them in spirits, cordials, jams and jellies. The recipe for elderberry jelly below can be adapted to both blackberries and sloes – just measure out the final liquid and add the same proportion of sugar. If you wish to make a blackberry liqueur, turn to page 199 and follow the recipe for raspberry ratafia.

BLACKBERRY ROLY-POLY

Roly-poly puddings are made with a suet pastry that has been spread and rolled up with a gooey sweet filling. They are usually boiled, as with treacle roll, jam roly-poly and spotted dick, but some are baked. This is based on a Warwickshire recipe and has a deliciously spiced jammy filling. (Serves 4)

340g/12oz blackberries	55g/2oz cold butter, cut into
85g/3oz soft brown sugar	small dice
½ teaspoon ground	85g/3oz shredded suet (beef
cinnamon	or vegetarian)
225g/8oz self-raising flour	140ml/¼ pint milk or less
pinch of salt	1 tablespoon granulated
	sugar

Preheat the oven to 200°C/400°F/gas 6 and liberally grease a baking sheet.

Toss the blackberries in the sugar and spice. If they still taste tart, add some more sugar according to your taste.

Sift the flour and salt into a bowl. Add the butter and, using your fingertips, quickly crumble it into the flour until it resembles fine bread-crumbs. (Or give it a quick whizz in the food processor.) Stir in the suet and then slowly add some of the milk, mixing with a fork until a rough dough is formed. At this stage turn it out on to a floured surface and lightly knead into a soft ball.

Roll the dough into a neat rectangle 1cm/½ inch thick. Strew the blackberries over it, leaving a good 2cm/¾ inch margin down the longer edges. Gently press them into the dough and brush the edges with water. Carefully roll the pastry up from the long side and seal all the edges together before sliding it on to the baking sheet. If you don't, the sweet blackberry juice will leak out and caramelize on the baking sheet.

Brush the roll with a little extra milk and liberally sprinkle with the granulated sugar. Bake in the preheated oven for 25–30 minutes until golden brown and puffy.

ELDERBERRY JELLY

The taste of elderberry jelly is vaguely reminiscent of port, so it is not surprising that elderberry juice was commonly used to adulterate both wine and port. The jelly makes an excellent addition to plum pies and game sauces.

1.8kg/4lb elderberries	2 lemons, juiced
140ml/¼ pint water	granulated sugar

Dip the fruit in plenty of cold water, as elderberries tend to harbour a lot of unseen insect life. Pull the berries off their stems and place in a saucepan. Crush thoroughly to release plenty of juice and add the water. Bring to the boil, cover and simmer for about 15 minutes or until tender.

Pour into a jelly bag and leave to drip overnight. Discard the berries and measure the liquid. Allow 455g/1lb sugar to every 565ml/1 pint of elderberry juice.

Place the elderberry juice, lemon juice and sugar in a jam or saucepan with a thermometer clipped on to the side. Heat gently, stirring occasionally, until the sugar has dissolved, then increase the heat and quickly bring to the boil. Boil vigorously, stirring regularly to prevent the jelly from catching, until it reaches setting point (106°C/220°F) on the thermometer.

Immediately remove from the heat and allow to cool. Skim off any scum and pour into sterilized jam jars and cover in the usual manner. See page 222 for general instructions on jam-making.

SLOE GIN

Many different flavourings can be added to sloes, such as lemon zest, cinnamon sticks, vanilla pods or even bruised almonds. Sloes are supposed to be picked for gin after the first frost, as this softens their tough skins. However, it is not worth waiting, since the birds will get them before you. The gin should be ready for Christmas, but improves steadily through the following year. Take a stout walking stick when you go picking, to help protect yourself against the ferocious thorns of the blackthorn.

455g/1lb sloes	3 strips orange peel, without
115g/4oz caster sugar	any pith attached
	850ml/1½ pints gin

Wash the sloes and patiently prick each fruit in several places with a darning needle. Carefully fill one or two sterilized bottling jars with the sloes, sugar and orange peel. Then cover with the gin. Seal the bottles and leave in a cool dark place, but remember to give them an occasional shake.

After 3 months you can strain and rebottle the gin if you wish, although this is not essential.

OCTOBER

GAME
Roast grouse
Roast partridge with bread sauce
Pheasant with orange and chicory
Mallard with elderberry sauce

PARTY FOOD
Chicory with crème fraîche and caviar
Moon and star biscuits
Spiced lamb pastries
Mini pizzas
Bacon sausages with tomato dip

MORE FISH
Grilled herring with pickled salad
Fish, chips and tartar sauce
Saffron fish pie

APPLES
Apple mousse
Baked apples
Rowan and apple jelly

SWEETS
Fudge
Peppermint creams
Coconut ice

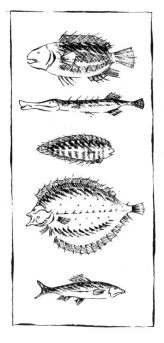

October is an interesting month for the British cook. The shorter days mark for many the recommencement of home entertaining, perhaps because, as Ambrose Heath states in his introduction to 'October' (*Good Food Throughout the Year*, 1932), 'The holiday season is over, and at last we have more time for our culinary contemplations.' Happily, October also brings a fresh influx of new produce ranging from game to fruit, so that modern cooks can still indulge themselves by using truly seasonal food.

By mid-October the game season is in full swing, yet the cooking of game is still regarded with great trepidation by many. I suspect that this is because it retains a certain social mystique from being cooked primarily by the rich for hundreds of years. Even when it became more widely available, it was a daunting task for the inexperienced cook to select a feather- or fur-clad animal under the eagle eye of the butcher. Now it is easy to walk into the supermarket and buy your chosen game neatly packaged, cleaned and ready for the pot. Not surprisingly the majority of recipes are still very traditional, but this may well change as increasing numbers of game are sold ready-portioned. For example, pheasant breasts are better when marinated and quickly pan-fried rather than roasted or stewed in the old manner.

As I have already said, the British are also notoriously conservative when it comes to fish and how to cook it. October is a particularly erratic month for native fish, as the autumn equinox brings storms and difficult fishing conditions. Consequently fish prices can fluctuate widely, so even

modern cooks have to be flexible in their choice of fish, despite the fact
that a wide variety is in season. In recent years, the revival of interest in
traditional British recipes among chefs has benefited many dishes, such as
fish and chips or fish pie, transforming them into fragrant modern dishes.
Even the humble herring, a favoured fish among the poor and middle
classes for centuries, has been rehabilitated on to the restaurant menu.

Cooking with apples also comes into its own in October. Every
farmhouse, every country cottage and even many a suburban house still
grows an apple tree. We love this fruit and use it for cooking throughout
the year. Different trees crop at different times, but September and
October are perhaps the most prolific months. Curiously, until recently
we grew only a few commercial varieties. Little was known about the
fruiting habits, disease-resistance and capacity for storage of the older
strains, so consequently only the redoubtable Bramley's Seedling, Cox's
Orange Pippin and the odd Egremont Russet were widely sold. Instead
we imported vast quantities of Granny Smiths, Red and Golden Delicious
and the like. At long last the older varieties are being grown and sold
commercially, so that even the most urban of cooks can enjoy rediscovering their different flavours and textures.

One area of British cooking that is constantly changing is the cocktail
canapé. Although they were first served between the wars, canapés did
not really become popular until after the Second World War. For some
reason, they have been the subject of much rivalry between hostesses. A
woman could be judged by the quality of her vol-au-vent and damned by
the fact that she served pineapple chunks with cheese on a stick. Nevertheless, the sudden boom in corporate entertaining in the eighties revolu-
tionized cocktail food by the introduction of truly suave catering firms
who specialized in producing witty nibbles. Vol-au-vents were thrown
out of the window in favour of new foods themed around the party.
Bankers were served miniature fish and chips in the *Financial Times* or
tiny Yorkshire puddings topped with roast beef. Anything could be
served provided it was tiny and looked beautiful.

GAME

The hunting and eating of game has always been an essential part of British country life. In Saxon times all and sundry were allowed to hunt game, but with the arrival of the Normans these liberal laws were changed to restrict hunting to the aristocracy. From then onwards the ordinary man has had a very uneasy relationship with both the hunting and cooking of most sorts of game. As the laws changed, sometimes in favour of the commoner, more often not, the tastes of the rich became increasingly refined. Sea birds and small birds such as blackbirds gradually went out of favour, while the popularity of pheasants and partridge remained undiminished.

The introduction of better firearms in the nineteenth century radically changed the British attitude to hunting game. Until then the majority of game had been caught with nets, hawks or dogs, but accurate guns introduced a new element of sportsmanship. The romantic image of the hunter was further helped by the adventurous writings of military characters like Colonel Thomas Thornton (1757–1823), who described his shooting escapades in *A Sporting Tour Through the Northern Parts of England and the Great Part of the Highlands*:

> It was now past five and a dreadful rain. No encampment to be seen; eight Highland miles home; in the very heart of game; my powder, which I had been preparing, well dried; shot sufficient in my holsters for a day's sport; my dogs well fed on two cheeses and a large bowl of milk – could there, to a sportsman be any better measure adopted?
>
> Matters thus adjusted, my landlady procured me a bowl of her best milk, to which I added a flask of very strong Jamaica rum; turned out of my canteen some ham and chicken, biscuits and Cheshire cheese, and, with fresh fuel, we became very merry.

As a result of this new image, shooting parties became an essential part of the social calendar. The rapid spread of the railways brought even the remotest estates within reach of any aspiring socialite. Thus it is not surprising that eating most forms of game still carries a certain social cachet. Consequently, few cooks have felt confident about challenging the way game is hung or cooked.

ROAST GROUSE

The fashion for eating grouse began only in the nineteenth century, when Prince Albert took up the sport. Traditionally, grouse was hung until the maggots fell out with its tail feathers. This degree of ripeness imbues it with a pungent flavour. Unhung, grouse tastes like a slightly gamy chicken. Young grouse is still thought to be best appreciated plainly roasted, although older birds can be gently cooked in game pies, puddings and stews. (Serves 4)

4 oven-ready grouse
½ lemon, finely grated and
   juiced
¼ teaspoon thyme leaves
115g/4oz softened butter
salt and freshly ground black
   pepper
4 slices thin streaky rindless
   bacon

Gravy
225ml/8 fl oz sweet dessert
   wine
225ml/8 fl oz chicken stock

Garnish
1 large bunch watercress,
   washed and trimmed

Preheat the oven to 220°C/425°F/gas 7.

Carefully wipe each bird inside and out with a damp cloth. Season lightly.

Beat together the lemon zest, juice, thyme, butter and seasoning. Liberally smear the grouse with the lemon butter and place a small nut of butter inside the cavities. Wrap a bacon slice over the breast of each.

Place in the centre of the preheated oven and roast for 15–20 minutes if you like your grouse pink and 25–30 minutes if you prefer a well-done bird. Remove the bacon 10 minutes before the end of cooking time. Baste the birds and allow to brown. Leave to rest in a warm place while you deglaze the pan.

Place the roasting pan over a moderately high heat. Add the wine and chicken stock and bubble vigorously while scraping any sediment off the bottom of the pan. Allow it to reduce until syrupy, then pour through a fine strainer and serve with the grouse.

Arrange a small bunch of watercress beside each bird and serve with the light gravy and game chips. (See three-flavoured crisps, page 287.)

Note: Traditionally, roast grouse is served on a round croûton of toasted bread, which is sometimes spread with its mashed fried liver. Otherwise it can be served with crispy fried breadcrumbs or with rowan and apple jelly, redcurrant jelly or bread sauce.

ROAST PARTRIDGE WITH BREAD SAUCE

The delicate flavour of the grey-legged partridge is perhaps more to modern taste than the expensive grouse. Partridge are at their best in October and November and are excellent roasted when young. (Serves 4)

4 oven-ready partridges	15g/½oz butter
salt and freshly ground black	2 tablespoons double
pepper	cream
115g/4oz softened butter	55g/2oz fresh white
8 sprigs thyme	breadcrumbs
4 slices thin streaky rindless	salt and freshly ground black
bacon	pepper
Bread sauce	*Gravy*
285ml/½ pint milk	225ml/8fl oz dry white wine
1 peeled onion, stuck with	225ml/8fl oz chicken stock
3 cloves	
1 small bay leaf	*Garnish*
a pinch of ground mace	1 large bunch watercress,
4 black peppercorns	washed and trimmed

Preheat the oven to 220°C/425°F/gas 7.

The art to making a good bread sauce is to allow sufficient time for the flavourings to infuse into the milk, otherwise it tastes very dull. Place the milk, onion, bay leaf, mace and peppercorns in a small pan and scald. Remove from the heat, cover, and leave to infuse for 30 minutes.

Carefully wipe each partridge inside and out with a damp cloth and season. Liberally smear the birds with the softened butter and place a small nut of butter inside their cavities with some of the thyme. Wrap a bacon slice over the breast of each and tuck the remaining thyme around the birds.

Place in the centre of the preheated oven and roast for 30 minutes. Remove the bacon 10 minutes before the end of cooking time. Baste the birds and allow to brown. Once cooked, leave to rest in a warm place while you finish the bread sauce. Make the gravy in the same manner as the previous recipe – but substitute a dry white wine for the dessert wine.

Strain the milk into a clean pan and reheat with the butter and cream. Whisk in the breadcrumbs over a low heat and stir occasionally until the sauce has thickened. Season to taste and serve separately along with the gravy. Garnish the partridge with watercress.

PHEASANT WITH ORANGE AND CHICORY

With the arrival of ready-portioned game, new quick-cooking recipes are being developed. Here is my favourite pheasant recipe – which includes the best way to cook Belgian endive. (Serves 2)

2 pheasant breasts	*Orange endive*
3 tablespoons olive oil	3 small heads Belgian
	endive (chicory)
Marinade	2 oranges, juiced
1 tablespoon olive oil	285ml/½ pint sweet dessert
3 tablespoons orange juice	wine
3 tablespoons sweet dessert	salt and freshly ground black
wine	pepper
2 sprigs thyme	55g/2oz butter, diced
3 sprigs parsley	

Place the pheasant breasts in a bowl with the marinade ingredients. Cover and chill for between 3 and 24 hours.

Prepare the Belgian endive by trimming its base and removing any battered outer leaves. Slice in half lengthways and place in one layer in a non-corrosive saucepan. Immediately cover with the orange juice and dessert wine. Season to taste and fleck with half the butter. Press some greaseproof paper over the Belgian endive and liquid to prevent them from discolouring. Simmer for 20 minutes or until tender.

Remove the pheasant breasts from their marinade, pat dry and season. Heat the olive oil in a frying pan over a moderate heat and fry the pheasant breasts for about 5 minutes on each side. As soon as they are cooked, set aside in a warm place and deglaze the pan with the hot liquid from the Belgian endive. Reduce it down a little, swirl in the remaining butter and strain into a sauce-boat. Serve with the hot Belgian endive.

MALLARD WITH ELDERBERRY SAUCE

The rich, almost currant-like flavour of the elderberries balances perfectly with the gamy flavour of the mallards. (Serves 4)

2 wild duck	30g/1oz softened butter
salt and freshly ground black	140ml/¼ pint good red wine
pepper	2 tablespoons elderberry
2 oranges	jelly
6 sprigs thyme	

Preheat the oven to 220°C/425°F/gas 7. Wipe the ducks inside and out with a damp cloth. Using a pair of tweezers, tweak out any feathers. Season the ducks inside and out. Cut one of the oranges in half and stuff each duck with an orange half and some thyme.

Rub the ducks with the butter and place in the centre of the preheated oven. Roast for between 25 and 35 minutes, depending on how well done you like your duck. Baste the ducks every 10 minutes.

Once cooked to your liking, remove the birds from the roasting tray and leave to rest in a warm place while you make the sauce.

Deglaze the roasting tray with a little red wine. Finely grate and juice the second orange and add its zest and juice to the wine. Reduce by half. Stir in the elderberry jelly and as soon as it has melted adjust the seasoning to taste and strain into a sauce-boat.

Carve the ducks and serve with the sauce.

PARTY FOOD

By the thirties new ideas regarding entertaining had begun to take hold of British society. It became fashionable to serve guests with drinks, even cocktails, before they were ushered into the dining-room. At the same time savouries, which until then had always been served at the end of the meal, began to be served, initially as hors d'oeuvre, but then as an accompaniment to the pre-dinner drink. The cocktail canapé had been created. Gradually a whole new range of 'small eats' began to evolve for the new 'drinks' parties. By 1963 the practice of serving 'nibbles' with drinks had become commonplace, as is illustrated by this extract from the *Penguin Cordon Bleu Cookery Book* by Rosemary Hume and Muriel Downes, first published in 1963.

Engagement Party Cocktail

Quiche (small)	Hot Frankfurters and French Mustard
Cheese Sables	Anchovy Loaf
Smoked Salmon Rolls	Egg and Prawn Croquettes
Small Tongue Sandwiches	Asparagus Rolls

And of course the usual nuts and olives and crisps.

Cocktail food had to be easy to eat with the fingers and never cause any unseemly or embarrassing mess. However, with the rise in corporate entertaining in the eighties, simple nibbles began to be ignored in favour of clever, showy food. Everything from sushi to mini pizzas was served. Although this extravagant fashion has become more subdued, it allowed cooks to rethink their party food and adapt many simple everyday dishes into attractive miniature versions.

The essential thing to remember when preparing cocktail food is that it always takes longer to prepare than one expects. Therefore it is wise to try and prepare as much as possible in advance. Allow ten nibbles per person for evening parties and fourteen for lunchtime drinks, as it is unlikely that your guests will go on to eat. If you just want to serve canapés with drinks before a meal, allow about three per person.

CHICORY WITH CRÈME FRAÎCHE AND CAVIAR

A perfect party dish, quick to make, lovely to look at and delicious to eat.
(Makes 24 portions)

200ml/7fl oz crème fraîche	2 heads red chicory (or trevisse)
2 tablespoons finely sliced chives	2 heads Belgian endive
1 lemon, finely grated	30g/1oz Sevruga caviar
salt and freshly ground black pepper	30g/1oz salmon caviar

Mix the crème fraîche with the finely sliced chives, lemon zest and
seasoning to taste. Cover and chill until needed.

Trim the chicory and Belgian endive and separate all the leaves. Wash
and gently pat dry. Wrap in slightly damp kitchen paper and chill until
needed.

When ready to serve, place a teaspoonful of the crème fraîche on the
stem of each leaf and top with a blob of caviar. Try the black Sevruga
caviar with the red chicory and the salmon caviar with the Belgian
endive. Arrange prettily on a plate and serve immediately.

MOON AND STAR BISCUITS

These are specially shaped cheese straws – with different savoury toppings
that give them an added bite. You can use other shapes such as hearts if
you wish. (Makes a total of 50–60 biscuits depending on the shape)

Cheese dough	Toppings
225g/8oz plain flour	1 tablespoon sesame seeds
salt	1 tablespoon poppy seeds
¼ teaspoon cayenne pepper	1 tablespoon yellow
115g/4oz cold butter, cut	mustard seeds
into small dice	
115g/4oz finely grated	1 tablespoon finely grated
Parmesan cheese	Parmesan cheese
1 egg	1 egg beaten with 1
	tablespoon cream

Preheat the oven to 200°C/400°F/gas 6 and grease several baking sheets.

Sift the flour, salt and cayenne pepper into a large bowl. Gently rub the
butter into the flour until it resembles fine breadcrumbs (or quickly whizz
in the food processor), then stir in the cheese. Mix in the egg and a little
cold water. As soon as the crumbs begin to hold together, turn out on to
a floured board and lightly knead until smooth.

Roll the pastry out to about 5mm/¼ inch thickness. Cut half the
dough into 5cm/2 inch stars and the other half into crescent moons. The
trimmings can be kneaded together and re-rolled.

As you cut, transfer the biscuits on to the greased baking sheets. Paint
all the shapes with the egg glaze. Sprinkle a quarter of them with sesame
seeds, a quarter with poppy seeds, another quarter with mustard seeds
and the remainder with the Parmesan.

Bake in the preheated oven for 8–10 minutes until golden brown.
Remove and cool on a wire cooling rack. They will keep for a few days
in an airtight tin.

SPICED LAMB PASTRIES

These can be made up in advance, spread out on a baking sheet and frozen. Defrost on the baking sheet, brush with egg wash and bake. Alternatively, bake the day before and reheat in a hot oven for 5 minutes before serving. (Makes 28 pieces)

Lamb filling
2 tablespoons vegetable oil
2 cloves garlic, crushed
1 small onion, finely diced
2 teaspoons chilli flakes
1 small stick cinnamon
¼ teaspoon ground cloves
¼ teaspoon dried oregano
4 tablespoons tomato purée
1 strip lemon peel
30g/1oz pine nuts

340g/12oz lean minced lamb
salt and freshly ground black pepper

Pastry
225g/8oz plain flour
1 teaspoon baking powder
½ teaspoon salt
115g/4oz cold butter, cut into small dice
1 egg beaten with 1 tablespoon milk

Heat the oil in a saucepan and gently fry the garlic and onion until soft. Add all the dried spices and herbs and sauté for a minute before mixing in the tomato purée, lemon peel and pine nuts. Heat through and then add the minced lamb. Keep stirring until the meat has coloured and separated, then add 140ml/¼ pint water and bring up to the boil. Reduce the heat to a simmer and cook for 30 minutes or until the mixture becomes dry and rich. Adjust the seasoning to taste, cool and chill until needed.

Sift the flour, baking powder and salt into a large bowl. Rub the butter into the flour until it forms fine crumbs. Mix to a fairly stiff dough with some cold water. Roll out on a lightly floured surface to 3mm/⅛ inch thickness and cut into 7.5cm/3 inch circles. Brush the rim of each circle with the egg wash and spoon the cold meat into the centre. Crimp the edges together to make mini Cornish pasties and brush with the egg wash. Chill for 30 minutes on a greased baking sheet, or freeze at this stage.

Preheat the oven to 200°C/400°F/Gas 6. Bake the pastries for 20–30 minutes and serve warm with lots of sour cream.

MINI PIZZAS

Mini pizzas are actually easier and less time-consuming to make than the usual toasted canapés. The dough can be made days in advance and frozen, while the toppings can be prepared either the night before or a few hours before they are needed. Once assembled, the pizzas can be stored in the fridge and baked as you need them. The toppings can also be varied – cherry tomato and Parmesan or caramelized onions with sage and cheese are also very good. (Makes 40 mini (5cm/2 inch) pizzas)

pizza dough made from
    225g/8oz flour (see page
    182)
olive oil
salt

*Roasted pepper and
    mozzarella topping
    Covers 20 mini pizzas*
½ red or orange pepper
½ yellow pepper
1 clove garlic, crushed
1 teaspoon finely chopped
    basil
1 tablespoon olive oil

salt and freshly ground black
    pepper
¼ Mozzarella cheese,
    diced

*Leek and blue cheese
    topping
    Covers 20 mini pizzas*
2 tablespoons olive oil
1 leek, finely sliced
¼ teaspoon finely chopped
    thyme
salt and freshly ground black
    pepper
30g/1oz Dolcelatte cheese,
    diced

For the first topping, preheat the grill to its highest setting. Cut the peppers into quarters and seed them. Place skin side up under the grill until the peppers begin to blister, then remove to a bowl, cover and leave to steam for 10 minutes. Peel the peppers and cut into small dice. Mix with the garlic, basil, a tablespoon of olive oil and some seasoning. Cover and chill until needed.

For the second topping, heat the olive oil in a small frying pan and quickly sauté the leeks with the thyme until they begin to wilt. Season to taste, cool, cover and chill until needed.

Several hours before cooking, you can roll out the pizza dough, cut into 5cm/2 inch rounds and place directly on to well oiled baking sheets. Brush them with a little extra olive oil, sprinkle with salt, and spoon the roasted pepper mixture on to half the pizzas, sprinkle with the Mozzarella cubes. Spoon the leek mixture on to the remaining pizzas and arrange the

Dolcelatte on top. Cover loosely with clingfilm and leave refrigerated until needed. They can stay like this for at least 6 hours.

Preheat the oven to its highest setting and bake the pizzas as needed. They cook in 8–10 minutes.

BACON SAUSAGES WITH TOMATO DIP

Everybody loves cocktail sausages, whether they are served plainly on their cocktail sticks or with a mustard dip. This is just one of the many variations. If you cannot buy any cocktail sausages, buy the same weight of chipolata sausages and twist each sausage in the middle so that they form an extra link that can then be cut. (Makes 32)

16 rashers rindless streaky bacon	1 tablespoon white wine vinegar
455g/1lb cocktail sausages	3 tablespoons olive oil
	¼ teaspoon caster sugar
Tomato dip	¼ teaspoon finely chopped basil or mint
4 large tomatoes, peeled, seeded and diced	salt and freshly ground black pepper

Stretch each slice of bacon and cut in half. Roll up each sausage in the bacon and place on an oiled baking sheet or store in the fridge until needed.

Peel the tomatoes by cutting a cross at the base and pouring boiling water over them. Leave for a few seconds and then quickly peel. Cut into quarters and place the seeds in a strainer above a bowl. Push the seeds against the strainer to extract as much juice as possible and then whisk into this the vinegar, olive oil, sugar and basil or mint. Neatly dice the tomato flesh and stir into the dressing. Season to taste and pour into a pretty bowl. (This can be made up to 8 hours ahead if necessary – just cover and chill until the party, then allow to come up to room temperature before serving.)

Preheat the oven to 200°C/400°F/gas 6. Bake the sausages for about 20 minutes or until crisp and golden. Roll in kitchen towelling to remove any excess fat before spearing on to cocktail sticks. Serve arranged around the tomato dip.

MORE FISH

By 1914 the monthly magazine *Home Cookery* was recommending unappetizing if economic fish pies such as herrings cooked in vinegar and topped
with mashed potato. Such fishy dishes were food for the poor. According
to Henry Mayhew, in his fascinating book *London Labour and the
London Poor* (1862), trays of fried fish were widely sold around the pubs
with bread and salt. The fish fryers would buy up cheap, unsold fish
from the fishmongers. These could range from 'soles, haddocks, whitings,
flounders, and herrings, but very sparingly indeed as regards herrings'.
They were then dipped in flour and water before being pan-fried in
rapeseed oil.

Fortunately, the current revival in traditional British food has also
benefited many of the poorer fish dishes by lavishing proper care on
them. Fried fish is now coated in a crispy batter or breadcrumbs and
served with an unctuous tartar sauce in the best of restaurants. Delicate
creamy stews of fish and shellfish are now topped with puff pastry or
fluffy mashed potato, while herrings are being reinstated plainly grilled
with a piquant accompaniment.

GRILLED HERRING WITH PICKLED SALAD

Over the last ten years, herrings have increasingly been served with Scandinavian-influenced sweet and sour sauces or dill-flavoured mustards. (Serves 4)

4 herrings, cleaned and
 beheaded
1 tablespoon olive oil
salt and freshly ground black
 pepper
1 lemon, cut into wedges

Pickled salad
4 sweet pickled cucumbers,
 diced

4 small cooked beetroot,
 diced
1 teaspoon finely chopped
 dill
1 dessertspoon runny
 honey
1 dessertspoon white wine
 vinegar

Preheat the grill to its highest setting.

Slit each fish from head to tail along its belly. Place a herring, cut side down, on a chopping board and gently but firmly press down along its spine until the fish flattens out. Lift up and pull away the spine and many of the attached bones. Repeat with the remaining fish.

Now inspect the flesh side of each fish and pull out as many bones as you can find, using tweezers. Trim off the fins and set aside.

Mix together the diced cucumber and beetroot. Stir in the dill, honey and vinegar and set aside.

Brush the fish with olive oil, season and place under the grill. As soon as the skin begins to bubble and colour, turn over and continue to cook. They usually take about 5 minutes per side. Serve with the pickle and lemon wedges.

FISH, CHIPS AND TARTAR SAUCE

Perfect chips need to be fried twice and cooled in between frying to get a
truly crisp-on-the-outside fluffy-on-the-inside chip. This has the advantage
of allowing the cook to prepare them ahead of the meal and then quickly
frying them along with the fish at the last minute. The tartar sauce can
also be made ahead and kept in the fridge until needed. Choose your
favourite white fish. (Serves 4)

Chips

4 large potatoes

vegetable oil for deep-
frying

Tartar sauce

2 egg yolks

2 teaspoons Dijon mustard

½ teaspoon salt

1 tablespoon white wine or
tarragon vinegar

285ml/½ pint vegetable oil

1 tablespoon finely chopped
chives

1 tablespoon finely chopped
parsley

¼ teaspoon finely chopped
tarragon

1 dessertspoon finely
chopped gherkins

1 dessertspoon finely
chopped, rinsed capers

Fish

285g/10oz plain flour

pinch of salt

2 small eggs, roughly beaten

285ml/½ pint lager

1 tablespoon olive oil

2 haddock or plaice etc.,
filleted and skinned

seasoned flour

vegetable oil for deep-
frying

1 lemon, cut into wedges

Peel and cut the potatoes into thin batons. Soak them in plenty of cold
water to remove the excess starch. Rinse well and either spin dry in a
salad spinner or pat dry in a tea cloth.

Heat the oil to 170°C/325°F and blanch the chips in batches. A
perfectly blanched chip should have a crisp uncoloured skin with a soft
centre. This will take around 3 minutes. Remove from the oil and leave
to cool and drain on kitchen paper. Chill until ready to serve.

Meanwhile, make the tartar sauce by placing the egg yolks, mustard,
salt and vinegar in a food processor or bowl. Whizz or whisk until pale,
then slowly add (or whisk in) the oil until it forms a thick emulsion. Fold
the remaining sauce ingredients into this and adjust the seasoning to taste
so that you have a tart, pungent sauce. Set aside.

Sift the flour and salt into a mixing bowl and make a hollow in the centre. Pour the eggs into the middle of this and gradually beat them in, before slowly adding the lager until the batter is smooth and has the consistency of double cream. Mix in the olive oil and leave to rest for 30 minutes. It is best to have 2 saucepans for deep-frying – one for the chips and one for the fish. Preheat the fish oil to 190°C/375°F.

Cut the fish fillets into neat portions and pat dry. Dip into the seasoned flour and shake off any excess before dipping them into the batter. Fry them in 2 batches until they become golden and crisp. Quickly drain on kitchen paper, sprinkle with salt and serve as soon as the chips are ready.

Reheat the chip oil to 180°C/350°F and cook the blanched chips in batches for about 3–4 minutes until golden and crisp. Drain on kitchen paper, salt liberally and serve piled high with the fish, tartar sauce and lemon wedges.

SAFFRON FISH PIE

The idea of covering a fish pie with mashed potato was introduced only in the middle of the last century. Eliza Acton gives a recipe for 'modern potato pastry' in 1845, and she recommends spreading it to the incredible thickness of 7.5cm/3 inches. However, the older method of covering a pie with pastry to my mind complements the texture of the fish far better and somehow raises the status of this luxurious dish. (Serves 4)

1.1kg/2½lb live mussels	455g/1lb ripe tomatoes,
2 shallots, finely chopped	peeled, seeded and diced
1 fat clove garlic, crushed	115g/4oz cooked peeled
3 sprigs tarragon	prawns
425ml/¾ pint Noilly Prat	2 tablespoons finely
3 saffron threads	chopped parsley
455g/1lb skinned monkfish	2–3 tablespoons lemon juice
fillet	salt and freshly ground black
1 bulb Florence fennel	pepper
3 tablespoons olive oil	225g/8oz puff pastry (see
425ml/¾ pint double cream	page 329)
	½ egg beaten with 1
	tablespoon milk

Preheat the oven to 220°C/425°F/gas 7.

Scrub the mussel shells clean and cut away their tough stringy beards. As you do so, lightly tap any open shells to see if they will close. If they do not respond throw them out, along with any damaged or floating mussels.

Place the finely chopped shallots, garlic and tarragon in a wide pan with the Noilly Prat. Cover and simmer gently for 10 minutes. Increase the heat to high and add the cleaned mussels to the boiling liquid, then cover once again and return to the boil. As soon as the mussels open, remove from the heat. Shell when cool enough to handle, saving any juices. Add these to the cooking broth in the pan.

Strain the broth through a muslin-lined sieve (or a rinsed J-cloth) into a clean pan. Check that there is no grit, then return to the boil and reduce by half. Remove from the heat, add the saffron and leave to infuse.

Cut the monkfish into large dice. Trim the fennel, cut in half and wash. Cut into thin fan-like slices.

Heat the oil in a non-stick frying pan until very hot. Season the monkfish cubes and sear until they are just coloured. Remove, reduce the temperature and gently fry the fennel for a couple of minutes.

Add the saffron-infused liquid with the double cream. Simmer gently for 3 minutes until the cream thickens a little, then add the tomato dice, monkfish, mussels, prawns, parsley, lemon juice and seasoning to taste. Transfer to a pie dish.

Roll out the pastry on a lightly floured surface. Cut a ribbon from the edge of the dough and press it firmly on to the rim of the pie dish. Brush the pastry rim with some of the beaten egg and milk. Then loosely roll the pastry on to the rolling pin and lift on to the pie dish. Using a fork or spoon, firmly press around the rim so that the pastries are glued together in an attractive manner. Cut off the excess pastry. Prick the lid with a fork and paint with some more beaten egg and milk.

Bake in the centre of the preheated oven for 20 minutes or until the pastry has puffed up and become golden.

Note: Mashed potato can be used instead of the pastry. Just cover the pie dish with a layer of fluffy mashed potato and bake in the oven for 20 minutes.

APPLES

Apples are perhaps one of the best loved British fruits, considering we consume around 4,368 million of them each year. Our adoration has led us to cultivate thousands of new varieties, including our unique cooking or 'culinary' apples. These large, highly acidic fruit will disintegrate into a delicious froth that is perfect for our apple sauces and purées but disastrous for such imports as French apple tart which need firm dessert fruit. Until recently only the redoubtable Bramley's Seedling was available from greengrocers, but now other good cookers such as Grenadier (fluffy and honey-flavoured) and Lord Derby (a firmer sharp fruit) can be bought.

Many of our native dessert apples were bred to reflect the economic standing of grand Victorian households. They were sampled as a delicacy at the end of a meal. Some of these are suitable for cooking and it is worth experimenting with different varieties. The well-balanced, sweetly acidic James Grieve, the lovely dry-textured Blenheim Orange and the juicy sweet Charles Ross are all excellent dual-purpose apples. Blenheim Orange is particularly good for apple tarts and compotes as it keeps its shape.

APPLE MOUSSE

Mousses, otherwise known as iced soufflés, which they were painstakingly made to imitate, were very popular in the seventies but have since slowly drifted out of fashion. Despite this they make a wonderful lighter-than-air pudding that is perfectly suited to the fresh flavour of apples. Choose your favourite variety. (Serves 4)

140ml/¼ pint dry cider	1 sachet (1 tablespoon)
2 tablespoons lemon juice	powdered gelatine
4 cloves	140ml/¼ pint crème
115g/4oz caster sugar	fraîche
455g/1lb cooking apples, for	2 egg whites
example, Grenadier,	pinch of salt
Bramley's Seedling or	
Golden Noble	

Place all but 3 tablespoons of the cider in a heavy-bottomed saucepan with the lemon juice, cloves and sugar. Peel, core and slice the apples. Mix them into the cider as you go to prevent them from discolouring. Place over a moderately low heat and simmer until they have disintegrated into a pulp.

Meanwhile, pour the remaining cider into a small bowl and sprinkle evenly with the gelatine. Leave to soak for 5 minutes, then place in a small pan of simmering water and wait until the gelatine has melted.

Remove the cloves from the apples and stir in the melted gelatine. Purée the mixture and set aside to cool. (If you are in a rush, rest the bowl in a larger bowl of iced water.)

As soon as the mixture begins to set and has the consistency of thick double cream, fold in the crème fraîche. Whisk the egg whites with a pinch of salt until they form soft peaks. Fold in a couple of spoonfuls to loosen the apple mixture before lightly folding in the remaining egg whites. Transfer to a serving bowl, cover and chill. Serve when set.

BAKED APPLES

Baked apples are comfort food *par excellence*. They can be stuffed with flavoured sweet butters, Calvados-soaked raisins, fresh blackberries, raspberries or a honey-bound mixture of nuts, butter and citrus zest. The possibilities are endless. The filled apples must be cooked until they have risen like a soufflé and are meltingly soft and fluffy inside. Although cooking apples are usually used, dessert apples are equally good cooked in this manner. (Serves 4)

4 tablespoons raisins or sultanas	1 lemon, finely grated
2 tablespoons Calvados or rum (optional)	115g/4oz softened butter
115g/4oz soft brown sugar	4 medium cooking apples, for example, Grenadier or Golden Noble
1 orange, finely grated	

If you have time, soak the raisins or sultanas in the Calvados or rum for a few hours.

Preheat the oven to 180°C/350°F/gas 4.

Beat the sugar, orange and lemon zest into the butter. Squeeze 1 tablespoon of lemon juice and 2 tablespoons of orange juice and beat into the butter along with the macerated raisins. Core the apples and score the skin around their circumference, so that they 'soufflé up' as they cook.

Arrange them on a small buttered baking dish and stuff their cavities with the raisin butter, smearing any excess over their tops. If any liquid has separated from the butter, pour around the apples.

Bake in the centre of the preheated oven for about 20–30 minutes or until they are soft. The time varies according to the size and variety of apple you use.

Serve with their gooey juices and lots and lots of cream.

ROWAN AND APPLE JELLY

Apples make excellent jellies and are often cooked with other fruit or flavoured with herbs such as rosemary. These can then be served with game, pork, ham or lamb. For most homes with a large apple tree, there is only a limited number of apples that can be stored over the winter, so other means of preserving them have to be found.

1.4kg/3lb rowan berries	1.4kg/3lb unblemished
1.14 litres/2 pints water	cooking apples
	granulated sugar

Thoroughly wash the rowan berries in plenty of cold water. Pick them off their stalks and place in a large pan with the water. Bring to the boil and cook gently until they begin to soften.

Meanwhile, roughly chop the cooking apples, pips and all. Crush the rowan berries with a wooden spoon, then add the apples and continue to simmer until they are reduced to a pulp.

Remove from the heat and drain through a jelly bag overnight. Measure the liquid and allow 455g/1lb sugar to every 565ml/1 pint of liquid.

Preheat the oven to low and warm the sugar along with the washed jam jars.

Pour the juice into a jam pan and clip a thermometer on to the side of the saucepan. Bring the juice to the boil, then add the warm sugar and stir until it has dissolved. Return to a high heat and boil rapidly until the thermometer registers 106°C/220°F – jam setting point.

Remove from the heat and allow to rest for 15 minutes. Using a slotted spoon, skim off any scum and pour into the warm dry jars. Seal as usual.

See page 222 for general instructions on jam-making.

SWEETS

The British have a very sweet tooth and they love their sweets with a childish affection. The eighties tried to make everyone grow up by serving sophisticated sweets such as home-made truffles or *petits fours* with the coffee. But the recession-hit nineties have allowed us to return to our old habits with the revival of traditional British sweets, sold in dinky packaging. These sweets are a uniquely British phenomena – who else makes liquorice all-sorts, lemon sherbets and chewy toffees? Since many of our traditional sweets are very easy to make, I have included a few of the most obvious recipes. Just the thing for a wet and windy afternoon when you have nothing better to do.

FUDGE

extra butter for greasing	255ml/9 fl oz milk
455g/1lb granulated sugar	1 tablespoon golden syrup
55g/2oz butter	1 teaspoon vanilla essence

Grease a shallow tray about 2.5cm/1 inch deep. Set aside.

Clip a thermometer on to a heavy-bottomed saucepan and add the sugar, butter, milk and syrup. Place over a moderate heat and stir until the ingredients have dissolved. Bring slowly to the boil and then boil hard until the mixture reaches 116°C/240°F/soft ball.

Immediately remove from the heat, add the vanilla essence, and beat vigorously with a wooden spoon until the mixture changes its consistency and becomes thick, pale and creamy. This will take a good 5–10 minutes.

Pour into the greased tray and leave to cool. As soon as it begins to set, cut the fudge into squares, otherwise it will be impossible to break pieces off later. Eat when hard.

PEPPERMINT CREAMS

These have to be the easiest sweets to make and were probably the first dish I ever made. (Makes 24)

340g/12oz icing sugar	peppermint essence, to
1 egg white, roughly beaten	taste

Sift the icing sugar into a bowl. Beat in the egg white, along with a few drops of peppermint essence, until the sugar forms a rough dough. Adjust the peppermint flavour to taste.

Turn out the paste and lightly knead until smooth. Either roll out to 5mm/¼ inch thickness and then stamp out into small circles, or pull off small pieces of paste, roll each into a ball and lightly flatten into discs. Leave to dry on a plate in a cool place for at least 24 hours. They are perfect at the end of a week, but it is unlikely that you will be able to resist them for that long.

COCONUT ICE

(Makes 24 tablets)

vegetable oil for greasing	140g/5oz desiccated
455g/1lb caster sugar	coconut
140ml/¼ pint milk	pink colouring or cochineal

Lightly oil a shallow tin 20cm/8 inches by 15cm/6 inches and set aside.

Place the sugar and milk in a saucepan over a low heat and stir until the sugar dissolves. Clip on a thermometer and increase the heat. Allow the mixture to boil gently for about 10 minutes or until it reaches 116°C/240°F/soft ball.

Remove from the heat and beat in the coconut. Quickly pour half of the mixture into the greased tray and spread it evenly, using a wet knife.

Stir a few drops of colouring into the remaining mixture so that it turns pale pink. Spread this evenly over the white coconut mixture. Leave to cool. As soon as it begins to set, mark the coconut ice into neat squares. Cut once cold and firm. Eat within a few days, as it is best enjoyed slightly moist.

NOVEMBER

STEWS
Lamb and barley stew
Beef casserole with horseradish dumplings
Pork with leeks and prunes

ROOT VEGETABLES
Mashed potatoes
Roasted root vegetables
Crispy potato cakes
Three-flavoured crisps

HAM
Honey glazed ham
Cumberland sauce
Bacon bubble and squeak
Cheese and ham scones

WINTER HERBS
Chick pea salad
Grilled field mushrooms
Rosemary lemon savarin

MORE WINTER PUDDINGS
Lemon rice pudding
Spiced pear granita

MULLED WINES
Mulled claret 1
Mulled claret 2

The cold November weather pulls most modern cooks back to their more conservative culinary past, with warming stews, roast hams and richly flavoured root vegetables. Many of our winter dishes revert to a more classical manner of British cooking, where flavours are simmered together and subtly layered one upon another, rather than being quickly assembled to contrast with one another, as happens in summer cooking. Thus hams are slowly simmered in a flavoursome broth before being further baked with a sweet glaze, and lemon savarins are baked before being saturated in a fresh rosemary, gin and lemon syrup.

Ham is perhaps one of the most traditional of British foods. Most British travellers miss the taste of bacon more than any other British food. Yet although we now tend to think of bacon and ham as being a highly commercialized product, even as late as the fifties recipes were still being published explaining to cooks how to cure it. *Farmhouse Fare*, a small book of country housewives' recipes collected by the *Farmers Weekly*, lists over twenty different cures, from Suffolk Treacle to Beer and Juniper. There are now signs of a return to some of the more traditional cures, as increasing numbers of modern cooks complain about watery bacon and tasteless gammons. This has meant that if you do not have the inclination to bake your own joint you can still buy some good varieties of sliced ham.

However, although many of our winter dishes are still regarded as epitomizing traditional British food, the manner in which they are served has changed totally. Meals have of necessity had to become simpler. A modern richly flavoured stew is served almost as a complete meal in itself, rather than as one element of a complex meal of roasts, boiled meats and vegetables. In the same way, despite revivalist movements, no 'traditional' recipe ever remains the same. The very nature of cooking means that it will continually evolve and develop with modern tastes and technology. Thus spiced pears in wines are now more likely to be served in the form of a delicate granita, topped with the tender poached pears.

Certainly modern British cooks have a great ability to adapt ideas around their ingredients. As soon as game chips became fashionable once again, every imaginable root vegetable was deep-fried, from celeriac to sweet potatoes or even beetroot. In the same way crispy cakes of potatoes were adapted to parsnips and carrots. The concept of serving different pulses such as chick peas or lentils as salads had a similar effect. Mediterranean and Middle Eastern ingredients were added to make hearty winter salads such as chick peas with roasted peppers and parsley.

But November cooking is marked mainly by the pleasure of rediscovering all the winter recipes that have been neglected through the summer months. It is a period for indulgence mixed with the anticipation of Christmas. Roast ham with Cumberland sauce, lemon rice pudding, mulled wine or butter-soaked scones bring a sense of comforting warmth.

STEWS

The modern interpretation of a stew tends to be a robust-flavoured meat dish that is associated in the common imagination with farmhouse kitchens. Recently many of the poorer cuts of meat such as oxtail, shin of beef and even pig's head have been enjoying a renaissance in restaurants, due in part to the fact that they are very cheap to buy and therefore make an excellent return for the restaurateur. This revival has been labelled peasant or rustic cookery, even after the transformations wrought to the homely dishes by modern chefs.

Stews originally developed from the early medieval pottages and have always formed an important part of the national diet. As fashions changed, they altered their names from pottage to mess to ragout, fricassée or stew and latterly to casserole. They embraced everything from vegetables to meat, fish and fruit. Their deepest influence came from the French, who were (and are) very skilled at the art of stewing, since it used to be said that the poor quality of their meat demanded much greater culinary attention than our own. These influences began with the arrival of the Norman court but have continued through the centuries, as French cooking comes and goes from fashion. So closely entwined have the two schools become within Britain that it is now very difficult to separate the different influences.

LAMB AND BARLEY STEW

There are certain British dishes that are fondly categorized as comforting, and lamb and barley stew is just such a dish. It warms and revives the eater in the most satisfying manner. You can vary the vegetables to taste. (Serves 4)

3 tablespoons olive oil or lamb dripping
salt and freshly ground black pepper
450g/1lb trimmed and diced shoulder or leg of lamb
1 medium onion, finely sliced
2 cloves garlic, crushed
1 large carrot, cut into half-moons
2 inner stalks celery, finely sliced
1 tablespoon flour

425ml/¾ pint lamb stock or water
285ml/½ pint dry white wine
1 tablespoon tomato purée (optional)
2 strips lemon peel
bouquet garni of thyme, parsley and bay leaf
pinch of ground mace
30g/1oz pearl barley
1 tablespoon chopped parsley

Preheat the oven to 170°C/325°F/gas 3.

Heat the olive oil in a casserole dish. Season the lamb dice and quickly brown in batches. Set aside. Add a little more oil if necessary and gently soften the onion, garlic, carrot and celery in the same dish. When soft, return the meat and mix in the flour, occasionally stirring for 2–3 minutes.

Add the stock, white wine, tomato purée, lemon peel, bouquet garni and mace. Bring to the boil and add the barley. Adjust the seasoning to taste. Cover and bake in the preheated oven for 1½ hours, or until the lamb is tender. Remove the bouquet garni just before serving and add the chopped parsley.

BEEF CASSEROLE WITH HORSERADISH DUMPLINGS

Stews are often served with some form of garnish such as tiny forcemeat balls, sippets of fried bread or dumplings. The latter are still a favourite accompaniment, despite the fact that many cooks are a little wary of making them. Happily, it does not matter what they look like, they still taste delicious soaked in the casserole juices. (Serves 4)

Casserole
680g/1½lb chuck steak,
   trimmed
seasoned flour
3 tablespoons olive oil or
   beef dripping
1 medium onion, finely
   sliced
1 clove garlic, crushed
2 carrots, cut into batons
3 tablespoons brandy
1 bay leaf, 1 sprig thyme
   and 1 sprig parsley
285ml/½ pint red wine, for
   example Pinot Noir
285ml/½ pint water

salt and freshly ground black
   pepper

Dumplings
½ tablespoon freshly grated
   horseradish mixed with a
   few drops of vinegar,
   mustard and caster sugar
   and 1 tablespoon double
   cream
115g/4oz self-raising flour
¼ teaspoon salt
½ tablespoon finely
   chopped parsley
55g/2oz shredded suet
extra flour

Remove any fat or tough fibres from the meat before cutting it into fairly large chunks. Toss the meat in batches in some seasoned flour.

Heat the oil in a heavy-bottomed saucepan or casserole dish and brown the meat on all sides over a moderately high heat. Cook the meat in batches to prevent it from reducing the temperature of the pan and thereby releasing a lot of juice.

Remove the meat from the pan. Add a little more olive oil if necessary and sauté the onion and garlic. As soon as the onion begins to soften add the carrot and continue to fry gently for 4 minutes before returning the beef to the saucepan.

Have some matches to hand before pouring the brandy over the meat. Immediately ignite and quickly stir the beef around the pan until the flames go out. Add the herbs, red wine and water. Adjust the seasoning. Return to the boil, then simmer very gently for an hour.

Make the dumplings once the beef has been cooking for a good hour. Mix together the horseradish, vinegar, mustard, sugar, cream, salt and pepper until it looks and tastes like thick horseradish sauce. Then mix together the flour, salt, parsley and suet in a bowl. Gradually stir in the water until you have a soft, pliable, but not sticky dough. Lightly knead, then divide the mixture into 8 small balls. Insert a large pinch of the horseradish into the centre of each ball and gently roll them into dumplings on a lightly floured surface.

The best way to achieve light airy dumplings is to poach them initially in plenty of boiling liquid, before reducing the temperature to a simmer. So add a little extra water to your casserole if necessary and then gently add the dumplings. Cover and boil briskly for 5 minutes before reducing the heat to a simmer. After a further 15–20 minutes they will puff up into succulent balls. Serve immediately.

Note: Plain dumplings can be made by omitting the horseradish filling. Extra herbs can be added to taste if wished.

PORK WITH LEEKS AND PRUNES

This stew is part of an old tradition of fast cooking ragouts, which allows the pork to stay very tender. Although the French influence is immediately obvious from the wine and prunes, these ingredients, along with leeks, have also been used in British meat cookery since medieval times. (Serves 4)

8 stoned prunes	225g/8oz sliced leeks
285ml/½ pint Vouvray	285ml/½ pint double cream
455g/1lb trimmed pork fillet	¼ teaspoon finely chopped
3 tablespoons olive oil	tarragon
seasoned flour	

Soak the prunes in the Vouvray for 12 hours.

Cut the trimmed fillet into 2.5cm/1 inch thick rounds. Heat the olive oil in a shallow pan. Lightly dust the pork with seasoned flour and then quickly fry to colour and seal the rounds. Set aside.

Add the leeks to the olive oil and gently fry. As soon as they begin to soften, add the prunes and their wine. Scrape any delicious crusty bits off the pan and let the wine come to the boil. Reduce by two thirds before adding the cream. Allow this to come up to boiling point, then season and return the pork to the pan.

Simmer very gently for 10 minutes, or until the pork is cooked through but still tender. If you overcook the pork it will become tough. Add the tarragon and serve.

ROOT VEGETABLES

The British have always been very partial to root vegetables, perhaps because they grow so well here. By the sixteenth century cooks of the rich were not only tentatively experimenting with new introductions such as sweet and ordinary potatoes, but also regularly cooking with parsnips, carrots, turnips and skirrets (now hard to find – apparently they are like a cross between a parsnip and a salsify). According to the chronicler Ralph Holinshed, writing in 1548, the latter group were eaten 'as deintie dishes at the tables of delicate merchants, gentlemen and the nobilitie who make their provision yearelie for new seeds out of strange countries'.

This thirst for new vegetables encouraged the introduction of Jerusalem artichokes and scorzonera in the seventeenth century, and salsify, celeriac and swedes in the eighteenth. Yet the British have had a strangely ambiguous attitude towards many root vegetables, since parsnips were also used to fatten succulent young piglets, and swedes and turnips became a popular form of animal fodder. They were food for the poor and yet they could be transformed into a fine dish, frittered, mashed with butter or delicately roasted. The swede is perhaps one exception to this, since south of the Border it has never been widely enjoyed. However, in Scotland, where it is commonly known as a neep or turnip, it is still made into a delicate mash, flavoured with butter and a pinch of ground ginger.

MASHED POTATOES

It has recently become very fashionable to serve mashed potato flavoured with olive oil – however, I feel there is still something sublime about fluffy mashed potatoes whipped up with lashings of milk, butter and nutmeg. (Serves 4)

680g/1½lb large potatoes	40g/1½oz butter
salt	freshly ground black pepper
3–4 tablespoons creamy milk	freshly ground nutmeg
or single cream	(optional)

Peel the potatoes and cut into quarters. Place in a pan with plenty of cold water and some salt. Bring to the boil over a moderately high heat. Continue to boil for 20–30 minutes or until the potatoes are tender, but not falling apart. Drain and leave to steam dry in the colander for 5 minutes.

Place the milk and butter in a large saucepan and bring to the boil. Add the potatoes and vigorously mash until they are smooth and fluffy. Never add potatoes to a food processor, as they will turn into wallpaper glue.

Season to taste with plenty of freshly ground black pepper and nutmeg and more salt if necessary. Add more cream, milk or butter to taste.

ROASTED ROOT VEGETABLES

The tradition of roasting root vegetables has remained popular since at least the sixteenth century. Their soft earthy flavours seem to suit the robust taste of roast and boiled meats. Modern interpretations draw on influences from all over the world. Just vary your ingredients to taste. (Serves 4)

2 red onions, sliced and separated into thick rings	6 sage leaves, finely chopped
2 carrots, cut into short batons	salt and freshly ground black pepper
2 parsnips, cored and cut into batons	2 tablespoons balsamic vinegar
4 tablespoons olive oil	2 tablespoons finely chopped parsley

Preheat the oven to 190°C/375°F/gas 5.

Prepare the vegetables and toss them with the olive oil, sage and seasoning. Place in a large gratin dish, cover and bake in the preheated oven for 30 minutes. Remove the covering, stir and then bake for another 20 minutes, or until the vegetables are soft and lightly browned. Season with the balsamic vinegar and serve with lots of freshly chopped parsley.

CRISPY POTATO CAKES

Another modern fashion – potato cakes, which are very easy to make. The essential element to binding them together is the starch in the potato, so although you can peel them ahead and leave them in cold water, they must not be grated until you are ready to cook them. But they can be cooked a few hours in advance, left to cool and then quickly reheated in the oven when needed. (Serves 4)

4 large potatoes	vegetable oil
1 small onion (optional)	30g/1oz butter (optional)
salt and freshly ground black pepper	

Peel and roughly grate all 4 potatoes and the onion. Season liberally and mix together thoroughly.

Place a large non-stick frying pan over a moderate heat. Once it is warm, pour in enough oil to cover the base and add half the butter. As soon as this begins to sizzle, roughly shape a round patty of grated potato and squish down in the pan. Repeat with 3 more cakes if you have room. Using a palette knife or spatula, press down on each cake and tuck in any untidy edges until it forms a round cake about 1cm/ ½ inch thick. Fry for 3–4 minutes until crisp and golden.

At this stage flip the cakes over, reshape if necessary, and continue to fry until crisp and golden on the outside. When they are cooked, quickly toss them in some paper towelling before transferring them to a low oven to keep warm (if serving immediately) while you continue with the remaining cakes.

Add more oil and butter and repeat until all the potato mixture is finished.

Note: Chopped herbs such as chives or parsley can be added to the mixture, as can other grated vegetables such as parsnips. If you are worried about them disintegrating you can always add a little beaten egg for confidence.

THREE-FLAVOURED CRISPS

Crisps can be made in advance and reheated in the oven. The celeriac crisps have a slightly smoky sweetness which is even more intense with the sweet potato. Further layers of flavour can be added by tossing the warm crisps in a mixture of finely chopped herbs such as thyme and salt. (Serves 4)

2 large potatoes	1 tablespoon vinegar or
2 sweet potatoes	lemon juice
1 celeriac	vegetable oil for deep frying
	salt

Peel the 2 types of potatoes and have 2 bowls of water ready. Then thinly slice the potatoes, using either a food processor or a mandoline. Immediately place the potato slices in a bowl of cold water and leave to soak for 10 minutes or so. Slice and soak the sweet potatoes in the same way.

Prepare the celeriac in exactly the same way, except that the cold water should contain a tablespoon of vinegar or lemon juice to prevent the slices from discolouring.

Heat the oil to 190°C/375°F. Drain the potato slices, rinse under cold water to remove as much starch as possible (as this causes the crisps to burn), and spin in a salad spinner. Pat dry on kitchen paper and add in small batches to the oil. Cook until golden, remembering that they will continue to colour a little even when removed from the oil. Repeat until finished. Toss on kitchen paper and set aside in a large bowl.

Cook the sweet potato and celeriac in exactly the same way. You will find that the celeriac slices will crinkle up as they cook but will not become crisp until they begin to cool. Mix together all the crisps and sprinkle with salt. Serve hot or cold.

HAM

Ham has to be one of the most adaptable of meats and perfectly suited to modern life. It is still a very economical joint, especially since every last trimming can be sliced up and added to all manner of dishes from vegetables, pies and stews to scones and sandwiches. Henry Mayhew actually gives an account of the first sale of ham sandwiches in 1862 in his book on *London Labour and the London Poor*:

> The ham-sandwich-seller carries his sandwiches on a tray or flat basket, covered with a clean white cloth; he also wears a white apron, and white sleeves. His usual stand is at the doors of the theatres.
>
> The trade was unknown until eleven years ago, when a man who had been unsuccessful in keeping a coffee-shop in Westminster, found it necessary to look out for some mode of living, and he hit upon the plan of vending sandwiches, precisely in the present style, at the theatre doors. The attempt was successful; the man soon took 10s. a night, half of which was profit. He 'attended' both the great theatres, and was 'doing well'; but at 5 or 6 weeks' end, competitors appeared in the field, and increased rapidly, and so his sale was affected, people being regardless of his urging that he 'was the original ham-sandwich'.

It is well worth boiling a ham or gammon since the meat retains far more flavour and succulence than the ready sliced varieties. There is often some confusion regarding the difference between hams and gammons. Both are the unfortunate pig's hind legs, but to cure a ham the butcher must first remove the leg from the carcass before salting, whereas for gammon, the hind leg remains attached to the carcass while being soaked in brine. As a result gammon is less salty than ham and need not be soaked before cooking. Uncooked hams, however, may well benefit from being soaked in several changes of cold water before cooking.

HONEY GLAZED HAM

Baked hams are good eaten either hot or cold. Their flavour can be altered by the stock ingredients and their glaze. The stock can then be used for split pea or lentil soup (in which case substitute water for the cider), while every last scrap of the ham can be used up. (Serves 8)

2kg/4½lb boned gammon or ham	whole cloves for studding
850ml/1½ pints cider	*Glaze*
1 large sprig parsley	2 tablespoons runny honey
1 sprig thyme	2 tablespoons soft brown sugar
1 bay leaf	1 teaspoon mustard powder
2 carrots, roughly chopped	pinch of ground cloves
1 fat leek, roughly chopped	
1 onion, halved	

Place the gammon in a large pan and completely cover with cold water. Bring to the boil then drain. Return the gammon to a large clean saucepan and add the cider, parsley, thyme, bay leaf, carrot, leek and onion. Add enough cold water to cover the meat and bring to the boil. Skim, then reduce the heat and simmer gently for 1 ½ hours.

Preheat the oven to 200°C/400°F/gas 6.

Remove the gammon from the stock and, as soon as it is cool enough to handle, peel away its tough skin and lightly score the fat in a diamond pattern. Stud the diamond corners with cloves. Place in a roasting tray.

Mix together the honey, sugar, mustard powder and ground cloves. Rub this sticky mixture all over the gammon. Then place it in the centre of the preheated oven and cook for a further 30 minutes or until the glaze has caramelized. As it roasts, baste regularly with the melted glaze. Serve hot or cold.

CUMBERLAND SAUCE

The origins of Cumberland sauce are unknown, although it seems likely that it began life as a sweet alcoholic sauce for game and brawn in the middle of the nineteenth century. It became very popular with the Edwardians, who served it with ham, chicken, goose, duck and venison. There are many variations on how to make Cumberland sauce. *British Cookery*, edited by Lizzie Boyd, suggests that it should be made with fresh cherries, while other recipes such as those by Soyer and Escoffier add blanched shallots. (Serves 8)

2 large oranges	salt and freshly ground black
2 lemons	pepper
8 tablespoons redcurrant	pinch of ground ginger and
jelly	ground cinnamon
2 heaped teaspoons French	(optional)
mustard (optional)	140ml/¼ pint port

If you possess a julienne zester then carefully remove the zest from the oranges and lemons. Otherwise thinly peel them, trying to ensure that you do not peel away any of the bitter white pith. Cut the peel into long, fine strips and cook in a pan of boiling water for about 4 minutes. (This is not necessary if you use a zester, since the strips are too fragile to be tough or bitter.)

Place the citrus zest, redcurrant jelly, mustard, seasoning and spices in a heavy-bottomed pan and set over a very low heat. Stir continuously until the jelly has melted and the sauce is smooth, but do not allow to boil.

Mix in the port and continue to cook gently for a further 5 minutes. Transfer to a clean bowl and leave to cool. As the redcurrant jelly resets the sauce will thicken. It will keep for several weeks in the refrigerator. Serve cold.

BACON BUBBLE AND SQUEAK

According to Mrs Beeton, bubble and squeak is a fried hash of yesterday's mashed potatoes and greens, flavoured with fried onion and vinegar and topped with fried slices of roast beef. But to me bubble and squeak has always been a much more appetizing dish, made with ham or crisp bacon and freshly cooked green cabbage, spring onions and creamy mashed potatoes. A comforting supper dish when you just don't know what you want to eat. (Serves 4)

455g/1lb potatoes	115g/4oz diced lean ham or
salt	bacon
170g/6oz green cabbage,	55ml/2fl oz milk
finely sliced	salt and freshly ground black
30g/1oz butter	pepper
1 bunch spring onions,	3 tablespoons vegetable oil
finely sliced	

Peel the potatoes and cut into large pieces. Place in a pan of cold salted water and bring to the boil. Continue to boil for 20–30 minutes or until tender.

Meanwhile, cook the cabbage in a separate pan of boiling salted water for 2 minutes. Immediately drain and cool with cold running water. Leave to drain in a colander.

Melt the butter in a frying pan and sauté the spring onions until they are soft. Add the diced ham (or bacon) and continue to fry for 3 more minutes, then stir in the cabbage and remove from the heat.

Drain the potatoes and cover with a clean tea towel. Leave to steam dry for a few minutes. Scald the milk while you are waiting. Place the potatoes in a large bowl and mash until smooth. Beat in the milk and fold in the ham mixture. Season to taste and shape into eight round cakes.

Heat the oil in a frying pan and carefully fry the patties until they are brown and slightly crisp on each side. Eat immediately.

CHEESE AND HAM SCONES

These are a variation of a savoury scone, and are lovely served either in place of bread with piping hot tomato soup or just plain for tea with loads of butter melting into them. (Makes 18 scones)

225g/8oz self-raising flour	55g/2oz finely grated
½ teaspoon salt	Parmesan cheese
55g/2oz cold butter, diced	85g/3oz finely diced ham
	140ml/¼ pint milk

Preheat the oven to 220°C/425°F/gas 7 and grease 2 baking sheets.

Sift the flour and salt into a mixing bowl. Rub the butter into the flour until it forms fine crumbs. Stir in the cheese and ham, followed by the milk. Quickly mix until it begins to form a soft dough.

Turn out on to a lightly floured work surface and very lightly knead to bind the dough together. Roll out to 1cm/½ inch thickness. Dust a scone cutter with flour and cut out the scones, as close together as possible, with a quick sharp movement. Place on the baking sheets and bake in the preheated oven for 10–12 minutes.

WINTER HERBS

One of the subtle changes in modern British cooking is the widespread availability of fresh herbs during the winter months. With the declining use of fresh herbs after the Second World War, cooks became increasingly dependent on dried herbs for much of the year, to such a degree that one reader wrote to Elizabeth David with the question: 'When a recipe says "herbs", when can I use dried and when must I use fresh ones (*must* because the latter are more difficult to get)?' Happily it is now easy to buy small packages of tender parsley, tarragon or chives long after they have died back in the garden, while more hardy herbs like rosemary, sage and thyme are now routinely used fresh throughout the year. As a result, many of our dishes have developed lighter, fresher flavours, since they are no longer dependent on traditional spices or dried herbs for added depth. Thus succulent field mushrooms are now tossed with butter flavoured with fresh parsley, chives and tarragon rather than mace and cayenne pepper.

CHICK PEA SALAD

Salads are increasingly served throughout the year as a healthy alternative to other dishes. Modern cooks now have a wide choice of pulses and fresh herbs to extend their winter repertoire of salads, all of which make excellent accompaniments to cold meats such as ham. Chick peas have a beautiful nutty flavour that marries well with herbs such as parsley or coriander. (Serves 4)

170g/6oz dried chick peas	2 tablespoons white wine
1 tablespoon vegetable oil	vinegar
1 red pepper, quartered and	6 tablespoons olive oil
seeded	salt and freshly ground black
4 ripe tomatoes, peeled	pepper
2 cloves garlic, crushed	5 tablespoons flat-leaf
	parsley leaves

Wash the chick peas and leave to soak overnight in plenty of cold water. Drain them the next day and place in a large pan of cold water with the vegetable oil. Bring up to the boil, skim off any scum, then simmer for 1 ½ hours or until they are tender.

Meanwhile, preheat the grill. Arrange the peppers skin side up under the grill. As soon as their skin blisters, remove and place in a covered bowl. Peel once cool, and cut into diamonds.

Cut the tomatoes into quarters. Carefully remove the seeds, placing them in a strainer over a bowl as you clean the tomatoes. Strain as much juice as possible from them and discard the pips. Neatly dice the tomato flesh and add to the peppers.

Whisk the garlic, vinegar, olive oil and seasoning into the tomato juice and pour over the peppers. Once the chick peas are ready, drain thoroughly and toss warm into this mixture. Add the whole parsley leaves and adjust the seasoning to taste. Serve warm or cold.

GRILLED FIELD MUSHROOMS

If you are concerned about using too much butter, simply mix the garlic and herbs with a few tablespoons of olive oil instead.

Herb butter
55g/2oz softened butter
1 clove garlic, crushed
1 tablespoon finely chopped
   parsley
1 tablespoon finely chopped
   chives
1 teaspoon finely chopped
   tarragon

1 teaspoon lemon juice
salt and freshly ground black
   pepper

Mushrooms
8–12 field mushrooms,
   depending on their size
olive oil

Preheat the grill to its highest setting or use a cast-iron grill top.

Beat together the butter, garlic, herbs, lemon juice and seasoning. Adjust any one of the flavourings according to your taste.

Peel the mushrooms and pull off their stalks. Save these trimmings if you are planning to make a stock, as they will imbue it with a lovely flavour. Season the mushrooms and drizzle with olive oil.

Grill on both sides until golden and tender. Just before you remove them from the grill, brush with the herb butter. Allow it to melt, then serve them piping hot with the remaining butter melting all over them.

ROSEMARY LEMON SAVARIN

Traditionally, rosemary, like marjoram and bay leaves, was used to flavour milk puddings and the sugar jar – just like a vanilla pod. However, some modern cooks now infuse sugar syrups with fresh herbs such as rosemary or thyme to impart a fragrant flavour to macerated dessert cakes and fruit salads. Combined with lemon or wine, they imbue food with a subtle scent that is very addictive.

Savarins belong to the sticky pudding brigade. They are very easy to make if you have a food processor or dough hook. The only thing they need is time to rise. This particular recipe cheats in the mixing, but still produces a light airy pudding. (Serves 8)

Savarin	Syrup
4 egg yolks	3 sprigs rosemary
1 small lemon, finely grated	1 lemon, finely pared and
30g/1oz caster sugar	juiced
115g/4oz butter	170g/6oz granulated sugar
225g/8oz plain flour	285ml/½ pint water
1 teaspoon easy-blend	1 tablespoon vodka or gin
dried yeast	(optional)
140ml/¼ pint lukewarm milk	

Beat the egg yolks with the lemon zest and sugar in the food processor until pale and fluffy.

Gently melt the butter. Strain through some clean muslin or a J-cloth to remove any sediment and leave the milky part in the saucepan. Beat this into the egg yolks.

Change over to a dough blade or hook. Sift the flour into a bowl and mix in the yeast. Transfer this to the food processor along with the warm milk. Process until the dough is well beaten but unbelievably soft and gooey. Scrape it into a large warm bowl and cover. Leave to rise in a warm place for 2 hours or until it has doubled in size.

While the dough is rising, make the syrup by placing the rosemary, lemon peel, sugar and water in a heavy-bottomed saucepan. Dissolve the sugar over a low heat and then simmer for 5 minutes. Add the lemon juice and alcohol and leave to infuse.

Preheat the oven to 190°C/375°F/gas 5 and oil a savarin ring or mould or even a cake tin. Liberally flour a work surface and your hands. Turn the dough out and knock it back as best you can. Then gently shape it into a sausage long enough to fit in a ring mould (otherwise just shape into a round). Tuck into the mould, cover once again, and leave to rise for about 45 minutes or until the dough has risen to just below the top of the mould. Remove its covering and place in the centre of the preheated oven. Bake for 30 minutes until firm and golden. Test with a fine skewer – just like a cake – to see if it comes out dry.

Turn it out immediately and place on a deep rimmed plate. Prick all over with a fork. Strain the syrup and spoon some of it over the savarin. Allow to soak in, then keep repeating until the savarin is saturated and the syrup is finished.

Transfer to a clean plate before serving with whipped cream.

Note: Savarins are usually served with fruit folded into whipped cream. Try the cranberry sauce recipe (page 316) folded into 285ml/½ pint whipped double cream.

MORE WINTER PUDDINGS

November is a time of year when comforting puddings vie with party pieces. Yet some of the more contrived dishes, such as spiced pear granita, have an ancient and honourable history. As early as the fifteenth century, wardens, a very large, hard old pear variety, were boiled before being further cooked in a spiced sweetened wine. Variations of this theme continued into the twentieth century, until we finally developed that wine bar favourite of spiced pears in red wine. Happily, somebody had the clever idea of transforming the wine into an exquisite granita.

Rice puddings, on the other hand, have suffered at the hands of school cooks. Once a delicacy for the rich, they continued to be lovingly cooked for at least four centuries. They were flavoured with cinnamon, nutmeg, rosewater or lemon, enriched with eggs, cream and currants, and some-times even topped with a delicate pastry crust. Then they were ruined by bad cooking and synthetic pink jam. However, food writers such as Nigel Slater are reinstating this pudding with sensitive new flavourings such as saffron, orange flower water, rosewater and cardamom.

LEMON RICE PUDDING

This pudding is left to bake slowly but in the process becomes infused with the lemon and spice. (Serves 4)

15g/½oz butter	285ml/½ pint single cream
3 tablespoons short-grain (pudding) rice	285ml/½ pint milk
	55g/2oz caster sugar
2 tablespoons roughly chopped blanched almonds	2 large lemons, finely grated
	salt
	freshly grated nutmeg or ground cinnamon

Preheat the oven to 150°C/300°F/gas 2 and liberally butter an ovenproof dish.

Mix together the rice, almonds, cream, milk, sugar, lemon zest and a tiny pinch of salt. Pour into the buttered dish and lightly sprinkle with either the nutmeg or cinnamon, according to your taste.

Bake for 2 hours until the rice is meltingly tender. Serve hot, warm or cold depending on your taste.

SPICED PEAR GRANITA

If possible cook the pears one to two days before they are needed, so that the wine can become imbued with the flavour of the spices and the pears. (Serves 6)

1 bottle Riesling	2 cloves
285ml/½ pint water	1 small stick cinnamon
3 strips lemon peel	1 vanilla pod
1 lemon, juiced	225g/8oz granulated sugar
6 peppercorns	6 small just ripe pears

Place all the ingredients except the pears into a non-corrosive saucepan. Dissolve the sugar over a low heat.

Peel the pears and carefully remove their cores, using an apple corer. When the white wine begins to simmer, add the pears. Place a folded sheet of greaseproof paper over the fruit and liquid, so that the pears are protected from the air and will not discolour. Simmer gently for 30 minutes or until they become soft and translucent.

Transfer the pears and wine into a bowl, cover once again and leave to cool. Chill until you are ready to make the granita.

To make the granita, remove the pears and strain the spiced wine. Pour into 2 shallow containers. Cover and freeze in the coldest section of the freezer. Leave for 1 hour then, using a fork, mix any ice crystals that have formed around the edge and bottom back into the main liquid. Repeat every hour for a further 3 hours until smooth ice crystals have formed throughout the whole mixture. As this granita is predominantly made from alcohol, it will not freeze as hard as a normal granita and consequently can be stored for several days.

To serve, spoon the granita into the base of 6 glass bowls. Arrange the chilled pears on top and garnish with a sprig of mint or a twist of lemon peel.

MULLED WINES

Mulled wines are still very popular in Britain, as is apparent from the annual appearance of dinky little spice bags in the supermarkets each winter. These are supposed to be infused into hot wine, just like a tea bag. This rather clinical approach somehow rather diminishes the romance of mulling your own wine, which after all dates back at least to the Normans with their spicy hippocras.

MULLED CLARET 1

A mild-tasting mulled wine. (Makes 8–9 glasses)

1 bottle claret	caster sugar, to taste
425ml/¾ pint water	freshly grated nutmeg, to
1 small cinnamon stick	taste

Slowly heat the claret, water and cinnamon stick in a non-corrosive saucepan to just below boiling point. Add the sugar and nutmeg to taste and serve piping hot.

MULLED CLARET 2

This is stronger and more spicy than the recipe above, but is very warming. (Makes 6 glasses)

12 cloves	3 strips orange peel
2 blades mace	1 bottle claret or a robust
4 allspice berries	red wine
1 small stick cinnamon	caster sugar, to taste
3 strips lemon peel	

Tie the cloves, mace, allspice berries and cinnamon stick in a small clean piece of muslin. Place with the citrus peel in the wine and slowly heat to just below boiling point. Allow to infuse for 15 minutes, keeping the wine warm but never allowing it to boil.

Sweeten to taste, remove the spices and peel, and serve piping hot.

Note: For a more powerful drink, add 285ml/½ pint boiling water and 55ml/2fl oz brandy at the last minute.

DECEMBER

SMOKED FISH
Smoked salmon
Smoked sturgeon with sour cream and chives
Smoked eel with horseradish sauce
Smoked trout salad
Kedgeree

BEEF
Roast beef and Yorkshire pudding
Steak and kidney pie
Steak with wild mushroom sauce

MORE WINTER VEGETABLES
Roast potatoes
Jerusalem artichoke gratin
Spinach and leeks
Brussels sprouts with bacon

CHRISTMAS
Champagne cocktail
Turkey escalopes with cranberry sauce
Roast goose
Roast pheasant with grape stuffing
Eliza Acton's Christmas pudding
Brandy butter

EXOTIC FRUIT
Lychee champagne jelly
Mango and clementine gratin
Pineapple romanoff

**D**ecember is dominated by the British obsession with Christmas. Before the first decorations are up, the shops are already beginning to fill with ready-made Christmas cakes and puddings, large Stiltons and boxes of fancy biscuits. Our food becomes a strange mixture of modern and traditional dishes, although the latter are unwittingly subjected to new interpretations.

Most cooks are keen to keep their Christmases as simple as possible, since they often have to cook for larger numbers than normal and produce more elaborate meals. Thus, much of the art of modern Christmas cooking is in producing easy, elegant meals. However, it has to be said that the fundamental changes in Christmas cooking are occurring as a result of shrinking family size. There are many households that consist of just two people and it is impractical to follow many traditional recipes rigidly. Happily, the supermarkets are now selling a wide range of different fowl, and even different parts of the ubiquitous turkey, so that a small family can dine on roast pheasant or turkey escalopes with all the trimmings.

December is a month of gastronomic indulgences – diets can only be contemplated with the arrival of New Year, and until then everyone is expected to enjoy themselves. Luxurious foods and old favourites such as smoked fish, exotic fruit òr beef are widely eaten. Smoked fish, in particular, is enjoying a revival of interest. Many of the older varieties such as smoked sprats, eel or buckling are being sold in the supermarkets, alongside innovations such as hot smoked prawns. Modern recipes tend to be very simple, so as to enhance the delicious flavour and texture of the smoked fish.

Perhaps roast beef still symbolizes prosperity and well-being to the British, but whereas it was once an essential part of every celebratory

meal it has become a rarity at the modern table. High prices and various
health concerns around eating red meat have reduced our consumption of
beef, forcing farmers to rethink how they market their meat. As a result
some are beginning to breed some of the older, traditional breeds, such as
Aberdeen Angus or Irish Dexters. Their meat is delicately larded with
fine fat, which not only imbues it with flavour but also bastes it as it
cooks, making it deliciously tender. Naturally, such meat commands a
high price and few domestic cooks will risk squandering its fine flavour
with experimental modern dishes. Old favourites such as roast beef and
Yorkshire pudding are still much loved, along with the occasional steak
that can be sauced according to whim.

One of the delights of Christmas shopping is the incredible variety of
imported fruit. Over the last twenty years the range of fruit available has
widened considerably, from pineapples, lychees and hothouse grapes to
mangoes, papayas, grenadillas and pitahayas, to name but a few. Our
native timidity with such foreign fruits is gradually lessening as they
become more commonplace. No longer are they just thrown into a fruit
salad or sprinkled with some lime juice or alcohol. Instead their subtle
textures and flavours are beginning to be explored more widely, so that
the luscious flesh of the lychee is set in an exquisite pink champagne jelly
while slightly sharp flavoured unripe mangoes are transformed into a
heavenly frothy dish of sabayon and fruit.

SMOKED FISH

Originally, smoking was used as an added preservative after the fish had been salted. Not only did it help to dry the fish in the damp British climate, but it also acted as protection against flies. As Dorothy Hartley explains in *Food in England* (1954), 'Nowadays, the salting is used for preserving, and the smoking chiefly to give a flavour. The old smoking took place in the farmhouse chimney or a specially built smoke-house. Frequently fir boughs and resinous woods were thrown on last to give a "tar" coating that would deter flies, and the open smoke-hold in the roof was the natural fly-proof flume.' Today, with all the benefits of modern refrigeration and transport, most smokers are more concerned with attaining the correct balance of smoky flavour to sweet succulence, rather than curing the fish to last the winter out.

There are two forms of smoking – hot (82°C/180°F), which will cook the fish, and cold (24°C/75°F), which leaves it raw. British cooks pay scant attention to which method has been used, since it makes little difference to their handling of the fish; (cold) smoked salmon is rarely cooked while (cold) smoked kippers usually are, it is merely a question of custom. The majority of modern smoked fish dishes are served very simply, with an appropriate sauce and thinly sliced brown bread and butter, though elegant blinis or a salad are becoming more common. Smoked fish pâté, or paste as it was originally called, has currently slipped from fashion, despite the fact that it makes a lovely snack eaten with hot buttered toast. But new salads and dainty dishes will no doubt gradually evolve as more varieties of smoked fish become widely available.

SMOKED SALMON

Most people agree that smoked salmon is best appreciated finely sliced and eaten very plainly with lots of thinly sliced, lightly buttered brown bread. Allow each diner 55–85g/2–3oz of finely sliced smoked salmon and two small lemon wedges (with no pips). A pepper mill with black peppercorns should be on the table.

If you are lucky enough to be given a whole half side of smoked salmon, lightly and evenly cut away the tough outer layer of smoked flesh. Then, using a pair of tweezers, pull out any small bones that run down the centre of the fish, usually near its head end. The side is now ready to slice, so keep it well wrapped and chilled until needed.

SMOKED STURGEON WITH SOUR CREAM AND CHIVES

If ever you see any smoked sturgeon, buy it. It is gorgeous and well worth the treat. It should be treated in the same manner as smoked salmon. Allow each person 55–85g/2–3oz of prepared smoked fish and arrange on the plate with a small dollop of sour cream and chives. Serve with finely sliced brown bread, or see note below. (Serves 4)

140ml/¼ pint sour cream	1 lemon, finely grated
2 tablespoons finely chopped chives	salt and freshly ground black pepper

Mix together the sour cream, chives and lemon zest before seasoning to taste.

Note: For a more elaborate starter either fry some blinis (see page 72) or make a small salad from a packet of mixed baby lettuces, which should be dressed at the last moment with 1 dessertspoon of lemon juice whisked together with 3 dessertspoons of olive oil and seasoning.

SMOKED EEL WITH HORSERADISH SAUCE

Although many people are squeamish about eel, it is excellent smoked. Either buy a chunk of whole smoked eel or buy it ready filleted. In the case of the former, peel off the skin and any excess fat before gently pulling the fillets away from the backbone. Allow about 10cm/4 inches of eel per person and serve with brown bread and butter and horseradish sauce.

HORSERADISH SAUCE

A jar of grated horseradish can be ordered from most greengrocers and will keep for a month or so in the fridge. Otherwise, horseradish is very easy to grow – in fact it has a tendency to run rampant through the vegetable garden. Its long tough roots have to be dug up, washed and peeled before grating. The heat of a freshly dug root will make your eyes and nose stream, but the resulting flavour makes it worthwhile. (Serves 6–8)

285ml/½ pint double cream
85g/3oz grated horseradish
2 tablespoons white wine
    vinegar

1 teaspoon made-up
    English mustard
1 tablespoon caster sugar
salt and freshly ground
    black pepper

If you like a thick sauce softly whip the cream, as it will thicken further when the remaining ingredients are added. Otherwise leave the cream as it is.

Mix together the horseradish, vinegar, mustard, sugar, salt and pepper and stir into the cream. Adjust any of the flavourings to your taste and leave chilled until ready to serve.

SMOKED TROUT SALAD

This lovely salad is more in the modern mode of combining smoked fish with a lightly dressed salad of lettuce leaves. Traditionally, smoked trout fillets were usually eaten either plain with bread and butter, horseradish sauce and lemon or as a fish paste. If you wish to make the latter, quickly blend the trout flesh with about half its weight in butter. Season with lemon juice and cayenne pepper and stir in a few tablespoons of double cream. (Serves 4)

1 tablespoon grated horseradish	225g/8oz fine green beans
1 teaspoon Dijon mustard	2 heads trevisse, red chicory or radicchio
½ teaspoon caster sugar	4 fillets smoked trout (that is, 2 whole smoked trout)
2 tablespoons white wine vinegar	½ lemon, juiced
6 tablespoons olive oil	1 tablespoon finely chopped parsley
salt and freshly ground black pepper	

Mix together the horseradish, mustard, sugar and vinegar in a small bowl. Whisk in the olive oil and season to taste.

Trim the beans and lightly cook in a pan of boiling salted water for 5 minutes. Drain and allow to cool for 5 minutes.

Place the beans in a large mixing bowl and liberally coat with some of the horseradish dressing. Meanwhile, prepare the lettuce by separating, washing and drying the leaves. Take the smoked trout fillets and run your fingers down the centre of the skin side of each one to remove the darker brown fat. Then break into large chunks. Drizzle these with a little lemon juice.

Once the beans are cold, add the parsley and any spare dressing. Carefully mix the lettuce leaves and smoked trout into the beans. Arrange on 4 individual plates and serve.

KEDGEREE

Kedgeree appears to have started life as an 'Indian breakfast dish' which, according to Eliza Acton, was made with equal quantities of cold fish (such as salmon, turbot, brill, sole, John Dory and shrimps) and freshly cooked rice, to which were added butter, cayenne pepper and, once hot, two beaten eggs. By the turn of the century Mrs Beeton is giving several distinct dishes, which include a 'kidgeree' (nearer the Indian original, which is made with dal not fish) and a breakfast kedgeree, which was made with dried haddock and hard-boiled eggs instead. Our modern version is as varied but is rarely served at breakfast. It makes an enjoyable lunch or supper dish.

Choose good smoked haddock, being careful to avoid anything dyed bright yellow. (Serves 4)

4 smoked haddock fillets	salt and freshly ground black
1 bay leaf	pepper
1 sprig parsley	4 hard-boiled eggs, peeled
565ml/1 pint milk	and roughly chopped
30g/1oz butter	285ml/½ pint double cream
225g/8oz button	225g/8oz peeled prawns
mushrooms, diced	2 tablespoons finely chopped
1 tablespoon lemon juice	parsley

Place the haddock fillets with the herbs in a saucepan and cover with milk. Simmer very gently until the fish is just cooked. Lift out the haddock and leave to cool. Remove the flesh in large flakes and place in a bowl, ensuring that there are no bones or skin remaining. Set aside.

Melt the butter in a small frying pan and quickly sauté the mushrooms. Add the lemon juice and season to taste. Once cooked, tip into the haddock bowl. Fold in the chopped eggs and cream. Chill, covered, until needed. When you are ready to serve, return the mixture to a pan and add the prawns.

Warm over a low heat, stirring frequently to ensure that the prawns do not over-cook and become tough. Adjust the seasoning and add more lemon juice if necessary. Toss in the parsley and serve with plenty of basmati rice.

Note: For truly superb smoked haddock search out either Finnan haddie (a traditionally cured split smoked haddock), Eyemouth cured haddock or Glasgow Pales (which are split and smoked after only 20 minutes in brine).

BEEF

Scarcely were the congratulations of the company to our hero, on his becoming a member of the Hit-im and Hold-im shire hunt over, ere a great rush of dinner poured into the room, borne by Peter and the usual miscellaneous attendants at an inn banquet; servants in livery, servants our of livery, servants in a sort of half-livery, servants in place, servants out of place, postboys converted into footmen, 'boots' put into shoes. Then the carrot and turnip garnished roasts and boils and stews were crowded down the table in a profusion that would astonish any one who thinks it impossible to dine under a guinea a head. Rounds, sirloins, saddles, sucking-pigs, poultry, &c. (for they dispensed with the formalities of soup and fish), being duly distributed, Peter announced the fact deferentially to Sir Moses, as he stood monopolizing the best place before the fire, whereupon the Baronet, drawing his hands out of his trousers pockets, let fall his yellow-lined laps, and, clapping his hands, exclaimed, 'DINNER, GENTLEMEN!'

This affectionate description of a lively and informal Victorian country dinner, as given by R.S. Surtees in *Ask Mamma*, somehow seems to exemplify how beef was considered an essential part of British feasting. Although modern beef is no longer served in so liberal a manner, we have retained many of our favourite recipes such as roast beef and Yorkshire pudding or steak and kidney pie.

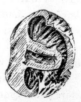

ROAST BEEF AND YORKSHIRE PUDDING

A classic British dish. (Serves 6)

2.3kg/5lb rib of beef	140ml/¼ pint milk
1 tablespoon olive oil	
freshly ground black pepper	*Gravy*
	2 tablespoons flour
Yorkshire pudding	140ml/¼ pint dry white
115g/4oz plain flour	wine
pinch of salt	425ml/¾ pint beef stock
2 eggs	

Preheat the oven to 220°C/425°F/gas 7.

Rub the beef with the olive oil and season with the black pepper. Place on a roasting rack if you have one, otherwise sit the beef directly on the roasting tray. Place in the centre of the preheated oven and roast for 15 minutes. Then lower the temperature to 170°C/325°F/gas 3 and roast for a further 1¼ hours if you like rare beef, 1 hour 40 minutes for medium cooked beef or 2 hours 5 minutes for well done beef.

Meanwhile, prepare the Yorkshire pudding batter by sifting the flour and salt into a bowl. Make a well in the centre and gradually beat in the eggs with some of the milk until you have a smooth lump-free paste. Gradually stir in the rest of the liquid. Once it is amalgamated, beat vigorously before leaving to rest for at least an hour.

Yorkshire puddings can be cooked individually or in one larger dish. In either case, take some of the hot dripping from the meat tray and spoon into the base of a dish or into 6 individual moulds. Place these in the oven, as the fat needs to be sizzling hot before the batter is added. Return the oven temperature to 220°C/425°F/gas 7. Allow 15 minutes for indi-vidual Yorkshire puddings and 30–40 minutes for a larger pudding. Time their baking to coincide with the serving of the beef, as they do not like to sit around. They are ready when they have puffed up and formed a crisp golden brown crust.

Allow the beef to rest in a warm place for 10–15 minutes while you make the gravy and finish the dinner. Pour off all but a couple of tablespoons of fat from the roasting tray. Place over a moderate heat and blend in the flour with a wooden spoon. Allow this to cook for a couple of minutes, then de-glaze with the wine. As the mixture thickens, stir in the stock and allow to bubble down and thicken. Strain and serve piping hot with the beef, Yorkshire pudding and horseradish sauce (see page 305).

STEAK AND KIDNEY PIE

Another classic dish. This recipe is adapted from Philippa Davenport's lovely book *Cooking for Family and Friends*. If you wish to make it into a pudding, follow the method for steamed savoury puddings on page 330. Non-kidney-lovers can use extra beef instead. (Serves 6)

680g/1½lb chuck steak, trimmed	1 bay leaf
340g/12oz lamb's kidneys	sprig each thyme and parsley
salt and freshly ground black pepper	1 teaspoon Worcestershire sauce
4 tablespoons beef dripping or olive oil	2 tablespoons olive oil
2 medium onions, finely sliced	225g/8oz button mushrooms, trimmed
1 clove garlic, crushed	squeeze of lemon juice
2 carrots, cut into rounds	225g/8oz puff or shortcrust pastry (see pages 327–29)
1 tablespoon plain flour	½ egg beaten with 2 tablespoons milk
425ml/¾ pint water or beef stock	

Remove any fat or tough fibres from the meat before cutting into chunks. Peel the fine membrane off the kidneys and slice in half to expose the tough white core inside. Using a pair of kitchen scissors, snip around each half core, until you have cut it out. Dice the kidneys. Season both meats.

Heat the dripping or oil in a heavy-bottomed saucepan. Brown the beef and then the kidneys in batches and set them to one side. Lower the heat and add the onions, garlic and carrots to the saucepan. Sauté for 5 minutes or until soft, then mix in the flour and cook for a further minute.

Return the meat to the saucepan along with the water or stock, herbs and Worcestershire sauce. Bring to the boil, adjust the seasoning, then simmer very gently for 1½ hours. Remove the herbs.

Heat 2 tablespoons of olive oil in a small frying pan and quickly colour the mushrooms. Add a generous squeeze of lemon to them and mix into the stew. Adjust the seasoning and transfer to a deep pie dish. If possible allow the mixture to cool before covering with pastry.

Preheat the oven to 220°C/425°F/gas 7. When you are ready to bake, roll out the pastry in roughly the same shape as your pie dish only larger. Cut a ribbon from the edge of the dough and press it firmly onto the rim of the pie dish. Brush this with a mixture of beaten egg and milk and place a pie vent in the centre of the filling. Loosely roll the pastry on to the rolling pin and lift on to the pie dish. Using a fork, firmly press around the rim so that the 2 pastries are glued together. Cut off the excess pastry. Prick the lid with a knife, ensuring that the vent has a hole, and paint the crust with some more egg and milk.

Place in the centre of the preheated oven and bake for 35 minutes, or until the pastry has puffed up and become golden.

STEAK WITH WILD MUSHROOM SAUCE

Wild mushrooms have become increasingly popular over the last few years, to such a degree that certainly one major supermarket chain has begun to sell small boxes of fresh mixed wild mushrooms. If you can't find any, replace them with shiitake and oyster mushrooms. (Serves 2)

115g/4oz mixed wild
  mushrooms
3 tablespoons olive oil
2 fillet or rump steaks
salt and freshly ground black
  pepper
2 cloves garlic, crushed

4 tablespoons dry vermouth
1 tablespoon finely chopped
  parsley
pinch of finely chopped
  thyme
30g/1oz butter

Carefully clean the mushrooms by wiping with a damp cloth and or brushing with a small brush. Remove any tough stems and rip into even-sized pieces. Set aside.

Place a frying pan over a moderately high heat. Add 2 tablespoons of olive oil. When the oil is very hot season the steak and pan-fry until cooked to your liking. Remove and keep warm while you quickly finish the sauce.

Add the remaining tablespoon of olive oil and the garlic to the pan. Fry for a minute, then add the mushrooms. Season with salt and pepper and fry briskly until the mushrooms begin to soften. Add the vermouth and herbs. Bring to the boil and reduce slightly before stirring in the butter. Remove from the heat and serve with the steak.

MORE WINTER VEGETABLES

December is not the best month for experimentation, as most cooks are too busy ensuring that each meal is cooked and served as smoothly as possible. Family peace takes precedence over every other activity, so fastidious elderly relatives should not be startled with unusual new dishes such as sweet potato game chips, and children must be kept happy with old favourites such as roast potatoes.

ROAST POTATOES

Traditionally, potatoes are roasted in the same tray as a joint of meat or a roast fowl, so that they absorb some of the flavours. However, if room is restricted or you wish to serve them with other dishes, just follow the instructions below. (Serves 4)

680g/1½lb potatoes	4 tablespoons dripping,
salt	olive oil or goose fat

If nothing else is being roasted, preheat the oven to 220°C/425°F/gas 7 – otherwise just add the potatoes 50–60 minutes before the roast is cooked. If the oven is low just allow a little extra time.

Peel the potatoes and cut into large pieces. Place in a large saucepan and liberally cover with cold water. Add salt, and bring to the boil over a moderately high heat. Boil for 7 minutes then drain.

While the potatoes are cooking, measure the fat into a roasting tray and place in the preheated oven. As soon as it is very hot, add the potatoes and coat thoroughly in the fat. Lightly season and roast, remembering to turn the potatoes every 20 minutes or so.

Note: Small sprigs of rosemary or thyme mixed into the oil with unpeeled garlic cloves add a delicious flavour to roast potatoes, especially if they are cooked in goose or duck fat.

JERUSALEM ARTICHOKE GRATIN

Jerusalem artichokes have a distinct, almost smoky flavour that slightly resembles that of globe artichokes. Although more commonly served as a soup, they have begun to be served in other ways, such as this simple gratin. (Serves 4)

3 tablespoons olive oil
1 onion, finely sliced
2 cloves garlic, crushed
2 inner sticks celery, finely
  sliced
1kg/2lb 3oz Jerusalem
  artichokes

salt and freshly ground black
  pepper
285ml/½ pint chicken or
  vegetable stock
15g/½oz butter, diced

Preheat the oven to 190°C/375°F/gas 5 and lightly oil a gratin dish.

Heat the remaining olive oil in a small pan and gently fry the onion, garlic and celery until soft.

Peel and finely slice the artichokes and arrange in neat layers, interspersed with the onion mixture, in the gratin dish. Liberally season each layer, then pour in just enough stock to reach beneath the top layer. Dot with butter and place in the centre of the preheated oven. Bake for 50 minutes or until meltingly soft.

SPINACH AND LEEKS

The British are partial to green vegetables and soon tire of plainly boiled cabbages, greens and spinach. This is a very pretty and fast recipe that I first came across while working at Sally Clarke's restaurant. Butter can be used instead of olive oil if preferred. (Serves 2)

2 tablespoons olive oil
2 leeks, finely sliced
200g/7oz cleaned young
  spinach

salt and freshly ground black
  pepper

Heat the olive oil in a large frying pan and soften the leeks. As soon as they are tender, add the spinach and seasoning and keep stirring for another couple of minutes until the spinach has reduced. Remove from the heat, tip off any excess juice and serve immediately.

BRUSSELS SPROUTS WITH BACON

According to Jane Grigson, although Brussels sprouts were recorded
growing near Brussels in the thirteenth century they mysteriously disappeared from any written records until the eighteenth century, when they
suddenly began to be grown in both English and French gardens. They
are best eaten when small and sweet. Cook lightly, otherwise they will
taste horribly bitter. (Serves 4)

680g/1½lb Brussels sprouts	3 tablespoons olive oil
salt	15g/½oz butter (optional)
6 slices smoked back bacon	freshly ground black pepper

Prepare the Brussels sprouts by trimming their stalks, peeling off any
tough outer leaves and cutting a small cross in their base. This is
supposed to help them cook quickly and evenly. (This last procedure is
not necessary if they are very small.) Bring a pan of salted water to the
boil and add the Brussels sprouts. Return to the boil and cook briskly for
about 5 minutes, depending on their size, until the sprouts are tender.

Meanwhile, remove the fat from the bacon and dice. Heat the olive oil
in a frying pan and fry the bacon until crisp.

Drain the sprouts. Place in a warm serving dish and dress with the
bacon, butter and a little black pepper to taste.

Note: Brussels sprouts can also be served in this manner with boiled
peeled sweet chestnuts, with or without the bacon.

CHRISTMAS

The British take Christmas very seriously: it is an institution. Every household develops its own rituals and recipes and these in time become almost sacrosanct. Fashions come and go – one year goose is the smart fowl to roast, while the next year it is bronze turkeys – but whatever food is served, most families try to re-create their own idealized vision of Christmas.

Since whole books, not to mention television series, have been dedicated to Christmas cooking, there seems little point in elaborating the theme here. As I mentioned in the introduction, shrinking families mean that many dishes have had to be readapted. One point that is worth making, however unethical it may seem, is that cooking should be a pleasure – rather than suffer agonies in a hot kitchen, trying to organise a three- or four-course meal, it is far better to cheat. Buy trimmed and washed vegetables or ready sliced smoked salmon or even a ready-made pudding if this allows you to cook what you enjoy.

CHAMPAGNE COCKTAIL

The ultimate weapon for creating Christmas cheer. (Serves 6)

6 sugar lumps	1 bottle chilled dry
Angostura bitters	champagne
brandy	

Place a sugar lump in each champagne glass and shake 2–3 drops of bitters on to it. Cover the sugar cube with brandy and then top with champagne, slowly as it will bubble wildly as soon as it touches the sugar.

TURKEY ESCALOPES WITH CRANBERRY SAUCE

Although we have come to think of both cranberries and turkey as recent American imports, cranberries have always grown wild in this country while the turkey was rapidly domesticated after its original introduction in the sixteenth century. But whereas the turkey soon replaced peacocks and swans in festive banquets, cranberries were regarded as a rustic food that was best made into tarts.

This simple recipe is the perfect solution for small numbers. If you want to have some cold turkey for the next day, just cook some extra escalopes and chill. They taste equally good cold, and you won't have to look at that forlorn carcass every day for the next two weeks. You can, of course, make bread sauce, sausages, crispy bacon and all the other trimmings if you wish, but they are not essential. (Serves 4)

680g/1½lb turkey
    escalopes, cut from the
    turkey breast
6 tablespoons olive oil
1 teaspoon finely chopped
    thyme
4 tablespoons finely
    chopped parsley
2 lemons, finely grated

Cranberry sauce
225g/8oz cranberries

85ml/3fl oz port
1 small stick cinnamon
1 orange, finely grated and
    juiced
115g/4oz caster sugar

Gravy
2 tablespoons plain flour
140ml/¼ pint dry white
    wine
425ml/¾ pint chicken stock

Remove any tough sinews from the turkey escalopes, then place each one between 2 sheets of clingfilm and carefully beat with a rolling pin until they flatten out.

Mix together the olive oil, thyme, parsley and lemon zest. Remove the escalopes from their clingfilm and marinate in the oil. (If you are making extra, double the marinade quantities.) Cover and chill for at least an hour.

Place the cranberries, port, cinnamon, orange juice and zest in a small non-corrosive saucepan. Bring to the boil and simmer uncovered until the berries begin to pop and soften. Stir in the sugar and adjust the sweetness to taste. (Sugar has the effect of toughening the cranberries, so do not add until this stage.) Remove the cinnamon stick and allow to cool before serving.

Heat a large dry non-stick frying pan over a moderately high heat. Liberally season the turkey slices, then sear for a couple of minutes on each side and keep warm. Add the remaining herb oil from the marinade bowl and stir in the flour. Allow to cook for a minute before adding the wine and stock. Dislodge any crusty bits and boil vigorously until the gravy reduces and thickens. Adjust the seasoning and simmer for 3–4 minutes. Strain into a sauce-boat and serve with the turkey and cranberry sauce.

ROAST GOOSE

Geese, like turkeys, were for centuries reared in huge flocks before being marched to market. Roast goose was usually served with an apple sauce (except in spring, when green or young goose was served with a goose-berry or sorrel sauce). But modern birds can be served with any tart sauce and there are countless different stuffings, from prunes with apples to green olives and sausagemeat. Tiny sage and onion forcemeat balls can also be made as an accompaniment if wished. (Serves 8)

4.5–5.5kg/10–12lb goose
   with giblets

Stuffing
55g/2oz butter
1 large onion, finely diced
1 clove garlic, crushed
2 dessert apples, peeled,
   cored and roughly grated
the goose liver, finely
   chopped (optional)
2 tablespoons finely
   chopped parsley
285g/10oz good quality
   sausagemeat

2 lemons, finely grated
55g/2oz white breadcrumbs
pinch of dried sage
2 eggs, beaten
salt and freshly ground black
   pepper

Gravy
4 tablespoons plain flour
285ml/½ pint dry white
   wine
850ml/1½ pints chicken
   stock

Preheat the oven to 220°C/425°F/gas 7.

Melt the butter in a small frying pan and sauté the onion and garlic until soft. Pour the buttery mixture into a large bowl and thoroughly mix in the remaining ingredients for the stuffing. Fry a small patty of the mixture to check the seasoning before you stuff the bird.

Wipe the goose inside and out with a damp cloth and season lightly. Pack the stuffing into the goose's cavity. If you have any left over, stuff and shape it into the neck, then fold the flap around it and tuck underneath. Secure with wooden toothpicks or a stitch.

Rub the goose all over with salt and lightly prick its skin. Season with pepper and place on a rack in a large roasting tray. Roast in the centre of the preheated oven for 30 minutes. Throughout the cooking time, baste the goose regularly with its own fat. Then reduce the temperature to 180°C/350°F/gas 4 and continue to roast the bird for 2¾ hours for a 4.5kg/10lb goose. Allow an extra 15 minutes for each 455g/1lb. To check the goose, pierce the thigh with a fine skewer. If the juices run clear your goose is cooked.

Remove from the oven and allow to rest while you make the gravy. Pour off all but 4 tablespoons of goose fat, making sure that you save the excess, as it is delicious with roast potatoes. Stir in the flour and cook for 3 minutes before gradually stirring in the wine and stock. Allow to boil and reduce down. Once the gravy has thickened a little, season to taste and allow to simmer gently for a few more minutes. Strain into a sauce-boat and serve with the goose.

ROAST PHEASANT WITH GRAPE STUFFING

Grapes have been used in stuffing for chickens since medieval times, but they also make a delicious stuffing for pheasant or turkey. (Serves 2)

Stuffing
200g/7oz grapes
55g/2oz butter
1 small onion, diced
2 cloves garlic, crushed
115g/4oz soft white
    breadcrumbs
3 tablespoons finely
    chopped parsley
½ beaten egg
salt and freshly ground black
    pepper

Pheasant
1 plump oven-ready
    pheasant
3 slices thin streaky rindless
    bacon
30g/1oz butter

Gravy
1 dessertspoon plain flour
85ml/3fl oz dry white wine
200ml/7fl oz chicken stock

Preheat the oven to 220°C/425°F/gas 7.

Peel the grapes by briefly covering them with boiling water – just as with tomatoes. Drain and peel before cutting in half and removing the pips. Set aside.

Melt the butter in a small pan and gently fry the onion and garlic until soft and golden. Remove from the heat and add the grapes, breadcrumbs, parsley and egg. Season to taste.

Wipe the pheasant inside and out with a damp cloth and remove any pin feathers. Season lightly and firmly stuff with the grape mixture. Liberally smear the butter over the breast before neatly covering with the bacon. Wrap the excess stuffing in some foil. Place this in the oven about 20 minutes before the pheasant is cooked.

Place the pheasant in a roasting tray and roast in the centre of the preheated oven for 50–60 minutes, basting every 20 minutes or so. Remove the bacon 15 minutes before the end of roasting to allow the bird to brown. Test the bird by inserting a skewer between its breast and thigh. If the juices run clear the pheasant is cooked. Remove and leave to rest in a warm place while you make the gravy.

Stir the flour into the debris in the pan. Allow to cook for a minute before adding the wine and stock. Dislodge any crusty bits and boil vigorously until the gravy reduces and thickens. Adjust the seasoning and simmer for 3–4 minutes. Strain into a sauce-boat and serve with the pheasant.

ELIZA ACTON'S CHRISTMAS PUDDING

Although plum pudding had been as essential a part of the eighteenth-century man's diet as roast beef, it was Prince Albert who popularized it as a Christmas pudding, along with the candlelit Christmas tree. Every family has its own favourite Christmas pudding recipe. Mine is Eliza Acton's. (Serves 6)

Use a 1.5 litre/2½ pint
pudding basin
170g/6oz raisins
170g/6oz currants
140ml/¼ pint brandy
85g/3oz plain flour
85g/3oz white breadcrumbs
170g/6oz shredded suet
115g/4oz peeled, cored and
roughly grated apple

140g/5oz caster sugar
55g/2oz chopped candied
peel
½ teaspoon mixed spice
pinch of salt
3 large eggs
3 tablespoons extra brandy
for flaming the pudding

If you have time, soak the raisins and currants in the brandy overnight. Beat together all the ingredients – not forgetting to make a wish as you do so. Lightly grease a pudding basin and fill with the mixture. Cover with a circle of greaseproof paper.

Lay 2 sheets of foil on top of one another and make a pleat in them before laying them on top of the pudding basin. Tie securely and lower the basin into a large pan of boiling water. Boil for a good 3½ hours. The pudding can be served at this stage. However, if you like a very dark pudding, reboil it every day until it is as dark brown as treacle.

Carefully turn out the hot pudding and place a sprig of holly (with berries) on top. Warm 3 tablespoons of brandy, then, when you are ready to serve, pour this over the pudding and set alight. March in with the flaming pudding but be careful not to serve anyone any holly berries. Eat with lashings of brandy butter.

Note: If you are short of cooking rings on Christmas Day you can always zap it in the microwave, where it will reheat well.

BRANDY BUTTER

You can substitute rum for the brandy if wished, in which case add the finely grated zest of 1 orange with the lemon zest. (Serves 6)

170g/6oz softened butter	6 tablespoons icing sugar or
1 lemon, finely grated	to taste
	4 tablespoons good brandy

Beat together the butter, lemon zest, icing sugar and brandy. Adjust each flavouring according to your taste. A few drops of lemon juice can be added if wished. This can be made in advance and chilled or frozen until needed.

EXOTIC FRUIT

The British have long adored tropical fruits, and from the eighteenth century, gardeners of the rich specialized in nurturing hothouse pineapples, bananas, grapes, mangosteens and guavas. So prized were these fruits that they were served in pride of place for the dessert course, where they could be admired by all. However, by the late nineteenth century many of the more hardy tropical fruits were beginning to be widely imported into the country. Gradually more fruits became available to ordinary cooks, initially in tinned form but later fresh. The improvements in shipping and air freight have meant that bananas are now considered as ordinary as apples, while mangoes are becoming an increasingly familiar, if expensive, fruit. Despite this, many of these exotic imports taste only a shadow of their native selves. A ripe, freshly picked mango has the texture of a peach and is unbelievably sweet and juicy – a far cry from the firm, slightly tart imports we often buy here. Consequently, careful cooking is needed for many of these fruits.

LYCHEE CHAMPAGNE JELLY

Fat juicy lychees are at their best in December and January, although they always seem very expensive. This fragile pudding is very refreshing after a rich meal. (Serves 6)

285ml/½ pint boiling water	115g/4oz caster sugar
4 teaspoons powdered gelatine	425ml/¾ pint pink champagne
1 lemon, finely pared and juiced	18 lychees

Pour 3 tablespoons of the boiling water into a small bowl and sprinkle with the gelatine. Place the remaining water in a saucepan with the lemon peel and sugar. Dissolve the sugar over a low heat then leave to cool.

Stir the gelatine, and if it has not melted place the bowl in a shallow pan of simmering water and simmer until it has dissolved. Remove the lemon peel from the syrup and add the liquid gelatine and lemon juice. Stir in the champagne and leave to cool in the fridge until it is nearly set.

At this stage peel and stone the lychees and divide them between 6 champagne flutes. Pour the jelly over them and chill until set.

MANGO AND CLEMENTINE GRATIN

Sabayons have recently become very popular among British chefs, who often use indigenous ingredients such as cider or sloe gin to flavour them. Although the sabayon has to be prepared at the last minute, this does not take long with an electric whisk. Satsumas or any other favourite citrus fruit can be used if wished. (Serves 6)

6 clementines	85g/3oz caster sugar
1 ripe mango	140ml/¼ pint Sauterne or
3 tablespoons Cointreau	another sweet dessert
3 large egg yolks	wine

The clementines and mango can be prepared in advance if wished. Using a sharp knife, cut away the pith and peel of the clementines. Holding each fruit over a bowl, to catch their juice, cut away each segment, leaving behind the fibrous casing. Stir in the Cointreau.

Peel the mango with a sharp knife. Cut the flesh away from the hard stone in 4 pieces. Cut each piece of mango flesh into elegant slices and add to the clementines.

Preheat the grill to its highest setting.

Whisk together the egg yolks and sugar in a mixing bowl. Once they are pale place the bowl over a pan of simmering but not boiling water. Keep whisking until the mixture becomes very pale and fluffy, then gradually whisk in the wine and continue to whisk until the sauce becomes very thick and fluffy.

Arrange the fruit in a shallow grill-proof dish and place under the grill for 3 minutes to warm through. Remove and cover with the thick sabayon before replacing it under the grill. Within seconds the sabayon will become flecked with golden brown spots. Remove immediately and serve.

PINEAPPLE ROMANOFF

There is still something luxurious about eating a pineapple, despite the fact that they are widely available for most of the year. Surprisingly, there are few outstanding pineapple recipes, most modern cooks preferring to serve them very simply, sprinkled with a little kirsch. This wonderful Robert Carrier recipe is an exception to the rule. (Serves 6)

1 large ripe pineapple	285ml/½ pint double cream
6 tablespoons icing sugar	3 tablespoons kirsch
3 tablespoons Cointreau	1 large orange
3 tablespoons rum	

Cut off the top and bottom of the pineapple before cutting straight down its sides to remove its skin. Then, using a small sharp knife, remove all the brown 'eyes'.

Remove the tough core by standing the pineapple on one end and cutting down the length of the core to give you 4 pieces of pineapple flesh and a square core. (Delicious to nibble as a quick snack.) Dice the pineapple flesh and toss in the sugar, Cointreau and rum. Cover and chill.

Shortly before you are ready to begin your meal, whip the cream with the kirsch until it forms soft peaks. Gently but thoroughly fold the cream into the pineapple and its alcoholic juices. Cover and leave in the fridge until you are ready to eat it.

At the last moment roughly grate the orange and sprinkle this on top of the pineapple. (It is important that you use the rough side of the grater, as for some reason it imparts a very special flavour to the dish.)

APPENDIX

Shortcrust pastry
Rough puff pastry
Puff pastry
Suet pastry and steamed pudding method
Vegetable stock

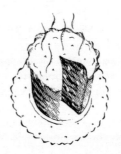

SHORTCRUST PASTRY

For some reason chefs have cultivated a certain mystique around all forms of pastry that is totally unfounded. Shortcrust pastry is not only very easy to make but it also freezes well. (Makes 225g/8oz pastry)

225g/8oz plain flour	115g/4oz cold butter
½ teaspoon salt	cold water

Quick method

Place the flour and salt in a food processor and give a quick whiz to mix and lighten. Cut the butter into small cubes and add to the flour. Start the processor, stopping frequently to check the consistency of the butter and flour. Stop as soon as the butter and flour have turned into fine crumbs. If you over-process they will become a paste, which will make your pastry very short.

Transfer the mixture to a mixing bowl and cautiously add a little cold water. Mix with a fork, adding a little more water if necessary, until the crumbs begin to form themselves into larger balls of dough. At this stage place the dough on a scantily floured surface and lightly knead by hand. Wrap in clingfilm, greaseproof paper or foil and refrigerate for 30 minutes. Roll when needed.

Manual method

Sift the flour and salt into a large mixing bowl. Cut the butter into very small dice and add. Using your fingertips, lightly rub the butter into the flour until it forms fine crumbs. Then add the cold water and continue as above.

ROUGH PUFF PASTRY

Rough puff pastry is a slightly quicker and less rich method of making a puff pastry. If you are apprehensive about making puff pastry it is a good recipe to start with, as it will build up your confidence. It can be used in place of puff pastry. (Makes 225g/8oz)

170g/6oz cold butter	1 teaspoon lemon juice
225g/8oz plain flour	140ml/¼ pint cold water
½ teaspoon salt	

Cut the butter into large dice. Sift the flour and salt into a large mixing bowl and stir in the butter. Gently mix in the lemon juice and enough water to bind the flour and water into a rough dough. Turn out on to a lightly floured work surface and lightly shape into a rectangle, but do not knead.

Roll out the dough on a floured surface into a long strip about 3 times as long as it is wide. Mark the pastry into thirds, fold one end up and then the other down over it. Using the rolling pin, lightly press down on each edge so that the pastry is sealed. Give the dough a half-turn clockwise.

Using short sharp strokes, roll out the dough so that it returns to its previous length but retains the same thickness. Then repeat exactly as before, before wrapping up in clingfilm or greaseproof paper and chilling for 15–30 minutes. Make a note of which way the pastry is facing before chilling, as you will need to continue with the clockwise half-turns.

After resting the pastry, replace on the floured surface in the position that you left off and continue with a further 2 rolls and half-turns. Refrigerate for another 30 minutes and then continue with 2 more rolls and half-turns. Wrap and refrigerate until needed or divide into 2 and freeze.

PUFF PASTRY

Puff pastry is my favourite pastry but it does require some organization, as you have to allow for plenty of chilling time. I usually make up the dough and give it its first roll the night before I need it, while making supper, and then finish the process the following day. (Makes 225g/8oz)

225g/8oz plain flour	225g/8oz butter
½ teaspoon salt	140ml/¼ pint cold water

Sift the flour and salt into a large mixing bowl and rub in 30g/1oz cold butter. This can be quickly processed in a food processor. Mix in by hand about 140ml/¼ pint cold water and then gently knead into a dough on a lightly floured work surface. Wrap in clingfilm and refrigerate for 30 minutes. Remember to leave out the remaining 200g/7oz butter so that it can soften.

Flatten the butter into a 2.5cm/1 inch thick rectangle. Roll out the dough on a floured surface into a rectangle that is 3 times the length of the butter and about 2.5cm/1 inch wider than the width of the butter. Place the butter in the centre of the dough and then fold over each dough flap, so that the butter is completely covered. Using the rolling pin, lightly press down on each edge so that the butter is sealed in. Give the dough a half-turn clockwise.

Using short sharp strokes, roll out the dough so that it returns to its previous length (3 times that of the butter) but retains the same thickness. Then fold over the 2 ends as though they were covering the butter, press the edges with the rolling pin and give a further half-turn clockwise. If the butter is breaking through the pastry or the pastry is becoming warm, stop, wrap and refrigerate for a further 30 minutes. If not, you can repeat the rolling process one more time before resting the dough. Make a note of which way the pastry is facing before chilling, as you will need to continue with the clockwise half-turns.

After resting the pastry replace on the floured surface in the position that you left off and continue with a further 2 rolls and half-turns. Refrigerate for another 30 minutes and then continue with 2 more rolls and half-turns. Wrap and refrigerate until needed or divide into 2 and freeze.

SUET PASTRY AND STEAMED PUDDING METHOD

Suet pastry should be made just before it is needed, never in advance, as water and heat trigger the raising agents in the flour. For a richer suet crust rub 55g/2oz cold diced butter into the flour and later stir in only 85g/3oz shredded suet instead of the 115g/4oz shredded suet listed below. (Makes 225g/8oz pastry)

225g/8oz self-raising flour	115g/4oz shredded suet
½ level teaspoon salt	140ml/¼ pint cold water

Check that your saucepan can hold the pudding basin(s) with a tight fitting lid. Then pour enough water into the saucepan to reach half-way up the empty basin(s). Remove these and bring the water to the boil. Carefully butter or oil the pudding basin(s) so that they will not stick on being turned out.

Sift the flour and salt into a mixing bowl. Thoroughly mix in the suet before stirring in the water with a fork. Turn the dough out on to a scantily floured work surface and lightly knead until the mixture becomes smooth and supple.

Remove a quarter of the dough for the lid(s). Roll this out to about 1cm/½ inch thickness and press the rim of the basin(s) lightly into it. Cut around the inside of this indentation and set aside, covered with a tea towel.

Shape the remaining dough into either a large circle or 4 smaller circles, but in either case large enough to line the pudding basin(s). Sprinkle each circle with flour and fold in half, and then half again, so that the pastry forms a triangle. Lift this over the basin and gently press against the sides, so that it acts as a neat lining. You may need to cut away the odd extra fold – if so just re-seal by firmly pressing the dough together.

Fill the basin(s) up to 1cm/½ inch of the rim with whatever filling you choose and then flip over the excess pastry. Brush this with water and then cover with the lid(s) and press firmly to seal. Place a fitted circle of buttered greaseproof paper on top.

To cover each basin, take a square of foil and fold a pleat down the centre so that the pudding can rise. Place over the basin and press down the sides. Then take a good length of string and loop it over so that double the length can go round the pudding basin, just beneath the rim. Thread the string through its own loop, pull back as tightly as you can and bring the string round to the opposite side. Tie in a firm knot.

Steamed puddings are extremely difficult to remove from a bubbling hot pan. One solution is to make 2 long strips of foil that have been folded over several times for extra strength. Place these in a cross, sit the basin on the cross and then pull up the foil ribbons over the top and twist together to form a handle.

At this point lower the pudding(s) into the pan of boiling water and cover. Keep the water at a gentle boil throughout the cooking time. You will need to check the water level regularly and replenish with boiling water. It must never run dry or the pudding will burn and the basin may crack when the water is added. Cook 850ml/1½ pint puddings for 2 hours and 285ml/½ pint puddings for 1 hour (if your savoury filling has already been partially cooked).

When you are ready to turn the pudding out, lift from the water and allow to sit for a couple of minutes before removing the foil and greaseproof paper. Place a warm serving plate over the top and invert the 2 together, giving a few gentle shakes until you feel the pudding slip out.

VEGETABLE STOCK

This is a delicious recipe that can be happily used as a replacement for chicken or fish stock. (Makes 2 litres/3½ pints)

2 litres/3½ pints water
2 litres/3½ pints dry white wine
4 ripe tomatoes
2 leeks, coarsely chopped
2 large carrots, coarsely chopped
1 celeriac root, peeled and coarsely chopped
2 large onions, coarsely chopped
1 head garlic, cut in 2
1 bouquet garni (parsley, thyme, bay leaf)
6 black peppercorns
2 cloves
salt

Put all the ingredients in a large saucepan. Bring to the boil. Skim off any scum, then gently simmer uncovered for 3 hours, stirring from time to time.

Strain the stock through a sieve. The liquid should have reduced by half. Add salt to taste.

SELECT BIBLIOGRAPHY

Eliza Acton, *Modern Cookery for Private Families* (1855), Southover Press, 1993.

Elizabeth Ayrton, *English Provincial Cooking*, Mitchell Beazley, 1982.

Lindsey Bareham, *A celebration of soup*, Michael Joseph, 1993.

Isabella Beeton, *Mrs Beeton's Book of Household Management*, Ward, Lock & Co., 1915.

Maggie Black, *A Taste of History*, British Museum Press, 1993.

Lizzie Boyd, *British Cookery*, Helm, 1988.

Arabella Boxer, *Arabella Boxer's Book of English Food*, Hodder & Stoughton, 1991.

Catherine Brown, *Broths to Bannocks*, John Murray, 1991.

Catherine Brown, *Scottish Cookery*, Chambers, 1985.

Robert Carrier, *The Robert Carrier Cookery Course*, Sphere Books, 1976.

Terence and Caroline Conran, *The Cook Book*, Mitchell Beazley, 1982.

Margaret Costa, *Four Seasons Cookery Book*, Papermac, 1982.

Philippa Davenport, *Cooking for Family and Friends*, Norman and Hobhouse, 1982.

Elizabeth David, *An Omelette and a Glass of Wine*, Penguin, 1986.

Elizabeth David, *Spices, Salt and Aromatics in the English Kitchen*, Penguin, 1970.

Elizabeth David, *Summer Cooking* (1955), Penguin, 1965.

Elizabeth David, *English Bread and Yeast Cookery*, Penguin, 1986.

Alan Davidson, *North Atlantic Seafood* (1979), Penguin, 1980.

John Farley, *The London Art of Cookery* (1807), Southover Press, 1988.

Farmhouse Fare, Hulton Press, 1950.

Theodora FitzGibbon, *A Taste of Wales*, J.M. Dent & Sons Ltd, 1971.

Hannah Glasse, *The Art of Cookery Made Plain and Easy* (1747), Prospect, 1983.

Ann Gomar, *Lancashire Country Recipes*, Ravette Books, 1988.

Pippa Gomar, *Dorset Country Recipes*, Ravette Books, 1988.

Jane Grigson, *English Food*, Penguin, 1981.

Jane Grigson, *Fish Cookery* (1973), Penguin, 1975.

Jane Grigson, *Jane Grigson's Fruit Book*, Michael Joseph, 1982.

Jane Grigson, *Good Things*, Penguin, 1977.

Jane Grigson, *Jane Grigson's Vegetable Book* (1978), Penguin, 1980.

Dorothy Hartley, *Food in England* (1954), MacDonald, 1964.

Ambrose Heath, *Good Food Throughout the Year*, The Cookery Book Club, 1966.

Simon Hopkinson with Lindsey Bareham, *Roast Chicken and Other Stories*, Ebury Press, 1994.

Deh-Ta Hsiung, *The Home Book of Chinese Cookery*, Faber & Faber, 1978.

Rosemary Hume and Muriel Downes, *The Penguin Cordon Bleu Cookery*, 1963.

Mrs C.F. Leyel and Miss Olga Hartley, *The Gentle Art of Cookery* (1929), Graham Watson, 1947.

Alastair Little and Richard Whittington, *Keep it Simple*, Conran Octopus, 1993.

Caroline Liddell and Robin Weir, *Ices*, Hodder & Stoughton, 1993, Grub Street, 1995.

Richard Mabey, *Food for Free*, Harper Collins, 1992.

Deborah Madison, *The Greens Cook Book*, Bantam, 1987.

F. Marian McNeill, *The Scots Kitchen* (1929), Mercat Press, 1993.

Sara Paston-Williams, *The Art of Dining*, National Trust, 1993.

Sara Paston-Williams, *Christmas and Festive Day Recipes* (David & Charles, 1981), Penguin, 1983.

Marguerite Patten, *Classic British Dishes*, Bloomsbury, 1994.

Molly Perham, *Norfolk Country Recipes*, Ravette Books, 1988.

Molly Perham, *Yorkshire Country Recipes*, Ravette Books, 1988.

Roger Phillips, *Wild Food*, Pan Books, 1983.

Readers Digest, *The Cookery Year*, 1981.

Elizabeth Rundell, *Modern Domestic Cookery*, 1853.

Rosanne Sanders, *The English Apple*, Phaidon, 1988.

The Scottish Women's Rural Institutes Cookery Book, 1946.

Nigel Slater, *Real Fast Puddings*, Penguin, 1994.

Delia Smith, *Delia Smith's Complete Cookery Course*, BBC Books, 1982.

Richard Stein, *English Seafood Cookery*, Penguin, 1988.

Katie Stewart, *The Times Cookery Book*, Pan Books, 1972.

Reay Tannahill, *Food in History*, Penguin, 1988.

INDEX